elsewhere

The author at twelve as sketched
by her piano teacher's son in Paris

elsewhere

A Memoir

Julia Schueler

Louisiana State University Press

Baton Rouge

Copyright © 1999 by Louisiana State University Press
All rights reserved
Manufactured in the United States of America
First printing
08 07 06 05 04 03 02 01 00 99
5 4 3 2 1

Designer: *Laura Roubique Gleason*
Typeface: *Abobe Garamond*
Printer and binder: *Edwards Brothers, Inc.*

LIBRARY OF CONGRESS CATALOGING-IN-PUBLICATION DATA:

Schueler, Julia, 1923–
     Elsewhere: a memoir / Julia Schueler.
        p.   cm.
     ISBN 0-8071-2376-5 (cl. : alk. paper)
     1. Schueler, Julia, 1923–   . 2. Jewish women—United States
Biography.   3. Jews—United States Biography.   4. Refugees, Jewish—
United States Biography.   I. Title.
E184.37.S38A3   1999
973'.04924'0092—dc21
     [B]   99-20909
                                                                            CIP

To my grandchildren
in order of appearance:

Reda and Amin Choukairi
Janelle, Janessa, Joel, and Joshua Schueler

in memory of the grandfather they never knew

Fred Warren Schueler

Contents

Illustrations

Acknowledgments

Thanks to the unrelenting support, constant reminders and endless curiosity of family, friends, former students, and colleagues, this book has come to an end and with it my search for Elsewhere.

Among the members of this informal booster club, Peggy Repass lent a finely attuned ear, came to listen when I stumbled over barely legible handwritten notes, asked incisive questions. Martine Alford, Simonne Fischer, and Sophie Gasser in New Orleans, Jacqueline Haguenauer, Cécile Raybaud, Colette Renard, and Juliette Touchard in France, helped corroborate disparate incidents in wartime France. Thussy Morphy, Mariana Scott, Sabine Seiler, and Bärbel Frenz in Berlin, provided a healthy perspective on the New Germany.

Tanya Schueler, my daughter, undertook the task of typing the major portion of the handwritten manuscript, peppering pages with questions, reminders and suggestions.

Carl Schueler, my son, and Reda and Amin Choukairi, my grandsons, patiently instructed me in the use of a computer. Eric Sanzenbach coached me in the basics of word processing.

My steadfast friend of fifty years, Julie Popkin, also my literary agent, offered to read the final copy with a keen and practiced eye.

André Liebich, author and historian (*From the Other Shore,* a scholarly treatise on the Mensheviks' triple exile), was kind enough to critique my manuscript with a focus on historical accuracy, validating my childhood memories.

A first anonymous reviewer responded to the story of my wanderings with great warmth and sympathy while making sure that dates, names, and places were correct.

Except as noted, names of persons are their real names. I ask the reader's indulgence for any small inaccuracies. All mistakes are my own.

Finally I wish to thank my "medical team," who encouraged me in this endeavor, mindful that, for me, writing was the best medicine.

New Orleans, December 1, 1998

elsewhere

Prologue

Papa and Mama grew up in the last quarter of the last century a scant generation after the abolition of serfdom in a crumbling Russian Empire racked by pogroms and rumblings of civil strife. They were not products of their past, but of a future they envisioned with certainty and, in their youth, helped shape.

Papa, the oldest of three boys, was born in Nesvizh, a small town at the westernmost fringe of Tsarist Russia. He was sent away to study in a Russian gymnasium, a school offering a stringent college preparatory curriculum. By the time he was fifteen, he had rebelled against his father's Orthodox Judaism. Steeped in politics, coached by the classic freethinkers of French and Russian literature, he honed his speaking skills, became a student activist painting a rosy picture of a socialist democratic Russia, and promptly landed in jail, a political prisoner. The First Russian Revolution of 1905, coinciding with the abysmal losses following the war with Japan, brought some measure of parliamentary reform and Papa's provisional liberty. His reputation as a speaker was henceforth to be reckoned with.

Papa continued his studies of law and economics at the University of St. Petersburg, became an active member of the Social Democratic Party, wrote articles, made speeches, and traveled the countryside. In 1908 he married Mama.

Mama grew up in Shklov, a lumber port on the Dnieper River, the oldest of nine children. Her father, a barber-surgeon, had broken with Jewish tradition, though he indulged his wife's strict Orthodox ways. Self-taught, widely read, he sent his oldest daughter to a Russian school at a time when many Jewish girls remained illiterate. As a girl, Mama did not help with the dishes, the baking, the diapering. Instead she dissected worms, collected insects, and in general followed a scientific bent, her heart set on medicine. That is, she fell hopelessly in love with a medical student, Papa's younger brother, whom she followed to Tiflis, now Tbilisi, the capital of Georgia, then a mere two or three days' train ride to the south in the heart of the Caucasus Mountains, wedged between the Black Sea to the west and the Caspian Sea to the east.

Mama stayed with her maternal aunt, a beauty by all accounts, who had married an Englishman, an engineer. The couple—childless, I believe—lived in relative ease and comfort, surrounded by handsome furnishings and a competent staff of servants.

Mama enrolled at the gymnasium for girls, waiting for my uncle to finish medical school and marry her. He graduated successfully, but promptly married someone else. Heartbroken, and sick with tuberculosis as well, Mama returned to Shklov, where my grandfather nursed her back to health. Eventually Papa arrived on the scene and married her.

My parents moved to Moscow, where Mama embarked on a full-time career as a student in the faculty of medicine, embracing a liberated lifestyle generations before the advent of women's lib in America. When Papa wasn't sitting in prison, which he considered to be a badge of honor, he wrote articles and broadcast the socialist ideal of democracy with vim and vigor in speeches, articles, at meetings, and eventually in his own journal. In 1913 he traveled the rim of the eastern Mediterranean for an extended reportage: Turkey, Syria, Palestine, and Egypt. Reluctantly he returned to Moscow at the start of World War I in 1914.

Mama served her internship behind the battle lines in Poland in military hospitals—interrupted, I presume, by Moscow interludes. When she found herself pregnant, she was sent back to Moscow, where my brother Max was born in June 1916.

The Revolutionary Party had split into Bolshevik (majority) and Menshevik (minority) factions. Papa, as a social democrat and a Menshevik, took an active part in the February Revolution of 1917. Tsar Nicholas II was forced to abdicate, and Kerensky, leader of the Socialist Revolutionary Party, presided over a moderate socialist cabinet. Papa assumed an official post in the Kerensky regime. Kerensky's experiment in democratic government collapsed a few months later when the Bolsheviks staged the October Revolution, after which their leader, Lenin, established the "dictatorship of the proletariat" and instituted a reign of terror against all opposition.

All the prominent Mensheviks were imprisoned, including Papa. After five years, they were given the option of permanent exile. They left, many for Berlin, in November 1922, where they set up a governing body for their party, the "Foreign Delegation." These were our friends, the Group, and the only family I came to know besides Mama, Papa, and my brother Max.

Berlin, 1923–1933

I don't know where the money came from. A photo taken shortly after my arrival in Berlin, June 1923, shows a prosperous, fashionably attired family vacationing on the Baltic. I am the bundle in the arms of my nurse, a young woman in a starched uniform. Later, when I was still very little, there was talk of money, packs of it stuffed in briefcases with a midmorning snack, paper notes that weren't worth picking up when they accidentally fluttered away; there was also talk of gold. I imagine that the Menshevik Group prudently sheltered funds as a safeguard against the ravages of inflation following the demise of the German Empire in the wake of a disastrous First World War. Perhaps there were private fortunes as well. There was talk about shipyards in St. Petersburg, lumber mills, banking. In those early years in Berlin, the Group was convinced the Soviet Union would collapse under the weight of its own ineptitude; it was only a matter of when, not if. "When we return to Moscow . . ." I remember how Mama constantly corrected herself, something like, "We got back to Moscow late last night, sorry, I mean Berlin," and "We're not leaving Moscow over the Easter holidays—I forgot, I mean Berlin." It is not hard to imagine that well-heeled, superbly groomed, imposing-looking gentlemen—I can think of three of them—of a kindly liberal persuasion would want to back a political group which would assure their financial well-being in a Russia restored to democracy.

I recall motor outings in one of our host's cars to a handsome villa on the outskirts of Berlin, a sure sign of wealth; this in the midst of the Great Depression, which hit the Germany of the Weimar Republic with a double whammy, sending thousands of embittered, idle youths to roam the streets, leaving the eyeless, the legless, the armless veterans to beg in public, while those fortunate enough to have survived the Great War intact, too proud to beg, retreated into hopelessness. This was the receptive audience for Hitler's magical solutions of instant pride, honor, and worship of an idealized pure Aryan race at the expense of those who did not fit that model, be they Jewish, retarded, or infirm.

Papa worked for a German publishing house as editor of its Russian-language editions; I seem to recall a Handbook of Economic Resources. *He*

*wrote occasional articles for Russian newspapers in Berlin and told me to say
"writer" when asked for his profession. Mama took up a residency in a well-
known hospital.*

    *By the time Hitler came to power in 1933, our family's bank account had
dwindled to nothing. Papa spent the last of his deutsche marks on suitable
clothes for our train trip to Paris, March 1933, where we arrived penniless,
once again beholden to the charity of the Group.*

I found a photo of me, a little girl, carrying a suitcase, smiling. I was not
a happy child, but in this photo I'm waving good-bye; I'm going somewhere else. My brown suitcase, not much bigger than a briefcase, is sturdy
and secure and all mine. Home has always been elsewhere, packed in a
bag; and that is pretty much the story of my life.

    When I was forty, we had lived four years in a two-story house with
custom-made drapes, wall to wall carpeting, carefully chosen furniture, a
library of books, two nice kids, two cars, two careers, and Fred (my husband) said, "When are you going to unpack? Our bedroom looks as if
you're ready to take off any minute." So it did. Furniture was just sort of
put there, of no consequence.

    The little brown suitcase was long gone, replaced by a steamer trunk
like the one my brother had retrieved from a basement in France after the
Second World War and which had held the family album with the picture of the little girl waving good-bye and a few other mementos. This is
where I kept letters, baby hand-knits, photos, embroidered cloths, a huge
pear-shaped amber pendant which my mother had kept in a silver jewelry box in the original steamer trunk which had brought her belongings
from Moscow on the three-day train ride to Berlin carrying a three-
month-old infant (me) and holding a seven-year-old boy (my brother
Max) by the hand.

    Fred was right. Home was always elsewhere, packed in the steamer
trunk, going somewhere where I could invent myself, choose to be someone else, lose myself in anonymous crowds, pretend to be French in Germany, Belgian in France, French in Italy. No one ever believed I was
American. There were many borders where my passport raised eyebrows:
Julia Schueler, United States of America, born in Moscow.

    On my first return to postwar Germany in 1953, I forgot not to an-
swer in German when asked for my papers at the Swiss-German border
control and got yelled at: "Schueler, geboren in Moskau, ja was ist denn

das! Amerikaner sind Sie nicht!" ("Schueler, born in Moscow, that's a fine one! You're no American!") One cannot yell like that in English, the accent doesn't fall heavily enough and sharply enough like a Nazi footfall. Never mind that my looks are the antithesis of my German accent, which matches Fred's family name, five centuries of Schuelers dutifully named Friedrich Wilhelm until Fred's father, born in America, was named Frederick William and Fred plain Fred after him.

When I was little, sitting on my very own suitcase getting ready to go on my very own trip, I wanted above all else to be like all the other little girls I saw: sturdy, pale, blond, and always a head taller than me. Strange that my mirror image never convinced me of the difference; that is, it took almost ten years, the advent of Hitler, to be exact.

I noticed that Mama (in Russian) or Mutti (in German) had lovely white, very white arms. I loved to stroke them with my own permanently tanned little hand both before I could talk, and later, when I learned to speak in German and refused to answer in Russian. Mama used to give me a hot bath at least once a week, in my own tin tub set on two chairs in the nursery to avoid the long chilly walk down the hall from the bathroom. She wrapped me in a huge white terry cloth blanket, enfolded me in her white white arms with her shirt sleeves rolled up, and called me Koshka. Not Julia, not Julka, not Julitchka; sometimes Lulu, which became my name in Berlin—for what reason I do not know.

Mama's friend, Sofia Ilyinitchna, called me Koshka also. When I was four and she had learned enough German, I asked her why. "Koshka, little kitten, where did you get those green slit eyes?" I looked in the mirror, and sure enough, my eyes were green and when I smiled they became tiny slits. They were the only green eyes in the family. I asked Mama and Papa if anyone else had green eyes, and they said no, no one in the family. "But you look just like your Papa, except for the green eyes."

Papa had a permanent tan just like mine, and high cheekbones, and slightly slanted eyes. He looked very foreign in Berlin and spoke German with a dreadful accent, so he was determined that I should speak German properly and hired a German nanny to take care of me. And that is how I learned to speak, to dress, to pull my socks up straight, to play in the sandbox without ever sitting down, and to hold my spoon properly without spilling the soup. I mastered this last feat by watching a trained chimp in the zoo, which was across the square from our house. I was fascinated by his table manners, and Nanny encouraged me: "See how he holds his spoon. See how careful he is not to spill his gruel." Every morning we went to the zoo and sat on a bench opposite the cage with the famous chimp. He wore short trousers and sat on a little chair just like mine, at a little table just like mine, and sat still while his trainer knotted a big white napkin around his neck. Then he grabbed an enormous spoon in his fist and carefully propelled mouthful after mouthful of gruel to his mouth without spilling a drop. He banged on the table for more; he made faces at the crowd; his trainer gave him a banana, untied his napkin, and led him away by the hand. We went home. I sat at my little table and practiced holding my enormous silver spoon, and spilled soup all over my big terry cloth bib.

Every morning, I went to the zoo with Nanny after Mama, whom Nanny called Frau Doktor and everyone else called Ida Osipovna, left in a blue serge suit with a briefcase under her arm, a small hat pulled tight over black bobbed hair, marching purposefully with shoulders squared and head held high to her full imposing stature of just under five feet. Sometimes Papa left also, wearing pearl gray spats, a hand-tailored three-piece suit, a carefully chosen bow tie, a felt hat over his glistening, thick, wavy black hair (which was my secret envy); he carried a cane, elegant and confident.

When Amin, my second grandson, first saw a photo of his great-grandfather Jeffim, he was puzzled, then said, "Like Mitzi." Mitzi was our Japanese American friend. Amin was perhaps three years old, but even as a toddler in Casablanca he had recognized the oriental look which was to puzzle me for so long until Aunt Mirrha returned to Berlin in 1930 and told me terrifying stories of Cossacks, Tartars, and other Mongols riding bareback on their horses, mowing down everything in their paths with their curved swords, burning and razing towns and villages. That was how, in some unfathomable way, Papa got his high cheekbones and I got my green slit eyes. (Mirrha could not have told me this in 1929—she spoke not a word of German then—so it must have been when she returned the following year from Vienna with baby Joshi, my very own cousin.)

My big brother, already nine years old, had left the house before our parents, riding his bike skillfully without touching the handlebars, his schoolbag strapped to his back. My secret ambition was to find out where they all went, but I never did. First I had to learn to open the door of my nursery, which, like all decent German doors, was kept closed. I struggled on my toes to reach the doorknob, which was not a knob but a handle one had to pull down, and by the time I learned to open the door and toddle down the long hallway, the apartment was empty, except for Nanny and Cook and the maid. Cook shooed me out of the kitchen; the maid, who was sanding the parquet floors of the huge living room on hands and knees, called Nanny; Nanny scooped me up and carried me, protesting, back to the nursery. When my family all came back after my afternoon nap, there was often company, and until I was two, when friends asked, "What does she speak?" meaning what language, Mama would mumble, "She doesn't speak," but after a while the awful truth had to be faced. Mama had to confess, "She speaks German."

So that is how "*ona ne govorit*" changed to "*ona ne govorit po russki*" ("she doesn't speak," and "she doesn't speak Russian"). "Shame! Shame! *Kak!* How could such an awful thing happen? And with her Papa's looks and her green slit eyes!" *Ona*, meaning "she," was my cue to listen, so unfortunately I only learned the third person: she is falling asleep, she dropped her spoon, it's time she went to bed. By the time I was three, my *r*s were hopeless, my *l*s worse, and any attempt at voicing the silent language became anathema to my ears. When I was seven, Mutti made a last, half-hearted attempt and enrolled me in private Russian lessons. My *l*s and *r*s remained raucous and unharmonious; verb endings and case endings required too much effort. I did master the Cyrillic alphabet, though, and never forgot the Russian of my preschool years. Irrevocable proof of this came some twenty years later when Fred and I were living in Iowa City in Finkbine Park. My husband, who could hypnotize everyone but me, sought my approval for an ingenious experiment: he would give one of his willing subjects the post-hypnotic suggestion that he could hypnotize me. It worked. As the young man gently prodded me back into my past, I dutifully regressed from English to French to German and spoke Russian when I reached age three. It was the first and last time I ever spoke Russian.

Recently, when I told my friend Julie Popkin, who had lived in the adjoining half of our Quonset hut, that I couldn't remember where this hypnotic session had taken place, except that it was not in our apartment, she laughed. "But Julia, I was there! You were in our half of the barracks' apartment." As I recall, our acquaintance with Julie and Dick Popkin was precipitated by a minor flooding, the result of neither Fred nor I emptying the pan underneath our icebox, each convinced it was the other's job.

The water didn't bother me—it was an excuse to give the cement floor an extra scrubbing—but Julie's new rug on the other side of the wall did not fare so well. Fred and Dick shook hands, discovered a common language of mathematics, and embarked on a lifelong friendship of easy banter and philosophical repartee.

That was almost fifty years ago. On Friday, I ordered a wheelchair and when Aunt Mirrha's oldest grandson, my cousin Joshi's son, came to visit from Washington, I asked him to take me for a "walk." He is tall and strong, and at forty plays basketball, jogs, bicycles twenty miles to work; yet he had a hard time managing the chair over our cracked sidewalks in New Orleans. Every oak tree's roots play havoc with the poured cement, a veritable obstacle course! I closed my eyes and remembered the weekend outings in Grünewald near Berlin, when I sat up in my green lightweight folding carriage as Mutti pushed me over the bumps on the path through the forest, the tall pines forming a canopy overhead, and I leaned over the side of the carriage and saw those dark twisted ropelike things which I was told were roots. We picnicked in a clearing where I ran around, picked flowers, and gathered pine cones and little twigs. I loved those outings. But mostly I loved going somewhere else.

Once Papa took me on a boat ride on the Spree River and explained about rivers and oceans. I could have stayed on that boat forever, just gliding smoothly past unfamiliar streets right through the heart of the big bustling city, underneath bridges, with people waving from the quays.

Across the square from our apartment house stood horse-drawn carriages for hire. There were also motorcar taxis, but I ignored them. My goal was to reach the horses, with their bags of oats tied under their chins, and to stroke their well-groomed, sleek noses; but I only just barely reached their tummies, and as I stood, awed, between their legs, Mutti grabbed me—the only time I recall her yelling at me in terror, caught between spanking the daylights out of me and hugging me tight. Years later, she told me about her youngest brother who ran away to the stables all the time, who loved horses, who once ran away with the circus. I tried to imagine this unknown uncle and secretly admired his spunk and spirit of adventure. His name was Yakov; he was perhaps eighteen years younger than my mother and the next to last of nine siblings, all of whom reached adulthood, which used to be the exception at the turn of the century—a tribute to my grandfather's devotion, self-taught liberal education, and scientific knowledge, as a result of which none of his children succumbed to diphtheria, scarlet fever, typhus, or tuberculosis; that is, they survived each of the dreaded diseases, thanks to his care and strict quarantine policy. Yakov was the black sheep of the family, who disappeared when he was a young man. He eventually resurfaced with a wife and three children, was drafted into the army, and fought on the eastern front in World War II. Later he spent time in a German prison camp, but disappeared for good after he returned to the Soviet Union in 1945. According to family lore, he, his wife and children perished in Siberia, since returning prisoners of war were automatically classified as traitors.

I tried to follow in his footsteps just once, the summer I spent in Brittany with my mother in a rented cottage with several of my friends for whom she provided supervision, plus room and board. We were all about eleven to thirteen years old, and had permission to go to the beach on our own and down to the village square. By that time, we spoke six different languages among us; most spoke three to my two and a half; and, although everyone had learned French, we often broke up into twos and threes to speak more privately in something else. "What shall we speak?" preceded "What shall we play?" When parents came to visit, it was a Tower of Babel, with Russian, Polish, German, Italian, Latvian, and Czech. Some were proud to practice their newly learned English.

The big attraction was a traveling circus, a modest, one tent affair. We all went to watch it being set up. There were perhaps half a dozen big sturdy horses; one of the stable boys offered us a ride, and he helped us get on the horses, bareback.

So I sat on this huge horse, grabbing onto his mane for dear life as he trotted dutifully in his assigned circle, and lost my balance and fell off, landing flat on my back, smack underneath the horse. I was knocked out, the breath scared out of me, incapable of movement. Luckily, the horse had been trained for just such an event and stood stock still while friends came to my rescue and pulled me out from between his legs.

My mother had worked mightily to instill in me a sense of balance, to no avail, and with disastrous consequences. Her approach was based on the laws of physics, which were self-evident to her but a mystery to me. How to hold a plate without dropping it had to do with concave and convex surfaces, how to transport and displace heavy objects necessitated an understanding of gravity, of focal point, etc., and how to walk on a low narrow iron railing had something to do with using outstretched arms like the wings of a plane, with explanations of air flow and basic

principles of aerodynamics. I continued to drop plates, to bang into re-
volving doors, to turn faucets the wrong way (hot for cold and cold for
hot, though in Berlin, hot was always hot and cold, cold, not like in
France where one could never tell), and to fall off the low iron railings
which bordered the immaculate lawns in the small parks which dotted
our Berlin neighborhood.

But there was hope. Again I was inspired by a circus, a large circus
poster on the way to school. If the little dog in the picture could stand
on two legs on a ball, so could I! (I should have listened to Mutti's physics
lessons more carefully: the dog was very small and the ball was very big.)
I was nine years old, enrolled in the first grade of gymnasium with classmates all a year older and a head taller than me. Since nursery school, I
had been accustomed to being the very last in every line, since children
were always lined up by height, the tallest one first and the shortest one
last. I was so used to being last in line that I seldom expected to see the
object of our wait. This expectation, or rather lack of it, came in mighty
handy when I spent my days standing in line in Toulouse during summer of 1940, never knowing what people were standing in line for.

But this was 1932. Every day I counted the swastikas hanging from the
windows; there were more each week. Hitler pointed his index finger at
me, stared me in the eye from huge posters that read, "You vote for me!"
Du, the familiar form of address; I knew it meant me. We had gym that
morning, which entailed a ten-minute walk from school to a playing field
where we changed into gym clothes in a locker room to play ball. Actually, regular gym classes were held in a beautifully appointed gymnasium
in school, with ropes to climb (I never got past the second knot), horses
to jump over, parallel bars, ladders, and so on. Playing ball on the playing
field was a special weekly treat. We lined up. I was as usual at the end of
the line. There was the ball just in back of me. So I ducked behind the
line, tried my balancing act on the ball, and crashed just as the teacher
blew her whistle as a prelude to explaining the rules of the game.

There was something terribly wrong with my right arm, which was all
crumpled up; a wave of nausea and pain hit me like a hammer. Classmates' faces leaning down swam before my eyes before I lost consciousness.

"This is what happens when you disobey. Get back in line, girls. Julia,
get up; it's just a sprained wrist, don't be a crybaby. Lotte and Gisela, help
her up and wait for me in the locker room." Supported by Lotte and

Gisela (I forget their real names), I reached the locker room not daring to look at my arm, which seemed to have sprouted a second elbow going the wrong way. The girls got me into my skirt, draped my sweater over my shoulders, and I marched, or rather was marched, still last in line, the ten minutes back to school, where I collapsed and was carried to the infirmary. Mutti was called at the hospital where she worked, found me in shock with a high fever, and took me home in a taxi—a form of transportation reserved only for going to the railroad station and emergencies such as this.

Eventually, I returned to school with a cast from my upper arm to the tips of my fingers, supported in a black sling, and to all who inquired I responded cheerfully, "It's nothing; just a sprained wrist." Writing with my left hand did not come naturally; my penmanship went from A to F, and my grades in German composition, French, and history plummeted likewise.

Two or three years earlier (we had just moved to the Regensburger-strasse where I went to second grade), Mutti was inspired to remedy my lack of balance by enrolling me in a modern dance class. She was a fan of Isadora Duncan, who danced barefoot covered in the flimsiest of veils, and who created the liberated, freestyle modern dance movement. My teacher, according to what my brother told me only recently, was one of Isadora's star students. I loved the music, the rhythm, and watched in awed admiration as my classmates arched their backs to touch their heels with their heads, bent their bodies halfway round, slid down gracefully for a grand split, flitted on their bare feet like butterflies, or stumbled purposefully across the floor in a lumbering bear walk with hunched shoulders and lolling arms. One of my friends could walk on her hands as easily and gracefully as on her feet, and fold her body in two with her hair sweeping the floor behind her heels. She danced effortlessly, as if made of rubber, creating stirring figures in the air. "Why can't you dance like that?" Papa said.

That was the end of my dancing career. But I did learn to turn cartwheels, not well, and could even stand on my head, though I could never figure out how to laugh while doing this, according to the popular saying, "Was sollen wir machen? Kopfstehen und Lachen." ("What shall we do? Stand on our heads and laugh.")

So when my big cast came off and was replaced by a small one, leaving my elbow free to bend and my fingers free to write, I was so giddy with this newfound freedom that I turned cartwheels for joy down the hill of a nearby park and promptly recracked the bones of my barely healed forearm. Since my orthopedic surgeon, a kind doctor with a sense of humor, had sent me off chuckling, "This small cast should hold you for a while, young lady; just don't turn any cartwheels," I didn't dare tell Mutti until the pain became unbearable. I had been a very disobedient child.

Many years later, in the summer of 1973, I spent three weeks in Berlin courtesy of a Goethe Seminar scholarship. I happened to be lodged in a boarding house which was a huge apartment laid out exactly like the one we had lived in across from the zoo, except that the boarding house had been divided up into smaller rooms to accommodate a dozen or so seminarians. It was located not three blocks away from the Fürstin-Bismarck Gymnasium where I had played out the broken arm scenario. The building, which had survived the World War II bombing almost intact, had been turned into a textbook depository.

One day I walked down the Leipzigerstrasse toward the Ku-Damm (Kurfürstendamm) from the direction where our playing field had been, then turned right into the cross street where my erstwhile school stood. I saw an ambulance, a child on a stretcher, a small car with a blood-spattered fender, police, a small crowd, and, sitting on the curb, hunched over and sobbing, a man in his forties. People on either side were trying to comfort him. "That boy had no business crossing the street in the middle of the block!" and "Terrible! Serves him right! It's not your fault. You couldn't possibly have avoided hitting him." There was no one by the side of the stretcher comforting the child, by all accounts badly injured. I felt sick all over again, the way I did when I was marched back to that very spot with my doubly fractured arm some forty years earlier.

I also remembered Papa's lessons in city walking. Papa started taking me on city outings when I was six so I could practice reading the big letters on billboards and storefronts. Papa adjusted his pace to mine, not walking briskly without looking to see if I could keep up on my short legs, the way my big brother did. For one thing, Papa wasn't very tall himself, not quite five feet five inches; and I suspect that his shoes, chosen for style and assiduously shined every morning, were pinching him. With his thick glasses, he wended his way carefully while giving me a running commentary on architectural features of balconies, drawing my attention to the many stone heads, flower garlands, and half busts of maidens à la

Isadora Duncan which then decorated the now smooth and blandly reconstructed house façades.

Carefully, Papa came to a full stop at each perilous street crossing. "Look to the left, look to the right, cross only in the pedestrian zone, and never, never get caught in the middle of the street by a policeman. He will ask you what you are, and you are nothing. You have no nationality. You have no country. You have no passport. You are not German. But you are not anything else, either. There is no one to protect you. So if you break the law, even just a little bit, it will be very serious." Jaywalking was a traffic offense; walking on lawns with little signs that read "Keep off the grass" was also punishable; so was throwing candy wrappers into fountains, or anywhere else for that matter except into their assigned receptacles under trees and lampposts. I became very serious, concentrated on pacing my steps evenly, and looked carefully at the pavement. Papa was right. There was not a stray cigarette butt or candy wrapper anywhere.

Of all Papa's negatives, the one that stuck in my mind was: "You are nothing." Papa had neglected to add that, as far as I remember, I had no birth certificate either. So technically, I didn't exist. My birth in Moscow was always shrouded in mystery. Papa had been imprisoned from the October Revolution in 1917 until the fall of 1922, when he was released and sent into permanent exile together with some two hundred other Mensheviks. (That story was confirmed to me when I went on the obligatory visit of the state prison in Leningrad, now again St. Petersburg, which was on my tour circuit, Christmas 1974. We were told, "Only one traitor to the Communist cause chose to recant his heresy and was allowed to stay in the Soviet Union.")

I imagine that Papa's long years of sitting in prison explain why my brother is seven years older than I am. My first cousin Vladimir, who came to America some fifteen years ago, asked me point blank if it was true that I had been born in prison! "Not to my knowledge," I told him. I did recall that Aunt Mirrha—who helped Mama bring me home, wrapped, I suppose, in layers of well-washed old pillow slips, flannel remnants, and a fur blanket—had once mentioned a "straw mattress on the floor," which I assumed to be in an overcrowded hospital during the height of the famine in April 1923. No, I was not born in prison, I told my cousin, but I may have been conceived there.

My brother told me a couple of years ago that Papa named him Max because that had been Papa's assumed name when he worked for the Social Democrats in what was to become the Menshevik Party in the February Revolution of 1917. Max also told me that Mama took him to prison to visit Papa. He must have been five or six years old and was allowed to play ball in the prison yard with Papa. There was a wall all around with four guard towers, each manned by a soldier with a machine gun. His ball went awry and hit one of the guards; he remembers Papa standing transfixed, but the guard broke out in a smile instead of shooting and, with a grin, threw the ball back to the little boy. That is how my brother came to believe in his own invincibility; and he has never been afraid of anything since.

I assume that Mama had visitation rights, and when Papa was exiled to join the rest of the Mensheviks in Berlin, she found herself pregnant and decided to stay behind in Moscow until the baby was born. I wasn't supposed to be born. People were starving and dying like fleas from hunger and cold, but Mama decided to carry the pregnancy to term, with Aunt Mirrha's help, who spent her days scrounging around for food between duty hours at her kindergarten.

When we were interviewed by the American consul in Marseilles in 1940 to receive our emergency visas to the United States as political refugees, we presented our Nansen passes, identification papers issued by the League of Nations to stateless persons, and our birth certificates. My birth certificate was a hastily concocted and notarized English translation of a French translation of a nonexistent German translation of a nonexistent Russian document, declaring that my father had registered my birth in April 1923 in Moscow. Since he was then in Berlin, this could not be true. I showed this "document" (a yellowed typewritten page) to my cousin Vladimir, who laughed, "This means nothing—bureaucracy—anything will do." Mama named me Julia after Julius Martov, whom she admired very much and who played an important role in the Menshevik movement.

Consequently, when people would ask, "Who are you?" I replied truthfully, "Nothing." I was able to amend, or rather embellish, this response to my entire satisfaction after four weeks spent in England during the summer of 1935. It took me that long to learn to understand and pronounce the English I had already learned to read and write in two years of lycée in Paris. "My name is Julia Israel. I was born in Moscow. I speak German. I live in Paris. I am traveling in England." This summarized my life history concisely and accurately, and I was rewarded with accepting nods and understated smiles: "So you are a traveler! Welcome to England!" Home at last ! An elsewhere of my own choosing, with my small, sturdy brown suitcase which Mama had helped me pack, matching available space and volumes of clothing with a trained mathematician's eye. Papa had long outworn his tailor-made silk shirts. When collars and cuffs became slightly frayed, Mama would expertly recycle them into my summer wardrobe of cool, sleeveless dresses. For the occasion of this first solo trip to England, Mama made me a real summer dress from scratch, cut from a brand new piece of baby blue cotton with tiny white flowers sprinkled all over it. Wearing this dress was pure wishful thinking. I had to borrow sweaters from my host's daughter and wait until my clothes dried every morning; they were draped over a laundry rack in front of the living room fireplace to take off the morning chill and dampness.

I had organized this trip all by myself! The previous summer, when I was eleven, Papa had sent me to camp, a sort of private, self-styled summer boarding school for vacationing high school students (lycée in France starts at age eleven), mostly boys who had flunked their year-end exams and needed serious supervised coaching to catch up in the fall. The camp was located somewhere in the north of France, but since the grounds were enclosed by thick stone walls, and I was confined to the despised *poulailler,* a little yard at the very end of the garden which was reserved for the younger kids, I never saw the surroundings. My French was still pretty wobbly. The bigger boys made fun of me, teased me mercilessly, and made life thoroughly miserable. My refuge and solace was in the branches of an apple tree. One day a young lady, tall and prim, all white and pink, looked up at me and introduced herself haltingly in French worse than mine, "I'm a teacher in grammar school in Cambridge. I'm here to learn French. And who are you?" We became friends. I actually helped her with her French pronunciation! "How would you like to come to England next summer? I'll ask one of my students. They may enjoy having a paying guest from France who also speaks German." Papa came to visit on a weekend. I introduced him to my new friend, addresses were exchanged, and the following summer, 1935, I was bound for England. Mama put me on the train in Brest, near our vacation cottage in Brittany, my suitcase securely at my feet.

Papa met me at the train station in Paris. I was introduced to Rudi, a tall, ruddy young man in his early thirties who spoke a funny kind of German, all softened up with little curlicue endings that rendered objects cute and took away the sharp edges. Papa explained that Rudi was my Uncle Karl's younger brother, from Vienna. He was going to accompany me on the trip to London and deliver me to the care of my brother's Latvian schoolmate from Berlin, then a student at the University of London, who would put me on the bus to Cambridge, where my British host family would meet me.

The Channel crossing was a disaster. Seas were rough. I was seasick the whole three hours, and as a result ate nothing. I recovered somewhat on the train ride to London, but not fast enough to ask for a sandwich from a passing tray. The problem was twofold: I had no idea what those neat little packages of white bread with cucumber and tomato slices sticking out from between the edges were called, and didn't know how to say "please" in English. So food passed me by. I recall that we arrived in London early in the morning, perhaps 7 A.M., so we must have taken a night train from Paris and embarked in the wee hours in Calais.

Papa had pressed upon me a tour book of London and a short history of England, but they didn't fit into my small brown suitcase. However, my assiduous reading and rereading of the many adventures of the Three Musketeers, *Oliver Twist,* and *The Prince and the Pauper* proved to be an invaluable asset.

Rudi delivered his charge with a sigh of relief at my brother's friend's apartment and disappeared with the barest of introductions (both spoke English fluently). I was left facing a disheveled young man in boxer shorts at a total loss as to what to do with a twelve-year-old girl until 6 P.M., when he was to put me on the bus to Cambridge. "What do you speak?" he repeated in several languages until we settled on his rather halting French. Then he took my suitcase, handed me a key, scribbled his address on a slip of paper, and told me to have a look at London and return by five o'clock.

I had no idea where I was, I had no map, I understood not a word of the English bandied about me, I had eaten nothing since six o'clock the previous evening. But I was determined to "have a look at London" and started walking, turning around at every corner to make sure I would recognize landmarks on my way back. In my head, I carried an imaginary skein of yarn, which, like Homer's hero in the *Iliad,* I unwound behind me to guide me back safely through London's labyrinth of streets. A veteran of the Berlin U-Bahn system, the Paris Métro, the German double-

decker buses, the French crazy cabs and unregulated traffic (I did not accompany my California grandchildren on their exhilarating "French Taxi-
cab" bumper car ride at MGM's theme park in Las Vegas last year for
good reason), I was not a bit disoriented by having to look right before
left. I took the red double-deckers in stride and took comfort in the sight
of the antiquated black cabs with old-fashioned running boards, which
reminded me of those stationed at the Wittenbergplatz in Berlin next to
my dear horse-drawn carriages.

I saw a big square tower with a huge clock, a giant compared to the
one facing the Seine on the Left Bank at the Conciergerie in Paris. I
walked across a large, imposing square with gentlemen impeccably attired, carrying canes and briefcases, tipping their bowler hats ever so discreetly without breaking their stride when encountering an acquaintance.
The street sign read Trafalgar Square. I walked and walked until I came
to a big park where I sat on a bench. There were lots of people, not all in
well-fitted suits and bowler hats, some in wrinkled work pants and rolled
up shirt sleeves and checkered caps at a rakish angle on unkempt red hair.
They were listening to some weird characters making speeches, standing
on soap boxes. I walked some more and came to an imposing palace, perhaps as big or bigger than the Louvre, with lots of space in front of it.
People lined up to watch the changing of the guard. So did I.

It was noon. I turned around and followed my imaginary unwound
red skein to find my brother's friend's apartment. It was five minutes to
five when I rang the doorbell. I had had a good look at London, I found
out years later: Big Ben, Trafalgar Square, Hyde Park, and Buckingham
Palace, without a map or a word of English. I had found elsewhere. I was
home.

For the first four weeks I was in England, I did not speak. I relished
the orderly pace of my English host family. Joyce was a friendly young
lady, perhaps sixteen years old, who introduced me to her pets: white
mice in a cage which she was breeding for biology class in grammar
school in Cambridge. I have forgotten their family name. Her mother,
an attractive brunette with hands roughed up by years of scrubbing without a maid, was called "Ducky" by her husband, a small mustached shy
man in a blue stationmaster's uniform, whom Ducky called "Mousy." It
was truly a fabulous experience, for we lived on the second floor of a
small railway station and had free rides on whatever train stopped! Some

that did not have a regular stop at our station stopped anyway to pick us up. I even rode in the engine and got to pull the bell as we approached a crossing. It was a forty minute or so ride to Cambridge (I tried to find the village on a map when I returned to Cambridge years later), where I occasionally accompanied Joyce to school. She took me to her Latin class, where her teacher's Anglicized Latin did not sound a bit the way my French teacher had pronounced Latin in France.

We visited the university and went punting on the Cam. Then we actually hitched a ride on the train back after walking several miles on country roads.

My heroine in Germany had been Bibi, a Danish girl in a Danish book, who had lost her mother and persuaded her father, a railway engineer, to take her along on his business trips. He agreed, provided that she write reports to her teachers on everything she saw, as well as keeping up with her schoolwork. I was entranced by Bibi's many adventures discovering fabled and not-so-fabled cities, mostly in eastern Europe, and her commentaries on people's strange demeanors and costumes. Tall for her twelve years, Bibi wore pigtails, which I imagined dark like my own arrow-straight, silky brown hair. But in fact her pigtails were blond, as I discovered when I reread the book for the last time in 1933 and it had been decreed that blond was the only acceptable Aryan hair color. Bibi was totally intrepid. I tried to emulate Bibi, to put the past behind me and keep my eyes open.

Papa had insisted I help Mrs. Ducky with chores in the house. He was aware of my total incompetence when it came to housework, as Mama had given up on teaching me to pull sheets straight, dry dishes without accident, or even wash a silk blouse, concentrating instead on my medical education.

Nearly everything I know about keeping house, I learned from Mrs. Ducky, with pride, in the four weeks of my non-English-speaking silence. She let me polish the legs of the dining table with furniture wax and buff them to a shine. She showed me how to hang up sheets, towels, and pillow slips on the line without wasting clothespins, so they would billow dry in the wind, and to fold them properly, which was quite an art. She let me practice ironing. She had no electricity, only a pump outside for running water. Several small irons were heated in turn over a small oil burner (there were two of them, with some sort of a square metal box used as an oven on top when needed). Each item of clothing, even socks, underwear, and towels, not to mention tablecloths and huge, heavy linen sheets, had to be pressed simply to be dry. Eventually I graduated to Mr. Mousy's dress shirts. To this day, ironing is a chore I enjoy doing with competence and pride.

I finally opened my mouth to respond in English just as Mrs. Ducky was ready to contact a child psychologist, fearing that I was either seriously retarded or badly traumatized. From that day on, Mrs. Ducky had to concentrate on my table manners and general good form, as I broke loose, spoke out of turn, interrupted, and gave unasked-for opinions and commentaries on subjects not always deemed appropriate table conversation.

The rewards were many. A motor trip in a new 1934 Ford for a weekend at Brighton Beach where the family had rented a tent. Another weekend in a remote, ivy-clad mansion with tennis courts and vast expanses of clipped lawn for cricket and golf, courtesy of a family member who was the caretaker and did the honors of his absent master's house. A weekend in London, including a memorable theater outing with vaudeville much like the performances at the Scala in Berlin, was spent at Mr. Mousy's brother's house in one of those red brick row houses that seemed to make up most of residential London, and which was the British version of Aunt Mirrha's house in Berlin when she returned from Vienna in 1930. There were two rooms, a small parlor reserved for visits of a serious nature, and a crowded dining room downstairs, two bedrooms upstairs. Toilet facilities and a water pump were outside in a small garden.

This was my formal introduction to the Great Depression. That's what everyone talked about. Coal miners out of work. Strikes. I gathered that Mr. Mousy was a lucky exception to have kept his job at the railway station; that Mrs. Ducky was slaving away from dawn to dusk, scrubbing sheets and floors and windows single-handedly, making plum preserves, canning vegetables from her garden, taking in paying guests like me to stretch a meager salary and help out less fortunate family members.

Of Germany I said nothing. Mrs. Ducky, a well-read, well-educated woman, was not far off base when she thought me too traumatized to speak. I could not, in English, in her ordered household, break the silence with pictures no child should have witnessed, with stories told daily of wild escapes and inhuman tortures. That is how I separated German and

English and French in their watertight compartments in my head. It was
to take decades to break down the walls.

Soon after we left our vast apartment near my beloved Tiergarten, when I
was not quite three years old, we moved to a different, more modest district in Charlottenburg on the Hauptstrasse (Main Street), early in 1926.
Recently, a friend sent me a photo book of the Berlin of my childhood,
and there I found the Wittenbergplatz as I remembered it, wide and
empty, with a lovely view of the Gedächtniskirche and its intact Gothic
spire at the end of a big shopping street, with KDW (*Kaufhaus des West-
ens,* the Department Store of the West) on the corner; not the present rebuilt nondescript structure, but the finely detailed palatial building of the
turn of the century. The next page shows the same square in 1927 with a
brand new U-Bahn station taking up the better part of it. I assume that
may have been the reason for our move. The noise, commotion, and dust
of breaking up the pavement must have been nerve-shattering.

Every time we moved, my small brown suitcase was packed with great
care and I was sent elsewhere to live with an assortment of friends, all
members of the Menshevik group of Russian émigrés. I remember the
Yugows, on the far left, politically speaking that is, since Papa refused to
speak to them. They were married to each other and living together,
which seemed to be the exception to the rule. Most married people I
knew were living with someone other than their spouse. The Yugows were
childless and bestowed upon each other all the tender loving care usually
reserved for offspring. Mr. Yugow even went into the kitchen to help his
wife with tea and sandwiches! I was perfectly happy in their small two-
room apartment, perched on two phone books on a kitchen chair.

After our big move to the Hauptstrasse, Mutti started taking me out
shopping, sometimes to try on shoes or choose gifts for various birthdays,
but mostly window shopping for dresses and coats, which she sketched
in a little notebook for execution at a later date She was a good seamstress, the first to operate a sewing machine, the pedaling kind, in her native town of Shklov. The sewing machine was a gift from her aunt, the
first in the family to have married a foreigner, a tall Englishman, an engineer. They lived in Tbilisi in comparative ease and comfort and were the
source of my mother's yearly brand-new dress. So, in the tradition of
"Don't feed him a fish, teach him how to fish," my great-aunt wisely
taught my mother how to operate this great wonder of the modern age.

This was 1901; my mother was ten years old. Friends and neighbors gathered round to watch her stitch up torn pillow cases in split seconds as she practiced guiding the fabric to achieve a straight and even seam. From then on, she made all of her own clothes and those of her little sisters as well, and became a whiz at recycling outgrown coats into fashionable smaller jackets, grown-ups' faded summer skirts into children's gay frocks.

For my third winter in Berlin, Mutti made me a beautiful cinnamon-brown wool coat, buttoned up to the neck, with a soft fur collar, fur cuffs at the sleeves, and a fur muff to match. I wore beige leggings over my wool stockings to complement the outfit and a hat with fur trim to match the coat. Beige wool gloves were anchored by a string around my neck which extended through the sleeves of the coat, so the gloves wouldn't get lost. It took a good long while to get me into this outfit and once I was in it, I didn't want to get out of it. Mutti had left a huge hem at the bottom and at the end of the sleeves, so the following year the coat grew with me, with the fur trim on the cuffs riding up a short distance on the sleeves. The year after that, I was going on six and getting ready for school when I found Mutti ripping my cherished coat apart with a razor blade! She explained that she was "winterizing" my coat for a long train trip to Leningrad, where my little cousins Manya and Masha would wear it to keep warm. She showed me the quilted fabric to be used as a third interlining, very much like the quilted stuff the Chinese used to use for their regulation winter jackets.

When—in the winter of 1974—I finally met those cousins in Leningrad, they were fashionably attired in elegant mink coats, fur hats, fur muffs to match, and boots I couldn't buy for less than $200 at Bally's. I felt positively dowdy in my borrowed light gray astrakhan fur coat, mismatched with a beige rabbit fur bonnet, also borrowed, and worn brown boots hastily acquired at a garage sale before my departure from New Orleans. Masha was much smaller than I. Neither she nor her sister ever reached their full growth after years of starvation and the siege of Leningrad, and grew to only four feet ten inches tall. Masha had studied German in preparation for medical school, German being considered the language of science, so we adopted the following rule of communication: we each spoke c l e a r l y and d i s t i n c t l y, she in Russian and I in German. I repeated in German what I thought she had said in Russian, and vice versa. We embraced in the Russian fashion, with big bear hugs, and Masha laughed and pointed at her clothes: hat bought in Finland, boots in Denmark, coat in West Germany, and so on. "We have money, but the stores are empty; nothing to buy here." That evening at my Aunt Doba's apartment, Masha and Manya thanked me for my coat, the one Mutti had ripped apart and winterized for the frozen north, which they had worn for a total of six years, one sister after the other.

But now, back to the Kurfürstendamm, about 1928, holding on to Mutti's hand on her window-shopping expeditions and my first lessons in gross anatomy. Along the wide sidewalk, leaning against the buildings between doorways and display windows, were beggars, mostly wounded veterans of the Great War, with their caps beside them for throwing in pennies. Unlike the *gueules cassées* in Paris, who kept away from public view except on Armistice Day, the German veterans, no matter how gruesome their injuries, were free to beg in public. This was before the advent of routine reconstructive and plastic surgery. These men had holes where eyes should have been, faces without ears and noses, bodies without arms; young muscular men propelled themselves on little boards on wheels because there was only half of them left.

I started checking to see if I still had two eyes, two ears, a nose, and I counted my fingers. At night, I counted my toes. This is not quite accurate, since my counting skills didn't reach ten yet, but I valiantly matched five fingers on my left hand with five on my right to make sure nothing was missing. On our next shopping expedition, I told Mutti I was practicing to be blind. I closed my eyes tight to avoid the sight of sightless men, legless men, noseless men. Mutti was to say "step down" and "step up" when we came to a street crossing, and "you can open your eyes now" when it was safe. Ever since that time, I have had a tendency to close my eyes to things that shouldn't be, to stick my head in the sand. That is why I didn't want to speak Russian, to hear the endless arguments about who had been shot and who had frozen to death, and how many people starved, and how many friends had disappeared. In Papa's vocabulary, Stalin was synonymous with the devil. Famed for his oratory, Papa could hold forth about the evils of the Stalinist empire in hellish detail.

When Papa wasn't raving and ranting about Stalin and the last mysterious guests had departed his home office, he invited me to sit at his desk. There was a small typewriter chair which I loved to push around when the maid had taken up the Persian rug to beat it in the courtyard downstairs. The chair glided easily over the buffed parquet floor, and I could pretend to be somewhere else, whizzing back and forth. I always landed at the desk, climbed on the chair, and surveyed Papa's puzzling treasures. There were reams of white paper, lots of colored pencils, a ruler, and a marvelous chrome instrument to punch holes in paper. There was another metal thing that fastened papers together. There was an inked pad in a little box and little wooden blocks with handles hanging on a rack. After you pressed them on the pad, they made funny lines of writing on paper. Best of all, there was a writing machine. Papa showed me how to press on the letter keys one at a time, and, sure enough, the machine flipped the letter onto a roller which moved back and forth. Papa typed only with his forefingers.

There were beautiful leather-bound books lining the walls and a small framed oil painting of a sailboat, seen from the front, tossed about on a wild and foaming sea. I recall people calling it the flying Dutchman, which puzzled me. There was also a telephone. It was black and had to be cranked up just like a car. When there was no one in the office, Papa spoke to unseen people on the telephone.

Papa handed me small colored sheets of paper to punch holes in and let me scribble to my heart's content with an array of colored pencils.

When we moved to the Hauptstrasse, I graduated from the zoo to nursery school. My brother dragged me the half mile or so down a wide and imposing avenue. I had to run to keep up with him. I am not sure he relished the thought of being seen by potential classmates escorting his little sister to nursery school. At any rate, he got me there, dropped me off without a word, and ran. (He told me recently that he was trying to get to school on time and I wasn't walking fast enough. I never found out where he went to school.)

I eventually caught up with Max, though I always needed two steps to his one stride. He grew only a couple of inches taller than Papa, which was the average height in France for the pre–World War II generation, but he kept his small frame tuned up and tightly compact, thanks to a regime of daily exercise ingrained from our ten years in Germany. As a result, my childhood memories of my big brother are colored by his early morning exercises in front of an open window, which left me shivering in my flannel pajamas, and which he has continued all his life.

Unlike his little sister—me—Max excelled in sports: swimming, tennis, skiing, mountain climbing. My brother tried to encourage me, and since he knew no fear, he threw me into the Marne River to sink or swim my way across. I was perhaps twelve, and Max and his friend Margot had kindly let me tag along on a weekend outing not far from Paris. I managed to stay afloat, dog-paddling, flailing my arms in a valiant imitation of a breast stroke, and reached the opposite shore. A swimmer I was not. A survivor, yes.

In April 1977, we had a rare family reunion of sorts in my brother's Paris apartment on the Left Bank. It was almost like old times, with people speaking five different languages and constantly forgetting what to speak to whom except for the monolinguists who had no choice. Around Danièle's (my brother's newlywed French wife) provincial dining table sat: my brother Max; my mother—Mama, Grandma, Grossmama, Mamitchka, depending by whom and in what language she was being addressed—whom Max had escorted from her nursing home in New Jersey to Paris; my daughter Tanya, who had joined us from her home in Casablanca; Danièle's former husband, on a business trip from Tunis; Danièle's parents; my niece Tamara, Max's elder daughter, who had come from Munich; Danièle's daughter Baya, perhaps eleven years old; and me, a vagabond from New Orleans. I was full of my latest adventures in the Caribbean, a journey to Senegal, and a memorable motor trip in Morocco over the High Atlas, the route of the Casbahs on the edge of the Sahara desert in the company of Tanya's sister-in-law, Halima. Halima had acquired a commendable mastery of basic French, the teaching of which I had observed in Dakar, so that we were able to communicate within the restrictions of her French vocabulary, my Arabic being totally nil. I actually had made an attempt to learn Arabic, even mastering parts of the alphabet, but I stumbled on the different sorts of *s* sounds, couldn't roll my *r*s, didn't perceive the difference between different sorts of *t*s, and was totally defeated by raucous aspirated consonants. My grandson Réda made fun of me and told me it was hopeless. When Réda was three, in Rabat, I had to rely on him to be my guide and interpreter. We were caught once at the top of his street, which ended on a roundabout facing the palace walls. There was a huge crowd gathered around what I assumed to be the king's honor guard, who were wearing marvelous white capes and mounted on shining black horses. Police were keeping the people back; and there was me, Réda on my shoulders, desperately wanting to know what was going on! "C'est le roi!" my little grandson whispered in my ear, "The king!" I was too short to see anything, Moroccans are quite tall, but Réda apparently had seen.

Each morning I took Réda by the hand to go down the street, through the Bab Er-Rouah, a southern gate that opened on the road to Casablanca. We went to sit in a little park on the other side of the medieval, crenelated wall. Most women—except perhaps secretaries in embassies and fashionable women tending high-class boutiques on Boulevard Mohammed V, which runs from the palace walls to the old medina, the old inner city within its own walled enclosure—still wore the djellaba, a loose outer garment with a hood attached. A veil covered their face, tied around the back of the head underneath the hood, so that only their eyes, heavily lined with kohl, remained visible. (I was reminded of my first day teaching at Ursuline Academy in New Orleans and being confused by the nuns, who still wore their habits as depicted in the famous painting of the Ursulines' landing in New Orleans in 1726. Like Moroccan women, they revealed only their eyes, minus the makeup, and a small part of their face to the outer world. All recognition had to be focused on the expression of those eyes!)

So when Réda let go of my hand, ran ahead, and jumped into the lap of a woman seated on a bench, who proceeded to enfold him in her voluminous, black-clad embrace, her eyes twinkling, I was in shock! Who was she, and how did Réda recognize her? Réda must have made some sort of introduction, telling her I was his American grandma, for she invited me to sit next to her and her eyes smiled at me. Eventually, after Réda's playtime in the sandbox, we returned home where the mystery was solved: the woman was a relative of a relative who occasionally babysat when Tanya's maid was not available.

So now we were gathered around Danièle's dinner table, food being brought in course by course, so that the menu remained a mystery to the very end. Much to my shame and in keeping with my disinterest in matters of the palate, I have not the slightest recollection of what was being served, though it must have been delicious judging by Monsieur and Madame Guillot's reaction. They are Danièle's parents, expert gourmet cooks and fine judges of the finest of French cuisine.

All of this had to be retold in German for Tamara, whose French was not very good then, and in Russian for my mother, since her efforts at mastering English had taken precedence over remembering French. All of this had to be translated into French for Danièle's parents' benefit, with Tamara interrupting to remind me that I was speaking French instead of German, and Danièle that I was speaking English instead of French, at which point Tanya and Baya's father decided to try out their respective Arabic—hers, Moroccan, his, Tunisian—which left the rest of the guests speechless.

The doorbell rang; Max went down the hall and returned mumbling something about an unexpected visit from a gentleman from Rome, as a result of which he had to prepare to leave for Italy on an urgent matter— all of my brother's affairs being urgent, mysterious, and classified. I envied my brother the huge maps lining his Paris office with little pins stuck all over them. My tiny study wall was too small for a big map. I had to keep a map in my head and repeat periodically the list of family members spread out over four continents, since keeping track of my family's whereabouts has turned out to be a major project.

My children always laugh. Tanya kids me, "You've been packing up your house since the day you bought it," and my son Carl—who managed to survive the sixties square and straight while his classmates totaled cars, succumbed to drugs, married and divorced—had to deal with his mother gallivanting around the world on a shoestring budget with a succession of brown carry-on bags, which had replaced my initial suitcase. I packed my last one for its last trip when I flew to Orléans to see Danièle's new grandson, Valentin.

In June 1996, in Paris, I had an hour's tour of Orly Airport, via freight elevator into the nether regions, bypassing custom and passport lines and escalators. Whizzed around by an unseen attendant, I picked up two blind hitchhikers who held onto my wheelchair, a middle-aged Algerian couple. I recalled how struck I had been by the comparative health of Algerians when we drove from Rabat to Tunis in 1971: no children with bowed legs, no protruding bellies, adults with all their teeth, far fewer blind people than in Morocco. Typically, a blind person would be led by a small boy, his hand on the boy's shoulder. I was fascinated when visiting the Hassan Tower in Rabat (remnants of a twelfth-century mosque) to see a young blind man walking surefooted around the retaining wall of the top of the tower, his hand on a young boy's shoulder. The boy gave him a running commentary on the sights he could not see! There was a poor blind man in Tanya's neighborhood who carried a poor cripple on his shoulders; thus the legless had legs and the blind had eyes, and the two were an inseparable pair.

For once my passport, Schueler, United States of America, born in Moscow, worked like a charm! Algerian border police saluted with a smile; some even tried out a few words of high school Russian. My son-in-law's name had a familiar ring; at any rate, whenever there was a glitch—reservations, border control—Ahmed started talking, and after a short time the problem was solved with smiles all around.

Réda, who was a year old, seated in his car seat next to me in the back, was a big attraction everywhere we stopped in Algeria. He had his father's looks, but a headful of loose blond curls and light eyes to match. Ahmed proudly carried his blond son on his shoulders, took care of having the kitchen help properly sterilize and heat his milk, did the necessary marketing for baby food where available and for bananas, crackers, and yogurt, always a safe standby. On the beach, he let Réda crawl without restriction. I was terrified that my grandson could be swept up by the rising surf with just a few pushes in the wrong direction, but it didn't happen. As Ahmed pointed out, Réda crawled around within the shadow of our beach umbrella, carefully retrieving a hand or a foot when they accidentally strayed into the searing sunlight.

Algeria looked spartan compared to laid-back Morocco. While fancy French villas on the seashore were dilapidated ruins, there were solid two-room structures of cement brick for every family in the countryside, a big improvement over the *bidonvilles* (shantytowns) on the outskirts of Casablanca. Everyone wore sandals or some sort of footwear; men swept the streets clean and did the marketing, since women in the countryside and small towns were heavily veiled in black shrouds called haiks with only one eye peeping out, and were not to be seen in public. Mao's little red book was prominently displayed in every stationery store. We all agreed, Tanya, Ahmed, and I: Algerians were the Prussians of North Africa.

There were no luxury hotels. Ahmed simply asked for "the best hotel," which turned out to be a drab affair, not unlike those Carl and I had experienced in East Germany two years earlier. So we were relieved to cross the border into Tunisia, with its smiling green verdant hills and laughing children, who turned out to be professional beggars and kept us hostage until Ahmed dealt with them, kidding and joking, with a few coins tossed in, I supposed.

My recollection of the drive from the Algerian/Tunisian border into the whitewashed bustling capital city, Tunis, consists of sharp twists and turns which threw me into Réda's car seat (not today's sturdy regulation affair, just a flimsy canvas seat on a light frame to keep a baby comfortable). Lurching from side to side, I held on to an open jar of baby food which I tried to feed Réda on the smooth stretches between descending hairpin curves.

We stopped on a palm-lined French-style avenue, crowded with busy shoppers, elegantly dressed business men, tourists in gay attire, and traditionally garbed Tunisian women enveloped in their white haiks to mid-calf, their small feet tapping, dancing along the pavement in high-heeled platform sandals, polished, manicured, and daintily stained with lace filigrees of red henna. With one hand they coyly retained the haik diagonally over their face, holding onto a small child with the other, and managed to look poised, regal, and infinitely charming.

Ahmed invited us to sit down at a fashionable café. We had an unimpaired view of the street scene, of the neutral ground planted in lush beds of gladiola, hibiscus in full bloom, and the white jasmine of lyric poems. As coffee was served, there was a sudden commotion: in front of us, on the sidewalk, a young man was seized by police and thrown unceremoniously into a blue wagon; a few young men tried to protest, were beaten; and as I opened my mouth to speak, half out of my seat, Ahmed calmly pushed me down. "Sit down. Nothing happened."

A brutal beating had turned into a nonevent.

I closed my eyes. I was nine years old. I was walking to school in Berlin in 1933, a few days after Hitler's posters had worked their charm, and he had been elected by a plurality of the German people. A year earlier, in grade school, my little schoolmates had been so proud in their Hitler Youth uniforms, demonstrating the many uses of their regulation knives. How I envied them trailing along long marches through the city, singing the "Horst Wessel Lied" (*"die Fahne hoch, die Reihen fest geschlossen, S.A. marschiert . . ."*), which brought tears to my eyes, as their fathers goosestepped in front of the line, heads held high, right arms extended in fervent Heil Hitler salutes which echoed from the houses on either side. And I was nothing. I wasn't German. I wasn't anything else. My teacher had said so. Sometime after my arm healed and I could use my right hand again, we had been given a list of foreign French words never to be used again. There was a piggy bank prominently displayed on Teacher's desk. Each time we said *Hotel* or *Telefon* or *Restaurant* or *Auto*, we had to march up front in full view of the class and put a penny into the piggy bank. Thus the German language was effectively purified in a span of two months. Teacher was sometimes caught saying nasty French words and had to put in her share of pennies, too. We learned to say things like *Fernsprecherapparat* and *Kraftwagen,* and were told to wear our swastika lapel pins. One day Teacher called on me. I had to leave my seat at the very back of the class and march up to her desk in front. "Julia, you don't have to be afraid. Class, Julia is not German. She has no country. She was born in Moscow. She is a refugee. [*Flüchtling,* 'refugee' in German, sounds much more ominous; rather like 'escapee,' someone taking flight, not someone seeking refuge.] Go sit down." And since I wasn't German or anything else either, I was officially dispensed from wearing my swastika pin.

A week later, as I turned the corner past the bakery with the fancy green-tiled walls, I saw red puddles on the pavement and lots of broken glass. The walls were streaked with red painted words, *Juda Verecke,* which I didn't quite understand except that they were despicable words calling for someone's death. All the shop windows had been smashed; all the fine clothes torn and strewn about. On the opposite side of the Olivaerplatz, as in a dreamy, slow-motion film sequence, brown-shirted Nazis were beating and stomping on a white-haired gentleman. That's what those red puddles were that I was trying not to step in: they were blood. For one long block, all the way to the Kurfürstendamm, I threaded my way between shards of glass and torn clothes and bloodied sidewalk; then I ran the rest of the way to school, up the stairs, to Teacher's desk. "All the glass is broken, all the stores are broken, there is blood on the street, and they are beating and stomping on an old gentleman!" I was out of breath; I was trembling; my orderly world had collapsed around me.

"Julia, pull yourself together and sit down. Nothing has happened. You saw nothing."

"But . . ."

"Sit down."

I sat down. When I got home after school and told Mutti, she said, "Don't speak to anyone. Not even our nice neighbors on the ground floor. Not your best friend at school. You have seen nothing."

"But I did! I did."

"No," Mutti said. "You must remember that you did not see it."

This, for me, was *Kristallnacht,* and I did see it. With my own eyes. Not in 1938. In March 1933. After that, there were rumors at school. Our sewing teacher was sick and never came back. Our art teacher disappeared. Everywhere, people disappeared, and friendly neighbors no longer smiled, and Papa and Mutti stopped speaking when I came into the room, even in Russian. "Not now. She can understand. Later."

Papa had taken me (was it shortly before or after my *Kristallnacht?*) to a big rally near the Reichstag. Hitler was to speak in person. All around a big square, buildings were draped from top to bottom in long flowing swastika flags. It was dark—night falls early in Berlin—and the square was lit with theatrical torch lights, a magnificent spectacle. S.A. and S.S. troops lined the podium. Papa stood in the back of the crowd and hoisted me on his shoulders; he probably couldn't see anything because he was too short, but I could. "Sieg Heil! Heil Hitler!" shouted the well-disciplined crowd. "Sieg Heil, Heil Hitler!" they chanted in unison as an unremarkable, mustached man in a brown uniform ascended the podium. He stood, he turned his head from left to right, stilling the crowd with his intense and mesmerizing glare, his right hand extended in his own salute. Then he started to speak, softly at first, then in rising crescendo, then down to a whisper, then exploding into a fury, and the crowd stood, not moving, held in awe, convinced, hypnotized.

That week, I got hold of Hitler's *Mein Kampf,* and since Hitler was no great writer and his book was written for everyone to understand at an eighth-grade reading level, I was able to read through it with ease. (I was in the fifth grade, but had already read a whole slew of Dickens, my favorite Bibi travel book, and the German equivalent of Nancy Drew stories.)

"Look, Mutti. He writes he is going to kill all the Jews!"

"That's just a figure of speech. Don't believe everything you read in a book."

But what else was I supposed to think?

And Papa ranted and raved about Stalin, the very devil, and Hitler being his best pupil.

The previous summer, my last summer in Germany, 1932, Mama had sent me elsewhere. Elsewhere with another of our little friends to stay with his teacher in a small town, perhaps an hour's drive from Berlin. His teacher was a young lady with a young husband and a beautiful German shepherd dog chained to a very long chain in their garden.

We were served healthy meals at precisely regular hours, were taught how to dry the dishes, and were invited to watch the dog—I forget his name—being fed. This dog was a recent acquisition, and apparently so homesick for his former owners that he howled all night and tried desperately to jump over the six-foot-high, chain-link gate. Eventually, he let me pet him and even feed him. It was the highlight of my day. Mutti had never allowed any animals in our succession of apartments.

We had moved again, from the spacious grand apartment on the Regensburgerstrasse where Mutti, due to Papa's reduced finances, rented out a large front room to a young Austrian university student and a tiny back room with a piano to an aspiring young lady concert pianist. I believe my brother slept in the minuscule maid's room next to the kitchen, and I occupied a strangely shaped room next to the bathroom; it seemed rectangular, with a wedge cut out of it, and a pattern of wildflowers climbed all over the wallpaper.

Mutti was trying to get along with only one maid, who also did the daily marketing and cooking. As a result, Mutti pitched in to sand the parquet floors or occasionally pluck a chicken. Needless to say, due to the lack of help, mealtimes were disastrous, with nothing arriving on the dining table on time or in the right sequence. The gentlemen retired to smoke in a smoke-filled room, which was no figure of speech. When I visited Papa in his office the following day after school, I had to cough my way to his desk in spite of the German wide-open window policy, which Mutti had adopted with great relish, no matter how freezing the temperature outside and how low on coal the fancy tile oven inside.

From these quite elegant quarters, we had moved to the Xantnerstrasse near the Olivaerplatz. (I found the restored façade of a house like ours in 1991, when I realized that the Kaiserallee had not completely disappeared after all, but had been rebuilt and renamed Bundesallee; of the neighboring street where my elementary school had stood, I found not a trace.) It was a truly modest affair, with five small rooms, no office, no gentleman's room, a living-dining room combination, and no help. There were no formal dinner parties. Mutti made jello and chocolate pudding. We ate a lot of mashed potatoes, frankfurters, and meatballs, with the occasional Russian borscht and stuffed cabbage—which was fine with me, but not with Papa.

The teacher lady's house in the country was even smaller than our apartment, but it was bright, with simple painted furniture, spotless windows covered by spotless white curtains, and an inviting, very neatly trimmed vegetable and flower garden.

We were not allowed to play outside, nor go down the main street to the town center closer to the railroad tracks, because of the "rowdies." I assumed they were the usual young men hanging out in beer parlors, but every time that part of town was mentioned, our hosts would frown and glance at each other with that "not in front of the children" look, and we felt the uneasiness of unspoken fear.

One night, the dog wouldn't stop howling. In the morning he was found half-strangled by his chain, hanging on the other side of the fence. He was nursed back to health with tender loving care, and I was actually deputized to dispense regular stroking sessions, softly petting his lovely gray coat.

"How would you like to ride in a moving van to Berlin?" the teacher lady asked one day. Oh, yes! Would I! This was better than Bibi riding on the train! This was a wild and true adventure. "My husband's cousin needs to move some furniture in his van, and we both need to visit some relatives while you are gone. I'll fix some sandwiches to take along, a thermos, and some fruit. But you must promise not to ask questions, no matter what happens. There are some real rough rowdies down by the tracks, the brown shirts. Just sit quietly next to the driver and watch the road."

I did. I sat in front, in the cab, between the driver and his helper, as straight as I could, and craned my neck to glimpse the road. The two young men, dressed in neat working clothes, their shirt sleeves rolled up, exchanged light banter in the local dialect, peppered with slang, so I had a hard time following their conversation. It was something about those ruffians giving themselves airs ever since they strutted around in their brown shirts. And Lisel's boy joining them, you'd think he had more sense than that, and Lisel afraid of her own son! Getting into fights, and the police standing by doing nothing.

Their conversation reminded me of second grade, when one boy snitched on another. All the boys in the class would beat him up at recess, while the yard supervisor just stood by, doing nothing. This was the traditional class beating meant to instill a fierce lifelong sense of loyalty and class spirit, as all the boys moved from grade to grade in the same class. The girls watched, and the victim, often severely injured, tried his best to stifle his screams. After that, he never ever snitched again.

When we moved to the Regensburgerstrasse, I attended a fine coed school, except that the boys all sat on benches on the left side of the classroom, and the girls on the right, and I sat in the last row, being the smallest in the second grade. Almost all of my classmates, being born five years after the Great War, had fathers at home, whereas my brother's classmates often had none. I am not sure that this was always to their advantage.

Our teacher was a tall, monocled, straight-backed veteran sporting a saber scar on his cheek and missing a finger, who kept the class spellbound with stories of recent and ancient history. He had a cane, a six-foot bamboo cane, standing in the corner in front of the class. After one or two beatings administered to hapless boys who had not turned in their homework, or who were folding paper airplanes underneath their desk tops or whispering when he talked, he only needed to glance at the cane to achieve perfect discipline.

The beating was an expected ceremony. The culprit, shivering with fear and wetting his pants, had to walk the gauntlet between the boys on the left and the girls on the right. In front of the class, he had to pull down his pants and bare his buttocks. The teacher proceeded to give him three, five, or ten strokes with the cane, expertly aimed, depending on the severity of the offense. The child, barely seven or eight years old, dared not scream in front of the girls; the girls, often the actual culprits, having egged the boy on to misbehave in the first place, had to suffer the humiliating spectacle.

Limping and whimpering, the child went home, terrified. I hoped his mother would dry his tears, tend to the bloody welts, and hide them from his father. If his father found out, he would give the boy another beating, *Ohrfeigen,* which are hard slaps on the ears, right, then left for good measure, and which often injured the eardrums. My classmates would boast of the beatings they got at home. They would embellish them: "My *Vati* is bigger than yours! He beats me harder!" since that was the expected punishment for the most imaginative of practical jokes or for fearless disobedience. I have often thought that only a generation of grossly abused boys could have grown up to revenge themselves by committing unspeakable horrors during the Nazi period.

So I closed my eyes on this fine day of summer, 1932, rolling along toward the outskirts of Berlin, trying to block out the talk about brown shirts, for it was very confusing. The smallest fellows in my fourth grade class had suddenly increased their standing among their peers by bragging about their father's gun, by wearing their own miniature version of the Nazi youth uniform on special occasions, and by demonstrating the many uses of their priceless knives. They were German; they would defend their fatherland; they would be strong.

When we moved to the Xantnerstrasse, I was still in fourth grade. I walked to and from school along the Pariserstrasse, a good mile and a half stretch. I counted flags. At first there was just a sprinkling, but each day a few more swastikas fluttered from the balconies. By the time I jumped a grade (big mistake) and was entered into the *Sexta,* or sixth grade, of the Kurfürstin Bismarck Gymnasium near the Kurfürstendamm, I had lost count; they fluttered from almost every balcony and window. Those that were flagless were suspect. The new school year started after Easter, so this must have been April 1932.

Geography was not my best subject. I struggled mightily to deal with a round earth that had people walking upside down in the New World, the result of Mutti's attempts at teaching me about gravity. In school, all the German rivers flowed up on the map, totally defying their natural inclination. Paris was practically off the map altogether.

I knew about Paris because Papa loved it. He had gone there many times by train, which was always a big occasion, because we took a real taxi to take him to the station, and he always brought back smart, elegant presents. For me, it was inevitably a silk dress, totally unsuitable for anything except having my picture taken, as I was not allowed to play in it, was afraid to crease it by sitting in it, and certainly did not dare eat anything while wearing it.

Rome was not on the map at all; it was too far south, but Papa loved Rome even more than Paris and told enchanting stories about oranges and lemons growing on trees, quoting Goethe about "the land where lemons bloom," and promising to take me there. Another omen? Fred took our family to Rome on a Fulbright in 1953, and even though Italy had not yet recovered from the scars of war, Papa's fantasies proved real.

I opened my eyes as we were rolling along a stretch of road lined by *Schräbergärten,* garden plots on the outskirts of Berlin where apartment dwellers could spend their weekends happily digging in the moist black loam, each garden dotted with a substantial shed for keeping tools. We were rolling along streets lined with modest apartment houses, tenements with blank walls, blind windows staring out unlit, unadorned with balconies or flower boxes; a section of the city that was foreign to me. Eventually we stopped. My young escorts leaped from the cab, installed a ramp, and moved heavy pieces of furniture while I watched, contentedly munching on my midmorning sandwich. They leaped back, glowing, in high spirits, invigorated by the hard physical labor. "Arbeit macht frei!" ("Work makes one free!") was a pretty good slogan, I thought. It certainly hit the spot where these two young men were concerned. Money in their pockets and plans to spend it were detailed with relish all the way back to my teacher host's house in the country.

There, tragedy had struck! The dog had made one final successful leap across the gate, pulling the chain from its mooring. He had run ten or so kilometers, dragging that enormous chain, all the way back to his previous owners. They returned him, bleeding and exhausted, the next evening. He was welcomed with hot chicken soup, fine smooth knuckle-bones, and lots of petting, but henceforth was confined by a short chain close to his comfortable doghouse. It really was a neat little house, with a pitched roof. I thought it would be quite suitable for a little girl as well. At nine, I was about the size of a normal German six year old. When I rode the trolley car, my head didn't reach the windowpane set in the upper part of the sliding door that separated the "standees" on the back platform from the privileged people seated in the interior of the tram. As a result, I didn't have to pay any fare because the *Schaffner* (ticket dispenser) couldn't see through the window and little kids rode for free. I also never sat, not only in the sense Papa used the word with pride, that is, spent time in prison as a political enemy of the state, but quite literally. I never got to sit down in buses, in the subway, in trolleys, or in trains, where I delighted in using the luggage net above the passengers seated in eight-person compartments as a comfortable hammock. Once I rolled over the edge onto the lap of an astonished gentleman. Grown-ups sat and little kids stood when there weren't enough seats, which there never were. I got so used to it that I automatically stood up in the bus when I spent three weeks in Berlin in 1973, forgetting I was now a fifty-year-old matron and a grandmother besides, with short graying hair. As a middle-aged *Hausfrau* approached to take the only remaining seat, I had just enough presence of mind to get even for all those years of not sitting down: "Excuse me, I'm older!" And I finally sat down for good.

I can't remember the name of the dog; we referred to him simply as Dog. I gave Dog a last good-bye hug and returned to Berlin, to serious learning: French, geography, history, German grammar and composition, singing, sewing, and art. My parents were unable to help me with any of my homework; I was the one asked to correct their grammar and pronunciation. Mutti's was pretty good, but Papa's was hopeless. In return, my parents undertook some serious educational programs of their own.

Papa attempted to introduce me to the world of finance. For the occasion, I was dressed up in my best Parisian outfit, brown Mary Jane shoes, knee socks, Chesterfield coat, felt hat, and gloves to match. We walked down the Kurfürstendamm, Unter den Linden, and other imposing avenues. Papa would drag me into enormous colonnaded bank buildings, where I could not see the tops of the counters, and try to explain transactions such as checking and saving accounts at a time when I was just trying to keep my change straight and was pretty proud of having mastered the decimal system. My personal finances consisted of figuring out the number of *Negerküsse* I could buy by not reaching the window in ten trolley car rides and saving the car fares. *Negerküsse* is a no-no word today, I'm sure, but that is what chocolate-covered marshmallow cakes were called, and I was very fond of them.

Papa's forays into art history and architecture were more successful, if very trying and exhausting. I kept up the pace of two-hour museum visits because there was a reward at the end: either a walk in my beloved Tiergarten or a visit to a fine pastry shop, where I had hot chocolate topped with mounds of whipped cream and my choice of truly yummy dessert cake.

We saw Egyptian and Mesopotamian temples in the Pergamon Museum. We visited palaces. Papa pointed out features of clothing in Renaissance paintings, details of baroque furnishings, decorative motifs on the finest porcelains. Mostly he stood and admired, whether it was a statue of some elder statesman in a park, or a young stone maiden perpetually pouring water from a jug into a fountain, or simply some sophisticated young ladies in the latest flapper styles showing off their dimpled knees when I was six years old, or their long midcalf clinging skirts when I was nine.

Meanwhile, Mutti continued my medical education, which had disastrous effects on my appetite and which Papa remedied by the rewards noted above, unknown but perhaps suspected by his nutrition-minded spouse.

I particularly recall my first traumatic lesson. Mutti called me to the kitchen when we were living in the Hauptstrasse, the kitchen being strictly forbidden territory, to observe her expert dissection of a chicken. The chicken had already been plucked by the cook; its head had been chopped off, and it was safely quite dead. Mutti slit open its abdominal cavity and retrieved a gruesome small bluish sac, which she neatly sliced open along a natural sort of seam. "You see all this gravel that this chicken swallowed with its food? This is the chicken's stomach, and you have a stomach like that also. We all do. That is where the food goes to be digested. Isn't that interesting? Look how the food reaches the stomach through this tube." I stared at the mess of the emptied chicken stomach and lost my appetite at the thought of what would happen to those lovely pastries Papa had treated me to. For one thing, my bites of food were much too big to get through that tube, and certainly that tiny stomach couldn't hold what I was supposed to eat for lunch, which was the big meal of the day. I had graduated to the dining table with the grown-ups, seated on two telephone books, bravely recalling my chimpanzee lessons on properly holding fork and spoon. The more I thought about the chicken stomach ("gizzard" in German is plain "stomach"), the more the food I ate seemed to get stuck on the way down, until I gagged and had to be excused. Mutti had neglected to inform me of the concept of relativity, or proportionate size and ratio, so that I literally believed I had a stomach the size of a chicken gizzard until I grew older.

I had a second lesson in anatomy. Again, Mutti's cheerful voice of discovery from the kitchen: "Come look at this rabbit!" I loved rabbit stew. I still do, and was able to purchase a rabbit on special order at our local meat market as recently as twenty years ago. Again, the rabbit was totally sanitized. It had been expertly skinned by the cook and now lay on a marble slab on the kitchen table. I should have paid closer attention; it would have helped a lot in my pre-med course on the anatomy of the rabbit.

Briefly, Mutti proceeded to dissect the rabbit to reveal its skeleton. Lo and behold, I too had just such bones in my hands, arms, and legs. That was how I could stand up and walk. Yes, Mutti showed me the spine. We all had one. Just like this rabbit. At the thought of those delicate, tiny rabbit bones in my arms and legs, I slouched, bewildered, back to the dining room. When the rabbit, in its culinary final grand entrée, was triumphantly carried to the table on a large porcelain platter, I shrank and slumped some more. How could that tiny spine keep my head up straight? How did our dinner guests all sit up, seemingly oblivious to the presence of bones and spine inside their bodies? I developed x-ray eyes.

(Mutti had explained the wonders of the Roentgen machine, into which she did not allow me to stick my feet when trying on shoes, because the long-term effects of frequent exposure to those magic rays were yet unknown.) From then on, I walked around trying to figure out how spine and bones all fit together inside the solid flesh of people around me. I lived in a perpetual sort of horror movie, where my best friends were reduced to Halloween skeletons. As I ate less and less, Mutti grumbled, "nothing but skin and bones." I would touch my left arm with my right: Mutti was right! My skinny arm was nothing but skin and bones. As in one of the gruesome stories of *Struwelpeter,* which my parents didn't know that my nanny had read to me, I would get thinner and thinner and melt down to nothing, a little puddle that once had been a healthy little girl.

My third lesson was breathing. Again, the call from the kitchen: this must have been in the Regensburgerstrasse. I was perhaps eight; skinny, but not melted down yet. On the marble slab atop the kitchen table lay a beautiful big fish, perhaps a carp. It was at least fifteen inches long and still breathing, rather, gasping for air, as it had been bought alive from a fish tank at the open market barely ten minutes earlier. Mutti proceeded to show me the gills, and explained how water went in and out to provide the fish with life-giving oxygen. I didn't have gills, I had lungs, hidden somewhere in my chest cavity, and I could breathe in and out through my nose and/or mouth (preferably the former), just like this shimmering fish was trying to do with his gills. The result of this breathing lesson was that I got my ears confused with the fish's gills and, since sound was unquestionably borne on some of Mutti's invisible magic waves through the invisible air we breathed, I found it much more comforting to think of music supplying me with "life-giving oxygen." But what happened when the music stopped? Simple. One hummed a little song, just like Pooh the Bear. I knew a large repertory of German folk songs, and when they gave out, I made up my own. Humming has become a lifelong habit of which I am quite unaware, as my California grandchildren constantly remind me to quit humming. I do not sing well and barely keep in tune. However, I was taking piano lessons from a liberated young Russian lady from St. Petersburg, who danced about stark naked in her modern, streamlined, sunlit apartment for the healthy benefits of nudism to the mind and body acquired during a recent Swedish interlude. She did put on a splashy Japanese kimono as she sat next to me on the piano bench. She spoke only a little German in strong Russian cadences, and gave me a fine grounding in music appreciation. When she returned to her beloved St. Petersburg, by then Leningrad, she was never heard of again. The golden Venice of the north, which matched her rich, clarion voice ringing with thrilling *r*s, softly muted *sh*s and *tch*s and *shch*s on a rising and ebbing tide of sound, swallowed her up.

I remembered the day my Aunt Mirrha arrived from Moscow with her Viennese husband, Karl, who was nicknamed "Handsome," *Der Hübsche.* We still lived in the Hauptstrasse. I had just started first grade, a week or so after my sixth birthday. I knew no relatives other than Mutti, Papa, and my brother Max. No grandparents came to visit me from the country, no aunts, uncles, or cousins from out of town. I refused to call our grown-up friends "Auntie" or "Uncle," which was very impolite, so when Mutti introduced her sister, younger by ten years, laughing and jolly in a huge loose garment which defied description, something one would not offer to a bag lady, as my real flesh and blood aunt, I tried to put my arms around her tremendously swollen belly, which kicked me right back! Mirrha explained that there was a baby growing in her belly, which would be my very own cousin. Since she spoke not a word of German, I hung onto her every word of Russian, with Uncle Karl coming to my rescue to avoid the direst of misunderstandings.

They left within a week for Uncle Karl's native Vienna, just in time for baby's birth; my cousin, Joseph Polzer, was named after my deceased grandfather in Moscow, whom I tried valiantly to imagine floating as a little angel behind every cloud. Mutti had cried as we were sitting on a bench in our favorite park a year or so earlier, interrupting her usual observations about drunks who in fact might be diabetics, rosy-cheeked maidens who in fact might be suffering from consumption, children with enlarged heads who would never learn to read, and children with matchstick legs who would never walk again. Mutti cried and talked about her father, my grandpapa, who was dead. She cried and cried. That night, I had nightmares about Mutti being a little doll that I had to lead by the hand, instead of trotting bravely by her side on our rare communal shopping trips. Somehow, I felt she had never meant to leave Moscow, her work, colleagues, and family, and that she had done so only to follow Papa into temporary exile, for the Mensheviks fervently believed in the rapid collapse of the Soviet regime. She was homesick, and I cried with her for the country and family she had lost and I had never known.

Mutti was apolitical, a true socialist who believed in "sharing the wealth," which she interpreted in a literal fashion. Most of her family had followed the new regime and were either Party members in good standing or were convinced that Stalin's five-year plans would eventually put an end to famine and economic distress. Only lately, when Papa's cousins emigrated to the United States, was I struck by the irony that the family whom he had left behind never suffered from political persecution and actually had prospered by Soviet standards, while Mama's family was decimated with the proverbial knocks on the door at night, deaths in the Gulag, famine, disease, and war—all too familiar and, as I learned on my visit to Leningrad, run-of-the-mill Soviet experience.

Karl Polzer, my cousin's eldest son, named after his grandfather, my Viennese Uncle Karl the Handsome, sat on my couch some time ago and solved the puzzle. It appears that his grandfather Karl, sent to the USSR in 1927 as a delegate of a printers' labor union and a dyed-in-the-wool Trotskyite, was soon disillusioned with the stark realities of the Soviet regime. True to his free and democratic upbringing in post–World War I Austria, he did not hesitate to say so in his precise, academically correct, and laboriously acquired Russian. He landed in prison—whether before or after he met my Aunt Mirrha at a celebrated dance at a Black Sea resort in the Crimea is not clear to me. According to family lore—Aunt Mirrha's richly embellished and theatrically rendered accounts—he was released and permitted to leave the "paradise of workers" with his new and very pregnant bride under the most suspect of conditions, one result of which was the series of tragedies that struck Mama's family out of the blue.

When we moved to the Regensburgerstrasse I was sent elsewhere with my little brown suitcase, to stay with friends named Wittenberg, like the Wittenbergplatz near the zoo, after the city of Wittenberg, which evoked foul weather as much as the Regensburgerstrasse evoked rain. The Wittenbergs lived in a sumptuous, richly furnished apartment, covered with vast expanses of precious Persian rugs. They had a concert-sized grand piano as well as a smaller upright piano for their eldest daughter, a concert pianist. Mr. Wittenberg was a jolly round man with a crown of graying hair who seemingly wrote letters to everyone in the whole world. He spoke an artificial language called Esperanto, the language of hope, which he believed would unite mankind, establish a universal means of communication, and guarantee global peace and friendship forever. He also wrote a newspaper in Esperanto, and carefully tore off the stamps from the letters he received from every country imaginable and put them in a little box on his enormous desk.

The Wittenbergs had a younger daughter, a serious student in mathematics, totally devoid of any teenage interests suitable to her age, and a little boy, three-year-old Alexander, who was to be my companion on our daily playground outings under the watchful eye of his nanny. Alexander possessed both a brand-new tricycle and a brand-new red fire engine with a seat and pedals, which put him in the enviable predicament of not being able to drive or ride both vehicles at the same time. The solution to me was obvious—Alexander would ride his tricycle and I, being six going on seven, could comfortably squeeze into the fire engine, which was designed for the average German child of four. No such luck. Alexander was adamant. This was his fire engine. If I wanted one, I only had to ask Father Christmas to bring me one, just like he had done. "I don't believe in Father Christmas. There is no such thing. That's just a fairy tale for little kids like you," I told him.

Well, I was wrong. Children need to believe, they need to learn to ask, which I never did, to my great sorrow. Never did it occur to me that something I very much wanted was there for the asking. My solution was to quit wanting it, for what was the use if there was no money to buy it? It took me a lifetime to learn to ask. The rewards in friendship, in closeness to my far-flung family, in the smiles and laughter of casual acquaintances, in the forthcoming help from people I depend upon for the simplest of favors—handing me a cup, posting a letter, guiding my faltering steps—have made up for the years of self-imposed denial.

Some twenty years ago, I ran into one of my former French students, now a successful lawyer. I barely recognized the self-assured young woman as the troubled teenager I had known, until she bubbled over in her inimitable fashion, "You know, I never forgot that red fire engine you rode in. Your stories were super!"

"I'm sorry," I answered. "I never rode a fire engine. I rode a big bus in Paris, but it was green, and I fell off the back steps as it drove away. Perhaps you misunderstood."

"No," she replied firmly. "You told us a story about a red fire engine." She was right. Alexander's fire engine had become a Christmas tradition, my very own version of "there is a Santa Claus." I told the story to countless classes in French and German during some twenty years of teaching after Fred's untimely death in 1964, and in this way learned to wish, to ask, and to hope again.

After my sojourn at the Wittenbergs, where I was treated to daily concerts courtesy of Sarah practicing at her grand piano and little Alexander picking up Mozart sonatas by ear, striking the keys with great relish and amazing accuracy, with Mrs. Wittenberg flitting from room to room in a constant state of distraction, her graying curls, becomingly unkempt, framing a worried face, I almost welcomed the relative quiet and orderliness of our new household on the Regensburgerstrasse.

I had learned to read, first out loud, then silently to myself, and was struggling with *Oliver Twist* in German translation, which was peppered with unpronounceable English names, unfamiliar cityscapes and street scenes. I systematically skipped complicated passages and long-winded descriptions, satire and humor totally passing me by, determined to follow the thread of the story, fascinated and horrified at the cruelty and misery inflicted upon the orphan boy. I woke up in tears, having fallen asleep during one of Oliver's particularly trying moments, and thought I was dreaming. Facing me at the foot of the bed was a big, fat, round-headed cherub of a baby boy and my Aunt Mirrha holding him up. I jumped up out of bed to hug my very own cousin, just like Mirrha had promised, and proceeded to adopt baby Joshi as my little brother. Mirrha let me help her dress him, not an easy task as he jiggled constantly. I fetched my doll carriage to take him for his outing in the park.

Mirrha was very proud of her newly acquired proficiency in German, having eliminated gender distinctions altogether by the simple expedient of adding diminutive endings to every noun, thus neutralizing it. The result was a world reduced to Lilliputian dimensions of leaflets, tablets, coverlets, little houses as well as little dolls, little boys, and little girls. My little carriage (I had followed Mirrha's diminutive instructions to the letter and was surprised at her stricken expression) proved a very tight fit for Joshi, a strapping one-year-old thirty-pounder. Since there was no larger alternative available, we went off to my favorite park across the Kaiserallee, pushing the diminutive carriage with Joshi vigorously bobbing his head right and left and inevitably falling down, backwards, the doll carriage on top of him. He had a very hard round head, but after several falls and clusters of consternated matrons and nannies viewing the spectacle with stern looks of disapproval, Mirrha retrieved her howling son and carried him in her arms, while I pushed my empty doll carriage back home.

Mirrha left Joshi in her sister's care to go to work, but since Mutti disappeared every morning and returned only briefly for a hurried lunch hour, and I was at school in the mornings, Joshi was pretty much left to our maid's sternly traditional notions of child care. The result was a howling, protesting baby whom I valiantly tried to distract with grimaces and funny faces. Our lunch hours became nightmares; Joshi missed his mother with inconsolable sobs. Eventually he was placed in a model Catholic child care institution where sobs were not allowed and little children soon developed a frightening, bland expression of total disinterest. The spectacle was too hard to bear; it was Mirrha's turn to sob and wail and cry her eyes out. Karl found a job just in time before irreversible psychological damage could occur; Joshi was returned to his parents' loving arms and continued to thrive.

Mirrha took him along to her own nursery school job, which happened to be entirely in Russian. I always presumed it was for children of Russian immigrants, but my brother told me recently that it was for children of Russian embassy personnel in Berlin. Mirrha had an exceptional sense of rhythm and beat. She knew endless songs, nursery tales, and games with which she entertained her charges with vim and vigor, making them dance and laugh until they collapsed blissfully onto their nap time pads.

By the time he was three, Joshi had learned to speak German with faultless grammar, and more importantly, to sing at the top of his voice. The Reichstag had burned, the city was fluttering with swastikas; Hitler had been elected. Joshi sat in the U-Bahn train behind his parents intoning the "International" and raising his little clenched fist in the Communist salute, chanting, "Freiheit und Solidarität!" ("Freedom and solidarity!") This was heavy stuff. People had been handcuffed and dragged away for less, never to be seen again. Karl hastily covered his son's mouth shut. Mirrha pantomimed her shock and total disapproval of her son's heresy. Joshi had to be muzzled at all costs; it was life-threatening to go anywhere with him in public.

Soon thereafter my "little brother" left Berlin to return to his native Vienna.

Several years ago, seated in my living room in Metairie, Louisiana, I heard the expression "Solidarität" pronounced in my own Prussian accent, with the same meaning and fervor, by a guest from the former East Germany, under the auspices of the United States Information Service. It brought back memories of our Menshevik group, wont to break out into long litanies of socialist songs which filled our eyes with tears, the same Russian Revolutionary songs translated into German in the blue book of the Thaelman Pioneers which I had acquired in East Berlin in 1973 when an International Communist Youth Festival happened to be going on. These songs were to be heard on every street corner as youngsters sang and discussed and propagandized and welcomed their counterparts from North Vietnam, North Korea, the People's Republic of China, Cuba, numerous African nations and, of course, every nation in the Communist bloc of Eastern Europe. I was particularly impressed that they knew all of these songs, the same ones Aunt Mirrha had taught her charges at the Russian embassy school, by heart. "One should be ashamed not to know our songs by heart," a rosy-cheeked teenager from Halle informed me politely. "You will find the official book at the bookstore on the Alexanderplatz." Which I did.

One song from my German repertory was missing: "Die Gedanken sind Frei" ("Thoughts Are Free"). It was to become the hummed password of recognition in the thirties and during World War II, in camps, at secret border points, undercover passages over the Alps and the Pyrenees, in Franco's Spain, and wherever freedom and resistance fighters were defying the Nazi Holocaust.

When I started teaching German early in the seventies, it had become indispensable to dispel the ghosts hidden behind every expression to free me from the unbidden associations which I had carefully kept behind invisible barriers in my head. The New Orleans school board had required proof of my knowledge of German to the tune of some eighteen credit hours, twelve of which I earned by translating a technical article for the head of the German language department. I ended up in a nineteenth-century German literature class, where the students and professor alike begged me not to answer any questions and to let the class proceed at its own slow pace. When I hesitantly ventured to participate in a "vocabulary enhancing" game of free word association, a sort of verbal Rohrschach test, the class was stunned. So was I.

Thumb? screw, I answered.

Nail? pincers.

Head? shave.

Arm? broken.
Eyes? blinded.
House? bombed.
Child? beaten.
Teeth? knocked out.
Face? disfigured.

There was no way I could face a class of eager American youngsters with that kind of tortured and hate-filled German. I had to go back and make my personal peace with the new Germany, learn the language of Goethe and Schiller all over again. I finally had to dry the tears I shed in March 1933 when Mutti—"Don't call me Mutti any more!"—pulled out her pocket German-French dictionary and told me, "From now on we must not speak German. We must learn to speak French." I was leaving the only country I knew, going elsewhere for good. I thought I would never hear German spoken again and cried bitterly for the loss of the language which was not my mother's tongue. I was not quite ten years old.

Elsewhere in Paris, 1933–1935

It was to take two years to overcome the uprooting from a relatively secure and ordered life in Germany; to recover from the profound shock of being thrust unto a scene devoid of a single familiar landmark; to shed all aspects of my adopted identity as a German-speaking little girl at a time when the historic animosity between French and German people had reached levels of palpable hatred, refueled by memories of the horrors of the Great War.

Eventually I was able to teach German, rewarding my students with the loveliest poems and my cherished folk songs. Every year in every class, we sang "Die Gedanken sind Frei," all three verses, and although I never rode in Alexander's red fire engine, he had taught me to believe in Santa Claus. I passed the word on faithfully, every Christmas, as my class gleefully recreated my childhood version of a Christmas tree: homemade gingerbread cookies, nuts, oranges, handmade paper chains, lots of icicles, and the indispensable sparklers.

Christmas 1984 was my last year of teaching. Fred had been gone twenty years. Our daughter lived in Casablanca, Morocco, raising her two boys and teaching English, the result in part of my successfully teaching her French, which was how she met her husband at the University of Southern California in Los Angeles and followed him, as far as I was concerned, to the end of the earth. My son Carl, a space engineer in California, was struggling with a heavy workload and family responsibilities in a model house, which his wife kept in immaculate order between bathing, feeding, and nursing the first two of four children who appeared in rapid succession within a six-year span.

For twenty years, I commuted between east and west, packing up my house every summer for rental to a succession of mystery tenants who fed my dog and watered my garden. I carefully packed my brown carry-on according to Mama's recipe of precisely calculated use of space, switching languages as needed, trying to get a handle on the new emerging postwar world. Blissfully I melted into crowds, a small, middle-aged, tanned little woman with high cheekbones and green slit eyes. Flea markets in Casablanca, Athens, and Madrid. Fish markets in Dakar, Las Palmas, Dominica, and Martinique. Flower markets in Paris, Strasbourg, Florence, Nice, and Rome. Floating gardens in Mexico. Black markets in Beijing. Department stores in Tokyo. Open markets in every village and small town as I crisscrossed the Pyrenees from France to Spain, the Alps from Austria to Germany; as I drove along the Loire, the Seine, the Rhône, the Rhine, the Danube, the Oder, and the Elbe.

This was my home, elsewhere: on a plane, a boat, a train, a hovercraft. The Tube in London, the Métro in Paris, the U-Bahn in Munich. I met Tanya in Paris, Munich, London, Madrid, southern France, and Switzerland. I shopped for my first grandson's layette in Gibraltar, a short ferry hop from Tangier across the Mediterranean strait. I baby-sat two memorable summers with my grandsons in Athens, while my daughter attended summer courses. My only Greek was retrieved from advanced math formulae, scientific nomenclatures, and similarities with the Cyrillic alphabet.

I arranged to live overseas during three sabbaticals, in 1969–70, 1973, and 1977, spanning the European continent from Berlin to Algeciras at the southern tip of Spain, French islands in the Caribbean, the west coast of Africa and the North African rim from Rabat to Algiers and Tunis. When my brother retired in 1981 and moved to Orléans from his work in Paris, I purchased a studio in remodeled seventeenth-century stables next to his eighteenth-century apartment with the vague idea of spending my retirement years half in the Old and half in the New World, that is, six months in old Orléans and six months in New Orleans.

But the best of plans came to naught as my gynecologist informed me, not too kindly, that I should have consulted him several months, preferably several years, earlier. He insisted that I call my son Carl in California from his office or he would do it himself, which he did in spite of my vehement protests, to tell Carl that I had an advanced case of breast cancer, I was to have surgery as soon as feasible, and he had better be prepared to come down when all the tests were in to discuss post-mastectomy treatment options, if any.

None of this came as any surprise to me, as I had postponed the inevitable doctor's appointment to visit my family in Morocco the day school let out for summer vacation. From there, I had joined a teachers' study trip in Rome, which earned me a much-needed increase in salary, and continued the tour by bus through northern Italy, Switzerland, and France, where I spent heartwarming days visiting friends and sightseeing to my heart's content. I returned to the United States only to fly to Calgary, where my cousin Joe had taken Mirrha to spend her waning years, her memory fading, her speech impaired, barely conscious of the spectacular mountain view from her nursing home window in Canmore, a mere thirty miles from Lake Louise.

I returned to New Orleans tired and spent, suspicious of an obvious mass, not lump, the day before school opened after Labor Day, exactly twenty years to the day that Fred died in 1964. But I had no time. Not now. I arranged to fly to California to meet my new number two granddaughter at Thanksgiving break. Réda, my eldest grandchild, was spending the school year with my son's American family in Santa Barbara. He was struggling with culture shock in a work-oriented household and a huge impersonal high school, desperately homesick for friends and cousins in Morocco, missing the easy conviviality and banter in Arabic and French, so I invited him to spend Christmas in New Orleans, after which I would consult my gynecologist.

I had just rented my spare bedroom to a medical student at Tulane University, whom I left in charge of house and garden. I had a neighbor drive me to the hospital, dropped the previous year's semester exams— five of them, two in French and three in German—in the mailbox at the hospital entrance, and checked out of the crazy rat race life I had constructed for myself.

Blissfully, all decisions were out of my hands. Biopsy, CAT scan, x-rays, uneventful surgery. I drifted in and out of consciousness to feel Fred's presence at my side, down from behind the clouds where he had joined Grandpapa, Papa, Uncle Karl, and Mama, and I knew I was not alone. But not now. I wasn't ready. A familiar face floated by me in the recovery room. "What are you doing here, Frau Schueler? I was in your German class eight years ago. I'm a nurse here."

Here! Not elsewhere. I had bumped into former students before. In Paris, eyes blinded by a speck of dust, "Pardon, Madame, que faites-vous ici? I was in your French class three years ago." In Quebec, getting on a bus, my head collided with the descending chest of a young woman. "Madame Schueler, que faites-vous ici? Je suis étudiante à l'Université Laval. I was in your French class four years ago." On planes, at assorted airports, bearded gentlemen in business suits: "Aren't you Mrs. Schueler? I was in your French class fifteen years ago." In London on the steps of the British Museum, in Berlin at a fashionable café, the same refrain. "Aren't you Mrs. Schueler?" I was here, elsewhere in New Orleans.

Cancer turned my life around. I could handle the mutilation, the hole under my arm that left me a bit lopsided. I had always considered my breasts a liability, too big for my small frame and narrow shoulders, downright unhideable and undressable for the "twiggy" look, undisguisable under the tight sweaters of the forties and fifties. Now, at my age, it didn't matter. I had a portrait at home showing my infant son nursing at my right breast, courtesy of my cousin Joe turned artist, by way of a thank-you for a year of raiding our icebox (not a refrigerator then) in our ex-army Quonset hut which served as married student and junior faculty housing in Finkbine Park in Iowa City.

Carl, my son, was standing by my bed, my surgeon at his side. This was the Thursday following the Monday of my operation. The verdict was in: "The good news is that we were able to remove the tumor mass. The bad news is that it has spread to the lymph nodes, fatty tissue, and skeletal tissue. Statistically this is an advanced stage III cancer; the odds are one in three for a two-year survival rate. I suggest you consult Dr. Sothern [not his real name] at Tulane as soon as you leave the hospital for treatment options."

Carl's face was drawn, tired: crises at work, two babies at home, and a sleepless flight had aged him overnight. He didn't need Mom struggling with cancer.

I had one clear choice: to live.

I recalled Verlaine's poem, taught year after year to each of my French classes:

Le ciel est, par-dessus le toit,	The sky above the roof
Si bleu, si calme!	So blue, so calm!
Un arbre, par-dessus le toit,	A tree above the roof
Berce sa palme.	Waves its palm.

It was so simple. Myriad decisions—what to wear, what to eat, whom to invite, what questions to ask, which books to assign, whom to recommend—paled into insignificance. Books not written, talks declined, expectations unmet, none of this mattered anymore. What mattered was to take a deep breath without pain, to learn to walk again, to enjoy the blue of the sky when it wasn't raining, the splash of water on roofs and side-

walks when it was. I learned to say "no" and I learned to say "yes." The
school secretary was dispatched to find me propped up in my hospital
bed. "We were hoping you could grade these exams in time for final semester grades before you are discharged."

"Thank you," I mumbled. Then I said, "No."

Friends came. "Don't hesitate to ask. A trip to the store. An errand.
Anything we can do for you." I learned to ask: talk to my son; bring my
mail; tell me a funny story; thank you for coming; I need to rest now.

I checked out with a fashionably thin, if lopsided, figure, from a size
twelve to a size eight petite: zipping in and out of skirts with two fingers'
width to spare, what a treat! I completely forgot about the limited mo-
bility of my right arm. I got stuck in overhead pullovers, a phantom grop-
ing her way to the neighbors' house with threatening uplifted arms, head
covered with a turtleneck collar without the benefit of a ski mask's eye
slits. After a few weeks, though, I could shift gears again and resolved my
next car would have automatic transmission. The reason for the succession of Volkswagens and Toyotas with manual shifts was the economic
advantage of double the mileage of a standard Ford. What I saved on gas
had bought me my yearly high-season airfare ticket overseas. Now I could
afford to fly when fares were low, in between checkups, bone scans, x-
rays, mammograms. I declined chemotherapy. The benefits then were
questionable and the risks too high. As soon as I recovered from a nasty
bout of bronchitis that left me gasping for air between uncontrollable fits
of coughing, and the ensuing antibiotic treatment which left me drained,
I booked the first of countless flights according to a vague schedule of
traveling to visit friends, family, and the world beyond. My little brown
bag, packed tight, whether for the weekend, a week, three weeks, three
months, fit under the seat in front of me. For cold weather, including
summer in England, I squeezed a couple of heavy sweaters inside my raincoat and put it in the overhead bin.

I settled for a silicon prosthesis, which proved ideal for carrying large
sums of cash, travelers' checks, and the like, wrapped in a soft hanky between my flat chest and bra. The thought occurred to me that I could
easily have hired out as a drug courier, which would have paid for all of
my trips, but I confess to a possibly misguided honesty.

Fred, too, had had one chance in a lifetime to make it rich. A mystery call at night, at home, from a horse racer, offering him half a million
dollars in 1960, easily the equivalent of three million today, if he would

design an untraceable drug to make a horse run faster. Fred first thought this was some sort of a joke, but it was not. Most tempting, and he knew he could do it. "I'll consider your offer and let you know in the morning." After much soul searching, his answer was unequivocal: No.

Sudden and early retirement left me with little more than half of the second lowest teacher's salary in the fifty states, plus a small check from Fred's Social Security earnings. I considered myself a veteran of living on practically nothing and I came pretty close to putting my retirement fantasy into action when Social Security advised me that I could not receive both a state pension and federal benefits. A loophole was found at the last minute so that I squeezed through a retroactive deadline.

My fantasy was this: I would live at school. My small brown bag, no bigger than what most boys lugged around for gym practice, would fit nicely in the locker in the teachers' lounge. I could keep a few essentials in the refrigerator, use the microwave to heat up cans of soup and beans, shower downstairs by the cafeteria, which doubled as a gym. I had my choice of healthily firm sleeping on one of two comfortable sofas in the lounge and a third one in the lady teachers' restroom. There were phones, copy machines, paper, and marvelous security. I could even afford the greatest of luxuries: living without a car! The school was located on New Orleans' historic St. Charles streetcar line, a scenic thirty or forty-minute ride to downtown and the old French Quarter. There were a plethora of little stores, boutiques, diners, coffee shops, and restaurants, all within walking distance, plus the levee along the River Road overlooking the Mississippi, and of course, the two university campuses, Loyola and Tulane, with their libraries, journals, professional resources galore, across from Audubon Park and the recently redesigned zoo. It all seemed so simple! Compared to living conditions as I had seen them on a study trip to China in 1982, this was downright cozy and comfortable. There was enough food left over after lunch, candy passed around, half-full cases of doughnuts left after special occasions. Sweaters, jackets, sneakers, scarves, were tossed unclaimed in the lost and found closet to clothe the needy (me?). I could read my way through centuries of literature in several languages, watch the news, read *Harper's, The Atlantic, Scientific American,* all in the evening hours after school was hermetically locked with me within. Early to bed and early to rise, before the gates opened to teachers still employed, would give me full days of walking, promenading, sightseeing, and visiting friends.

A judicious perusal of social events in the daily paper would guarantee receptions, gallery openings, and special lectures, all with welcome and succulent refreshments. Without house payments, utilities, insurance, and car maintenance, my half salary would stretch to cover my program of travels. Thus I would fashion a life of quality on practically nothing.

But then again, with my newly acquired Amazon status, I no longer worried about a long stretch of useless aging and diminishing faculties eating up my hard-earned savings. I splurged. I sent a friend to buy a TV for me with a remote control, the best, not too big and not too small. I dragged myself to the Persian Cat, a fancy feast of expensive imported yarns, and bought $100 worth of my favorite colors with no particular aim in mind. Eventually, I spent contented hours watching popular murder mysteries on television, comfortably ensconced against armrest pillows on my bed, crocheting unneeded afghans for surprised members of my family. Tamoxifen's ability to stop the spread of my kind of cancer was still in doubt, but I decided I had to do something. The first unexpected side effect of the drug was a caffeine high. I was not a morning person; I needed a good strong cup of coffee plus an energetic sprint up the stairs at school to get me going at the start of the day. No more. I felt as if I was jumping out of my skin. No more coffee for me! When I was strong enough to meet friends "for coffee," I was shocked to find my appetite for chocolate and pastry had vanished as well. So much for my best intentions of splurging on superfluous desserts. Eventually, I made my first hesitant foray into a shopping mall and actually purchased a London Fog raincoat I didn't need. I already had a blue one hanging in my closet, but this one, in my favorite shade of rust with a becoming mandarin collar, was irresistible. By the time I could manage two hours upright between two hours lying down, I booked a flight overseas with a stopover in New York to meet my newly arrived cousins from Georgia, then still part of the Soviet Union.

Unlike Mama, Papa seldom spoke of his family. I knew he had two brothers, one of whom had been my mother's first love. Papa also had three sisters he never mentioned. I still have a mental image of the only childhood memory Papa shared with me: a desperately homesick little boy of nine being driven in a troika through a snowstorm to the nearest railway station, some five or six hours away, to take the train to boarding school.

By the time he was fifteen, in 1902, he had made numerous speeches, and had earned a reputation as a student leader and activist, a member of the growing intelligentsia preparing for the failed Revolution of 1905. He sat in jail under the Tsar when his mother died of scarlet fever. She was thirty-five. It was the only time I recall Papa expressing grief and remorse: being in prison when his mother died.

It took me a week to decipher and translate my cousin Vovo's letter, thanks to Mama's last-ditch attempt at Russian lessons in Berlin. The letter informed me that he and his sister Maya (which unfortunately was the name I had chosen for my third dachshund) were new immigrants to the United States, living in Queens, New York. Vovo was accompanied by his second wife, Rita. Maya's husband Raffi, tall, blond, and blue-eyed, drove a taxi. Her older daughter, married to a handlebar-mustached Armenian, worked as a receptionist; her younger daughter was enrolled in high school. There was a little granddaughter. Maya and Vovo's father was Papa's youngest brother, Naum, of whom I had heard nothing.

A good friend in Long Island picked me up at Kennedy Airport. After hesitantly negotiating the few winding steps up to his comfortable house, I asked to "please lie down." This was to be my refrain wherever I stopped on this first journey after illness forced me into retirement; but I was determined to see friends and family.

Raffi provided free taxi service for his family and picked me up to meet them at a nearby restaurant which served what I thought was a pretty elegant meal. (I learned better when the family invited me back the following year; the Armenian, already established in a brisk antique trade in the depths of Brooklyn, drove me in his car to a feast punctuated with ample toasts of vodka, prepared by the three grown women in three minuscule kitchenettes, with every imaginable delicacy, caviar not excluded, which must have set them back a month's combined food stamps and salaries!)

I recognized Vovo immediately: a vigorous fifty-plus gentleman with the unmistakable high cheekbones and matte skin tone, the same flair for elegance, the same assured walk, a slightly taller, slightly broader and younger version of Papa in his sixties. Maya was a handsome, fair-skinned, dark blonde matron; her daughters were aglow with natural charm, radiating confidence and curiosity, obviously experimenting with the myriad possibilities of beauty products of the West. Only the little granddaugh-

ter, perhaps five, was attired in true Russian fashion, at least as I conceived
of it, with a big fabric bow on top of her head and a nice party dress for
the occasion.

After hefty hugs and embraces, we all sat down to settle the problem of
language. I was a bit unnerved as I understood practically nothing; even
my early childhood Russian seemed to have deserted me. Then Vovo told
me in what he remembered from his high school German, "We don't
speak Russian; we speak Georgian. My niece's husband is Armenian, he
speaks Armenian. The girls have learned some English, but for us it is
very hard."

Our dinner party turned into a good-natured guessing game: namely,
who was this newfound American cousin with a German name and a German accent who drank no vodka and recoiled from any physical closeness (which threatened the yet-untested resistance of a silicone breast ready
to collapse, its two-year warranty notwithstanding, and a precarious equilibrium)? This on top of lifelong habits of keeping a certain distance. I
was suddenly thrust into the midst of a close-knit family, of which I was
a bona fide member and yet a total stranger. It was incomprehensible.
How could I live alone, with grown children a continent away? To live
alone was a state to be pitied above all others, the ultimate deprivation,
the ultimate poverty.

I recalled the same reaction when I first met Tanya's "instant family" in
Casablanca some twenty years earlier, in the summer of 1965. Transported
into a childhood vision of the *Arabian Nights,* primly seated, a feat which
defied the low soft couches or, worse yet, softer pillows cast atop piles of
blankets, shamefully aware of my exposed knees when Ahmed's sisters,
aunts, and cousins were gracefully reclining in glimmering layers of garments, assuming poses depicted in Delacroix's romantic paintings. My
grandsons frequently refer to their twenty-five or so brothers and sisters,
an endearing term for cousins, even friends. At the time I first met the
family, there were only some thirteen or so assorted children, from babies
to early teens, all politely kissing my hand, kissing my cheek, mute and
big-eyed, silently seated at their mothers' feet.

No words were needed as each proceeded to her assigned task to honor
and welcome the mother of their brother's fiancée. Bending straight from
the hips, they offered tidbits from low round tables, daintily filigreed,
henna decorated feet padding softly on thick carpets, masses of hair in

auburn tresses, deep black eyes lined with kohl, a body language of un-
dulating, waving, swaying motions which kept their outer garments aflut-
ter in softly changing patterns, catching the play of light and shadows filtered through the louvered windows, a flowing continuum of
imperceptible movements which came to rest in a composed attitude of
peaceful silence.

Tanya's Arabic, still halting, sufficed for the most rudimentary of polite exchanges. "Keep your voice down, speak softly." I felt that I was indeed an object of pity, deserving of the deepest sympathy, alone without
husband, family, or children in the bustling American wilderness, fend-
ing for myself, exposed daily to all eyes, an existence which I gathered the
poorest of beggars would not exchange for the fabled riches of the United
States.

Family members unobtrusively disappeared; others as silently took
their place; mint tea was served, prepared with what looked like basketfuls
of fresh mint leaves stuffed into polished silver teapots, huge volumes of
leaves mysteriously reduced to the confines of potbellied containers holding no more than a quart of steaming water.

Deftly, the tea was poured in delicate arcs of liquid, nonchalantly
aimed with unlikely precision into small, colored, gold-trimmed glasses.
My sense of space and time deserted me. There were no defined spaces
anywhere, no separate seats, no two walls that met at precisely right angles,
no individual plates. Mounds of wondrous undefinable foods on huge
platters were shared by four, or seven, or thirteen; numbers shifted and
didn't matter; people came and went in costumes spanning centuries of
fashion.

Drawn by a promise of clear azure sky, I ventured to the open window to behold a biblical scene: open fields dotted with stones, shepherds
clothed in long brown cloaks herding their flocks of woolly sheep with
the traditional crooked staff of children's Christmas plays; "Marys" in blue
djellabas mounted sideways on docile donkeys, heads modestly downcast,
hooded and veiled, propelling their charges with swift taps of their bare
heels. There were no assigned paths, no enclosures; cows, mangy dogs,
sheep, and some goats were wandering about; small girls walked with babies tied securely to their backs; here and there lay prostrate figures, which
I took to be cows at rest until they got up and turned into unlikely scare-
crows: beggars covered in cloaks so torn that pieces of them were flap-
ping in the wind.

Tanya's "instant family" was housed in several apartments in what once had been a French apartment complex, appropriately named a *cité* since it covered several blocks carved out of the stony fields, incorporating a small shopping strip with post office, grocery store, dairy, butcher, and expanses of what had once been well-kept lawns.

The airport was an ancient army hangar, little more than a landing strip, with chickens scooting out of the way, about an hour's drive to Tanya's home over partially paved roads that skirted lush green fields radiating from whitewashed flat-roofed buildings.

Traffic was a miscellany of horse-drawn carriages fitted with car tires; bicyclists (sometimes two or even three on a single bike); motorbikes with sidecars containing a whole family; *mobilettes* (bicycles fitted with little engines); donkeys all but disappearing beneath heavy loads of straw or sacks of grain; taxis with trunk lids precariously tied down over unlikely mounds of unwieldy cloth-wrapped packages; ancient buses with baggage piled a meter high pell-mell on the roof, threatening to slide off at every jolt, and passengers squeezed tight inside, unable to move.

No speeding here, as cows and people nonchalantly crossed our path oblivious of oncoming traffic. How far? How fast? When and where? were questions I learned not to ask over twenty-odd years of summer and winter holidays in a land where time and space were defined by traditional rhythms unknown to me; where people sat under the same tree for hours or for days waiting for a bus, walked a mile or two, or ten or twenty, to visit a friend; waited a year, three years, ten years for a brother to return, a son to write. I would catch myself looking at my watch to see how close it was to lunchtime, a nonsensical gesture according to Ahmed's maxim, "Eat when you are hungry, sleep when you are tired," and marveled at the delight his people took in each morsel of delicately steamed lamb, each bite of just-so ripe cantaloupe, for "hunger is the best cook," another of Ahmed's maxims. Bread was broken in the traditional gestures of the Last Supper, lovely home baked (well, home kneaded and baked in the public ovens) large, round, fragrant, crusty, warm loaves of whole wheat bread, broken up in wedges to scoop up one's share of steaming vegetables and meats from amply laden common platters.

That first summer of 1965, Tanya and Ahmed, who were staying with the family, had rented a room for me at a small European-style hotel in Anfa, overlooking the beach, a mile or two south of the old port of

Casablanca, a half hour's drive from Bournazel, where most of the family lived.

During the heat of the day, the city closed down. Shutters shut tight at noon against the sun, and streets emptied as all went home to eat and sleep. When shadows lengthened, awake again and fortified by late afternoon mint tea, people ventured out to work, shop, visit, or promenade until every quarter of the city was bursting with crowds, streams of motor traffic held up by horse-drawn carts, donkeys, the occasional stray herd of sheep, pushcarts, women with babies on their backs, all merrily ignoring every common sense rule of the road.

Tanya, her tight polka dot sleeveless summer dress well-hidden beneath an ample djellaba, led the way, her golden-brown locks of hair shamelessly exposed, a head taller than most women. I hung onto her arm, or at least a fold of her cover-up garment, with her future sister-in-law, Halima, at my side, a diminutive figure discreetly garbed from head to foot, hood carefully adjusted, veil artfully arranged, leaving her sharp brown eyes free to view the world.

Tanya's father, Fred, was broad and strong, but not tall; Fred's grandfather, the original Wilhelm Schueler from Germany, was downright small; yet Fred's Aunt Wilhelmina, whom I had met quite by accident when I visited a girls' reform school near Boulder, Colorado, for a project in sociology where she worked as a nurse, was of formidable Wagnerian proportions.

Even more surprisingly, when I took Grandma Mabel, Fred's mother, to Greenville, Missouri, where she was born, not a single Poor cousin (that was her maiden name, Poor; her sister, Betty, ten years her junior and not tall either, married a farmer in Loveland, Colorado, named Cash) was under six feet tall, ladies included! So I guess Tanya came by her height from the German side of the family. The Poors traced their ancestry back to the early 1700s as Pennsylvania Dutch, with a bit of Scotch and Irish mixed in.

Every second generation, the eldest son packed his family in a wagon and headed west to homestead. After three such moves to the Virginias and the Carolinas, the family settled in Missouri well before the Civil War; I think it was in 1838. Once again, the eldest son, Grandma Mabel's grandfather, packed his family into a wagon and headed west, this time

all the way to Texas, to homestead his own farm. All of this Grandma
Mabel told me on our drive to Missouri from New Orleans in the summer of 1961 in our new white Ford. We had moved to our big new house
in Metairie. By the driveway I had planted a row of rose bushes, which
Grandma Mabel insisted on watering every morning, in spite of more
than ample rainfall.

Tragedy struck in Texas. Grandma Mabel's grandfather surprised a
bunch of horse thieves, who shot him dead. Her grandmother packed her
seven children, the oldest boy—fourteen—helping her, into the wagon
and drove back to the family farm in Missouri. That is the real stuff of
westerns, and I cannot begin to imagine the trials and hardships of that
journey. Grandma Mabel said of her grandmother that "she was strong
and tough." She remembered her well.

Greenville, a small, southern, tree-lined town, was dotted with Poors:
pharmacy, beauty parlor, diner, and lots of Poor headstones in the ceme-
tery. Grandma Mabel, the eldest of six children, had left with her family
when she was nine, before the end of the nineteenth century. She never
forgot the lush green fields, the white houses trimmed with bright green
shutters, washed down by heavy rains. Water is what she remembered
best, standing behind the rain-streaked window of her parents' small cottage, waiting for the train to whistle past the railroad station a block away.
Year after year, she waited for the train to take her west, away from diapers, away from crawling, spitting, howling, scrapping little brothers.

We stayed at a motel overnight to get up at dawn. "Follow the trail of
the old gray mare," Grandma Mabel said, as she directed me, ignoring
the newly paved wide streets, along the well-trodden paths of her childhood memories. Streets gave way to country roads, then to lanes, then to
barely marked ruts between woods and fields, where the car came to rest
halfway across a shallow creek; and there it stood, the old homestead, perhaps half a mile away on top of a hill, lush lawns sloping gently down-
ward, a large, neat two-storied rectangle of a wooden house painted white
with green shutters. With difficulty, I extricated the car, no longer white,
from the shallow water back onto the muddy stretch of narrow rutted
roadway, while Grandma Mabel called out to some big trees she remembered as saplings when she was a little girl. Somehow, we wound our way
back to town, stopping twice in front of little houses where Grandma
Mabel would confront tall spry septuagenarians with a level-toned, "Hi!
I'm your cousin Mabel; we left sixty-two years ago. This is my daughter-

in-law, Julia." "Why, come in, Mabel," was the laconic reply; whereupon we sat down for an exchange of essential information with no wasted words, punctuated by long silences.

I was directed a few miles further west, marveling at Grandma Mabel's innate sense of direction, until we found the four-room, square house—abandoned, roof caved in, shutters askew—where she and her four brothers had been born and raised.

I had met her parents once, Fred's grandparents, on their farm near Fort Collins; they were both in their eighties. Her father, a still active six-foot-plus, her mother bedridden. This was in the forties; Tanya was perhaps two, a happy little cherub of a girl with golden curls.

Now, some eighteen years later, in the old medina of Casablanca, in the summer of 1965, as in my childhood nightmare in Berlin in which Mutti turned into a doll I led by the hand, our roles were reversed; I was desperately following my grown daughter's lead, barely reaching her shoulder, Halima's veiled figure indistinguishable from those of eager shoppers crowding about us, through a crooked labyrinth of narrow alleys steeped in shadows, imagined dangers lurking behind every colorfully tiled recess in whitewashed walls, pulled back in the nick of time to let a caravan of heavily laden donkeys pass us by. I dreaded the dead looks of the blind, the uneven steps of cripples, often the result of simple fractures left unset, of dislocated hips untreated, of club feet uncorrected; I shied away from the festering wounds of professional beggars, exposed to buzzing flies. One more turn, one more passageway through walls and courtyards with narrow steps leading nowhere, and I lost all sense of balance, of direction, of up and down, of inside and out: this was the ultimate elsewhere, with not a single familiar clue to hang on to. Overcome by a wave of nausea, I started shaking and vomiting. Somehow, Tanya and Halima held me up, got me beyond the walls of the medina, into a taxi and back to my hotel, where I collapsed in a classic case of culture shock. Tanya spent the day at my bedside; Halima spent the night. Nonstop fever, vomiting, and diarrhea for three days left me a welcome size thinner, very much humbled, weak as a kitten, and forever in Halima's debt, who had nursed me, bathed me, and spoon-fed me healing liquids, all without a word, her eyes alone conveying sympathy and understanding. No, Halima was not mute: I understood no Arabic.

I spent the balance of these first ten days or so in Morocco in the more

familiar atmosphere of my French hotel, overlooking the oceanside promenade, the Corniche, with a refreshing view of the sea and huge ships gliding close to port. There were a few timid forays with Tanya to the business
section of Casablanca, the French-built city of the thirties with wide, tree-
lined avenues radiating from roundabouts; coffee shops and restaurants,
gentlemen in business suits alternating with others elegantly clad in snow-
white djellabas. The focal point was a newspaper stand opposite the
Casablanca Hotel, then white as its name implies, where Tanya purchased
the *International Herald Tribune* every day and I had my choice of a dozen
French dailies, half a dozen German dailies, the same in English, Spanish, Italian, Portuguese, and Greek, not to mention the many papers from
the Middle East and I don't know how many of the newly emerging countries of sub-Saharan Africa.

Censorship, I learned, was very strict. In the Moroccan papers, articles were cut out at the last minute, leaving a blank space. As to the foreign press, papers mysteriously disappeared before they hit the newsstand,
a sure sign that something controversial and interesting was happening
not to His Majesty's liking.

I had arranged a stopover in Paris, and had booked a minuscule room at
a minuscule price in a small hotel on the Right Bank, hidden behind the
rue de Rivoli, just a block from the back entrance of the infamous Hotel
Meurice, which faced the Tuileries Gardens and had served as German
headquarters during the Occupation. This according to my number one
travel principle, which has proved itself over the years: use small, cheap,
but safe lodgings within easy reach of a well-known luxury hotel, which
would assure restful surroundings for the occasional meetings with friends
and new acquaintances, plus all the information needed about the city,
travel, entertainment, and so forth.

Thundering traffic, hurried shoppers, blinking lights, luxury shops
displaying enough cameras, perfumes, and high-fashion clothes in half a
block to equal all of Casablanca's resources, gave me a giant headache. It
took me three days to venture forth beyond the relative quiet of my street,
face the well-dressed, immaculately groomed crowd (this was before the
events of 1968, micro-minis, flared pants, and dirty jeans) and seek the
open familiar surroundings of the Tuileries.

I was stopped by barricades. Since I had not read the papers (travel
principle number two: always read the paper before landing in Paris to

find out which trains and buses are running and which utilities are not functioning), I assumed there might be a protest march or perhaps a new excavation project. Something was definitely wrong. Beyond the barricades, German soldiers were running about; there were jeeps, trucks, machine guns, and a few cannon. In the distance, toward the Place de la Concorde, there was fire and smoke. After twenty-five years I was back, smack in the middle of occupied Paris! Unobtrusively, I walked around the barricades. There was something not quite right about the German soldiers; their movements were too smooth, their faces too relaxed, their eyes suppressing a twinkle. I must be dreaming. A canvas-covered khaki-colored pickup truck had stopped nearby. Incongruously, jolly pink pigs escaped down a makeshift ramp, merrily scurrying toward the nearest water basin, German soldiers in hot pursuit. Pigs are agile, intelligent creatures; these were glistening, well-groomed animals; they slipped out of each soldier's grasp. A furious voice was shouting orders in French— "Right! No, left!"—soldiers were colliding with each other, in standard Gallic confusion. I had walked into a movie, not a nightmare. A gendarme at the Concorde end of the Tuileries, in his blue cape and distinctive blue kepi, confirmed my suspicion. *Is Paris Burning?* was to be the title of the film. Back in New Orleans, I took my French classes to see it the following spring at the Saenger Theater. As I recall, the pig sequence was reduced to thirty seconds—one soldier, one pig—symbolizing the German army feeding itself off the land.

Unlike the British, who fought on despite the Blitz, France refused the risk of Paris burning; it was unthinkable that the treasures of French art, civilization, and architecture be reduced to rubble. Paris was declared an open city and occupied on June 15, 1940.

I could sympathize with this point of view. My love affair with Paris was not one of love at first sight. On the contrary, it took hard work, years of disciplined reading, hours and hours of walking in the footsteps of my favorite authors, book in hand; leisurely weekend promenades along the Seine, crossing every bridge; leisurely walks in parks; untold hours visiting museums and attending classic plays; savoring street scenes from the now defunct Halles (the central market) on the Right Bank to the open markets in the Latin Quarter.

Papa and my brother Max were not on the same train with us, me and Mama, no longer Mutti, from Berlin to Paris. I was clutching my teddy

bear, whispering in German in his ear, as spring unfolded this last week of
March 1933, just a few days short of my tenth birthday, speeding past
greening fields, trees that were sprouting fresh new leaves until the chestnut trees were ready to burst into bloom in Paris.

The train was filthy, crowded with poor Jewish families speaking Polish, crying babies, toddlers, coughing children. Mama carefully wiped our
seats with disinfectant and made sure that I wore my gloves and did not
touch anything.

Of Paris, I knew nothing except that Papa loved it and our French
teacher in the gymnasium despised it. "Girls all wear black smocks in
school. The French eat everything, snails, frogs, and nasty things. They
use their hands to talk; they laugh and kiss in public; they're not civilized," she told us. "They hang out their wash from the window; they talk
and talk and waste time." I concentrated on the French I had learned—
Où est le restaurant? Où est le parc?—and tried to give Mama the emergency speed course she asked for.

Papa met us at the station; it must have been the Gare de l'Est. All
around us as we descended from the train, people were hugging and kissing each other. Papa took us to our lodgings deep in the Latin Quarter: a
small hotel on the rue Cardinal Le Moyne. It was all true! Horribly gray,
dirty-looking narrow streets with wash hanging out at the windows.
Houses that were so old their walls buckled. Not one roof, one window,
one door was at the same level with another! And, yes, children wore black
smocks, and most of the older women wore nothing but black: black
dresses, black vests, black hose, black shoes. No one walked at the same
pace; everywhere, people stopped to talk with their hands, shouted or
laughed, and kissed right in front of everybody!

I was tired, totally bewildered, lost. The charm of a seventeenth-
century fountain set against a wall covered with finely detailed, hand-
painted flowered tiles at the back of a shaded courtyard was lost on me; so
was an elegantly curving stairwell, steps sagging in the middle, worn down
by several centuries of footfalls.

Mama and Papa had separated. Mama and I shared the legendary tiny
room, wallpapered with huge roses, while Papa shared a similar room, I
believe, with my brother. There was no bathroom, at least not on our
floor. I was terrified. The toilet was in a small dark recess between two
floors, the bathroom on another floor below. And there was no roll of

paper! Just little tiny squares of tissue paper or, worse, half pages torn from catalogs.

The next day, I dressed in a brown knit outfit with matching knee socks and sturdy Buster Brown shoes, Papa having insisted on spending his last marks in Berlin on a new wardrobe for his children, to go for a walk down the street. This turned out to be a perilous undertaking, "down" meaning a descending forty-five-degree angle on huge uneven cobblestones, the same cobblestones that students in 1968 merrily broke loose to throw at the "pigs" of policemen. There was an ancient gutter running down the middle of the street, and no sidewalks to speak of, or sidewalks so narrow one could just barely squeeze against a bulging wall to avoid a descending cart, clattering perilously on huge iron-rimmed wheels, or worse, a speeding taxi. People said *pardon* as they bumped into you, followed by a long flow of unintelligible remarks.

I was shown the bakery. Even with my atrophied sense of smell, I could tell fresh loaves of bread had just come out of the oven. They were strangely shaped, long narrow loaves of white bread, which people carried away holding them in the middle by the same sort of square tissue paper that served as toilet paper! Papa showed me some French money, which was called *francs* and *sous*. One franc would buy a loaf of bread, which was to be my chore twice daily. Next, we turned left on a busy, relatively wide thoroughfare to look at the Panthéon where Papa told me that famous people were buried. Somewhere behind the Panthéon, on a narrow street behind an ancient, gray, crumbling stone wall, stood the public school I was to attend.

We were not alone in Paris. The whole Menshevik group that had sought refuge in Berlin had left for Paris at the same time we did, to rejoin those Mensheviks who had headed directly for Paris when they were forced into exile in 1922. The Group was like a family, providing help, advice, food, and perhaps money to the less fortunate ones among them. Mama must have appealed to one of her Parisian-based—that is, French-speaking—colleagues to accompany us to school the next day and act as interpreter. It was explained to me that I would sit in a class of third graders, children perhaps eight years old, and that I would not be expected to write tests or answer questions until I had picked up enough French to do so. Eventually, I would be moved up to my proper grade level. Of course, I would have to wear a black smock, acquire a regulation notebook with funny narrow lines, a slate, ruler, pen, pencils, and eraser. Textbooks were furnished free. I am sure that Mama was relieved at such a sensible solution. The school was only a ten-minute walk from our hotel. I could return for lunch, pick up a loaf of bread on the way, rest a bit, and spend the remainder of the afternoon in school. On days when no one was at home, I could stay in supervised study hall until six o'clock.

The next day, I was shown my seat in a class of some forty little girls, all clad in identical black smocks, and since I was by far the tallest, being two years older (I had noticed with great satisfaction that most children in Paris were just about my height at my age), my seat was at the back of the classroom. In Paris, children lined up with the smallest in front and the tallest at the end of the line. My world had turned upside down! No one stood up when the teacher entered the classroom; everyone was speaking at once, giggling, laughing, waving their hands about, shaking their heads, leaning in all directions, until a sharp tap of the ruler on the teacher's desk brought silence. Notebooks were opened, pens readied, everyone listened, arms folded on their desks. I understood nothing. Teacher, a bosomy middle-aged lady dressed in black, had written a paragraph on the blackboard which everyone copied. So did I, laboriously, without understanding any of it except the occasional article, or a common verb form of *être, avoir,* or *aller.* Nothing made sense. I concentrated on penmanship. Those mysterious lines between lines in my notebook were to assure the proper height of small *t*s, capital *t*s, tails on *q*s and *p*s in cursive writing, which was new to me. I had learned to use capital Roman letters and small Roman letters as an alternative to the German gothic script. French children devoted much time to practicing penmanship, with the result that ledgers two hundred years old could be read as easily as the grocer's daily accounts, all in cursive handwriting adhering to the same strict standards of legibility.

There was much reciting by heart, repetition of senseless phrases, speech without a clue as to where words started and ended, or where phrases began; there was no emphasis; consonants were dulled, vowels drowned in undefinable nasal singsong, words flowed together in long ripples of uninterrupted sound. I had been taught clarity, precision, terseness. For my single, distinct "Danke," the French used a string of words— "Merci beaucoup, Madame, je vous remercie; vous êtes bien aimable"— which one meant "thanks?" "Bitte" became another litany: "Je vous en prie, Mademoiselle, vous êtes bien gentille," or "Il n'y a pas de quoi, je vous assure," or the mysterious "S'il vous plaît, Madame," which seemed to precede almost every question addressed to a grown-up.

Only years later did it occur to me that the majority of the class did not make any more sense out of the mindless repetitions than I did, even though they understood the words.

As I recall, we each had an individual desk, not jammed together four or five on one bench as we had been in grade school in Berlin, and there was much changing of seats each time test papers were returned. It was a regular musical chairs, with some children taking front row seats as their names were called, happily gathering books and miscellaneous belongings, others dragging their feet, dropping pencils and pens, as they slouched miserably toward their newly assigned desks in the back of the room. It took me a while to figure out the French grading system, which turned out to be the exact opposite of the German one. The number one, as in the English expression "A-one," always expressed excellence; hence it was only logical that 1 should be the best grade, corresponding to the American A. The numeral 2 was a B, 3 a C, 4 a D, and 5 denoted total failure. Very clear and simple. French test papers had two numbers on them, one cardinal and one ordinal. The cardinal number reflected the objective grade from the unattainable perfection of 20 down to the zero of a blank paper, with 10 the ironclad passing average. The ordinal number reflected rank in class, according to which students were seated and re-seated, the best students in front, the laggards in back.

This had the advantage for the teacher of automatically being able to direct her gaze and remarks to those students most in need of clarifications, or to call on the best for a model recitation, concentrating on the front rows for more advanced explanations lost on the poorer students. In classes of forty to fifty students, this served as an automatic tracking system and ensured that the best had a chance to aspire to the highest level of academic achievement. There was no compunction about putting the dullards in their place. There was no such thing as a curve. Standards were the same nationwide, regardless of neighborhood or background. It could happen that the best grade was an 11, barely above the passing average of 10, with most of the pupils falling below the passing line, doomed to repeat a grade and to academic failure.

There was no help for me at home, our bower of paper roses sparsely furnished with two cots, a chair, an armoire. Mama counted on me to help *her* with *her* French. All I could do was burst into tears. I understood nothing. I would never understand anything. Tearfully I went to bed, tearfully I was dragged out of bed in the morning, tearfully I went to school. On the playground, curious little classmates gathered round. They pointed at my shoes, my funny knee socks with a neat contrasting band just below the knee, my knit dress which seemed to be the wrong length, as it showed beneath the hemline of my smock. They mispronounced my name. I didn't realize how lucky I was. Julia, pronounced in French, was a perfectly acceptable name which connoted nothing Germanic, unlike my reticent gestures, my clunky shoes, my habit of curtsying whenever a teacher went by. My downfall was "Berlin." At the mention of the city where I grew up, smiles froze, bodies stiffened. "Boche!" (French pejorative slang for "German") a pupil spat out at me; "boche," repeated her classmates; "sale boche" (filthy kraut) was flung at me as the girls left me standing forlorn, turning their backs on the archenemy.

I learned never to mention Berlin again. I learned to pronounce Moscow properly in French. Mama reverted to speaking Russian when we were out walking. I could speak German only in the privacy of our hotel room, and even there the walls were thin. Learning French without a German accent became a matter of survival in the country that had welcomed us as the first wave of refugees from Nazi Germany.

Shortly before we left Berlin, I had learned of the sudden death of Dog, my beautiful German shepherd friend, in a short cryptic note from the young lady teacher where I had spent my last summer in Germany. Dog had apparently been poisoned, but by whom or why was not clear. I had tried to correspond with Dog in care of the young lady teacher, asking her to pet him for me, to talk to him, to read him my letters. Now, in Paris, I cried for the loss of the only language I knew, which was not mine, and for the loss of Dog, whom I had fed, who was my friend, my solace. I wrote a letter of condolence and sympathy, which Mama refused to post. (It didn't occur to me then that receiving a letter from Paris with my name on it might jeopardize the recipient's safety.) I had been sworn to silence the last six weeks or so in Berlin. "Do not talk to anyone, not even your best friend, not even the nice people next door." I was no longer allowed to play marbles at the Olivaerplatz just down the street where I used to meet one or two of my German classmates from the gymnasium.

Now the last tie with Germany was cut, irrevocably, and henceforth I learned never to mention German things or Germany in my new French surroundings.

Mama literally had to pull me down the street each morning. I was sick to my stomach! I wanted so badly to understand, to do well. School had always been a safe haven where I knew my place, knew what was expected, when and where and how, even when I had to struggle to keep up the last year because I had jumped a grade and was younger and smaller than everyone else in the school.

I knew my multiplication tables by heart, and when the class recited in unison in a lulling singsong what I assumed rightly to be 3 times 3, 3 times 4, 3 times 5, and so on, having learned my numbers in French class at the gymnasium, I confidently joined in. Since counting to twenty in French pretty much covers all of the diphthongs, nasals, and other basic sounds of the language, this was an excellent exercise in pronunciation and intonation, one that I have used successfully in my French teaching years to introduce the sound of French to my absolute beginners. I took heart. I had always loved arithmetic. The last year in Berlin we had mastered horrendously huge numbers, building thousands, hundreds of thousands, millions, and billions by the wondrous expedient of adding zeros, each representing a factor of ten. I prided myself on a solid grasp of the decimal system and could handle long divisions of very large numbers. There were no calculators, although Papa's abacus had helped me to visualize numbers graphically. The teacher wrote simple problems on the blackboard: additions, subtractions, multiplications. This I could do very well, until a real puzzler appeared: two numbers separated by a weird half rectangle, the smaller to the left, the larger to the right of the vertical line. Which went into what? In German, fifteen divided by three, for example, would be written as 15:3. Had the divisor and dividend changed places? A bit of my secure world of numbers came tumbling down.

Teacher saw my puzzled look and took pity on me. She came to my desk, let go a cascade of words which confused me even more, and then tried to console me, as I burst into tears, by hugging me. The more she hugged, the more I cried. The more I cried, the more she hugged. It was a no-win situation.

Teacher returned to her desk while I continued to sob in quiet desperation.

That evening, after Mama tucked me into bed before leaving for her night class at the Alliance Française (the cultural arm of the French government designed to teach French, French civilization, and Cartesian logic all over the world as a matter of foreign policy), I burst into audible sobs, out of anger and frustration. Everything was wrong: the shape and color of the bread, walls that bent, steps that sagged, streets that curved. Boys in smocks that looked like dresses. My shoes, my stockings, my dress, the way I curtsied, the way I walked, the way I spoke, the way I wrote, and the way the divisor and dividend had changed places. Nothing made sense any more. I couldn't stop crying. I was clutching my soggy pillow when the door opened. My big brother walked in with heavy, threatening steps and gave me the first and last spanking of my life. It stopped my hysterics cold. "You're a spoiled brat, a crybaby. I'm the only one to earn a little money selling rugs, like a peddler. Mama is running around all day trying to find work, and so is Papa. You're too big to cry because Mama left you to go to sleep alone. Papa won't spank you, so I have to do it for him."

It was a sobering speech, but my brother had misunderstood the source of my misery. The next morning, I refused to go to school. And the next. I had a tummy ache. I was nauseated. I stayed in bed. Finally one morning I woke up to see Mama leaning over my small brown suitcase, set on a chair next to my bed, carefully folding my few belongings. "Where am I going?" I asked hopefully, recalling the many happy interludes in Berlin when I was sent elsewhere each time we moved. "I am taking you to the railroad station. A nice lady who is a teacher agreed to have you stay with her family for a month or two. She lives in the country, in a big house, near the city of Orléans." "Does she speak German?" "She is a very educated lady. I think very educated ladies in France speak German."

Thus reassured, I took my assigned seat in the train compartment, my very own brown suitcase safely stashed in the overhead baggage rack, facing my hostess, who smiled encouragingly and said, "Bonjour, Julia," without any unintelligible embellishments, without any provocative attempts at hugging, keeping her distance.

I cannot recall her looks, nor her name. She was simply a middle-aged woman of average stature and average looks, in a sober, well-tailored suit, with a bearing of unmistakable confidence. "Sprechen Sie Deutsch?" I ventured. "Non, Julia, je parle français." She spoke simply and clearly. I could understand every word. Thus started my rigorous and disciplined introduction to all things French—words, gestures, food, games, customs—until every trace of my German accent and behavior was suppressed and I was no longer the enemy, just a poor little girl without a country.

When my brother retired from his work in Paris, he and his wife

Danièle settled in Orléans. A few years earlier, they had bought a four-room house next to the one Danièle inherited from her grandparents in Meung, a twenty-minute drive downriver from Orléans. I used to stop by fairly regularly every summer on my way south to the Midi and/or Morocco, and/or on my way north to Germany. There we puzzled over maps and drove around the countryside, to no avail. I had no clue as to precisely where I had spent those months learning French in a two-room public school which Madame directed with faultless expertise within a ten-mile radius of Orléans.

I recall that Madame had a car, *ma voiture,* that we drove a short distance to her domain, a big sand and gravel covered yard, with two symmetrically aligned buildings on one side, Madame's residence and Madame's schoolhouse. On the opposite side were rudimentary sanitary facilities since there was no plumbing, one serving Madame's residence and separate ones serving the schoolchildren.

There were no children in Madame's family, only four or five adults. Their relationships were not clear to me. Sisters? Aunts? A mother?

Madame showed me my room upstairs, unpacked my suitcase, and shook her head as she held up my brown knit dress, my black smock, my knee socks, and my ankle socks with their multicolored borders. These she took away. I was shown the *toilettes* outside. It was imperative that I learn to say, "La toilette, s'il vous plaît, Madame," to get permission to leave the house in case of urgency. For night emergencies there was an old-fashioned chamber pot underneath the bed.

Dinner was served in the dining room. I was handed a cloth napkin case with a large white napkin folded inside—"Ta serviette, Julia,"—and told to say, "Merci, Madame." Wine was poured, soup was served, everyone said *bon appétit* and began to eat. There were chunks of bread in a straw basket, but no butter to spread on them. The basket was passed around, people took a piece of bread, daintily broke off a small bit of it, and popped it in their mouths, followed by a spoonful of soup. There was talk. Talk between bites, talk between mouthfuls, talk between soup and fowl or fish, talk between fish and potatoes, talk between potatoes and salad, talk between salad and fruit and cheese, as each course was served separately, plates carried away, new plates taking their place, the meal stretching on and on well past my bedtime.

There was no pillow on my bed! Only a long cylindrical bolster, *un traversin.* There was no quilt, no featherbed. I got into my pajamas, clutched my teddy bear, and crawled into bed with blankets loosely laid upon the sheets, not buttoned down, threatening to slide off at every turn. Madame fixed that as she said *bonne nuit* and "bordered" me in so tightly and snugly on my back that I couldn't move. The blankets and top sheet were tightly drawn and deftly tucked underneath the mattress. I slept, transfixed.

In the morning, after a breakfast of steaming coffee, that is, hot milk diluted with a spoonful of coffee (I learned that French children never drank milk; they drank coffee or hot chocolate, just enough to disguise the white of the milk), bread, and yummy homemade marmalade, Madame drove me to town with perhaps two of the other ladies. It must have been a Thursday when school was out, and a market day, the kind where clothes and pots and pans were sold from open stalls, as well as vegetables, fruits, meats, eggs, live chickens, dead rabbits, and crawly things our French teacher at the gymnasium had warned us about. I had to stand very still—"Tiens-toi tranquille, Julia"—while Madame held a pleated navy-blue skirt against my waist, then chose a cardigan to match. Two blouses, two checkered school smocks in baby blue and pink on white, and several pairs of white knee socks almost completed my new wardrobe. The most difficult was yet to come: a pair of shoes. My feet were long and very narrow, the exact opposite of the average French girl's foot, which tended to be short and wide. There were no different widths in store-bought shoes then. People with money had their shoes made to order, just as most families had their seamstress or favorite sewing aunt whip up their clothes in fall and spring. I had to settle for a pair of black shoes with straps, with a piece of felt under my too-narrow heel. A pair of warm slippers, *pantoufles,* was another essential. I was not allowed to wear shoes in the house. There was a sharp shoe-scraper bar next to the entrance door on which to scrape the mud off the soles of one's shoes before entering, after which one put on slippers.

The next day, I went to the schoolhouse next door, and unobtrusively took a seat in the back of the room, equipped with notebook, pen, and colored pencils. I was given to understand that I could do anything I pleased, as long as I was quiet and didn't disturb the class. This I proceeded to do with a vengeance. I neatly copied a tree with branches, leaves, and roots which the teacher had drawn on the board, as well as the words that went with it. Every part of the tree—the trunk, the bark, the veins on the leaves—was pointed out, as the class repeated in unison

the botanical vocabulary. Madame added clouds on one side shedding
rain and a sun on the other. Everything was labeled. There followed an
explanation of how the tree grew. I picked up the French words for "rain,"
"clouds," "sun," and "sky." And as Madame pointed to the labels, I was
able to match the sound of the words to their written equivalents, a task
not to be taken lightly as many letters remained silent! *E*s were squashed
between consonants, and final consonants were left dangling unpronounced, especially the letter *s,* which appeared and disappeared at the
end of the same words for no apparent reason.

The room was airy, bright, freshly painted. Girls of different ages and
sizes, perhaps spanning grades three to six, wore checkered smocks just
like mine. Diligently I copied. Diligently I drew. At recess I was surrounded by a crowd of eager little teachers. "I'm Giselle. I'm nine." "She's
Jeanne, she's eight. How old are you?" I understood. I could answer. "Julia
is ten," someone repeated. The same phrases were slung about over and
over again. "Look! Watch out!" "She's got the ball." "Get out of the way!"
"Run!" "Let's skip rope!" I loved to skip rope; I thought I was pretty good
at it. These French girls skipped nimbly, elegantly, each taking her turn
without a break in the rhythm of the swinging rope as the two girls who
swung the rope kept count each time the rope came down. "You want to
jump?" I was asked. "Yes, jump," I responded eagerly, and was greeted
with an outbreak of giggles. Fingers pointed at me, and "*sotte, sotte*"
(which rhymes with "not") was repeated with renewed laughter until one
girl relented and gently corrected me: *saute* (which rhymes with "note").
Henceforth I had to watch my short and long *o*s to stay out of trouble.
It took some time before I learned that *sotte* was pretty much of an idiot,
a silly goose, but I had made a dent in the language barrier. This was a
real breakthrough.

Each day I copied everything on the board, sang out the multiplication
tables with the rest of the class, listened attentively as the same La
Fontaine fable was recited over and over again. Something about cheese,
a fox, and a mean blackbird. Cheese was served after every meal, or rather
many varieties of cheeses, so I had been taught *fromage,* along with everything else on the table, and *merci,* to signify that I didn't want any. Surviving in France without eating cheese, which for some reason I never
liked (though my family ate it after meals, before meals, and in between),
along with yogurt, cream cheese, cottage cheese, and generous dollops of
sour cream on beet soup and cold spinach soup, presented somewhat of a

problem. Most servings were small. Fresh fruit in season—berries, cherries, plums, peaches, grapes, apples, pears—was plentiful, temptingly succulent and delicious. Together with twice daily servings of salad greens in vinaigrette sauce expertly tossed at the table by the head of the household, soups of infinite variety, and fresh garden vegetables, cheese was an essential part of the diet to prevent having to be excused to run outside, rain or shine, more often than one would wish. Cheese eaters simply consider cheese delicious. Gourmet cheese eaters, and every French person is one, savor every bite of every kind of cheese, each of which has its own distinctive texture, coloring, its known origin and flavor, all of which is a source of ever renewed satisfaction and lengthy discussion. Even in Berlin, my parents' guests used to exclaim, "What, she doesn't eat cheese!" with the same tone of disapproval as, "What, she doesn't speak Russian!" On my first trip to China in 1982, I felt vindicated. One billion Chinese and a hundred million more since then do not eat cheese. I believe that is one fifth of the world population. I am not alone.

I made up for my cheese phobia by eating chocolate. Hot chocolate, chocolate pudding, chocolate mousse, chocolate cake, chocolate frosting, plain dark baker's chocolate, Belgian, Swiss and French chocolate.

After school, when all the girls went home, I returned to Madame's dining room for the traditional after school snack, a chocolate sandwich: a lovely six-inch crusty white loaf of bread, into which was stuck a piece of dark chocolate, the size of a Hershey bar, but infinitely better tasting. This with a bowl of warm pretend coffee sent me off with enough renewed energy to practice skipping rope in the yard until dinnertime. An alternative to the homemade chocolate sandwich was the store-bought *petit pain au chocolat,* a sweet roll with a piece of chocolate baked in. But I liked the real thing better. Visiting my brother two summers ago between chemotherapy treatments, I managed the few steps to the kitchen and had a real chocolate sandwich, butter spread on both sides and dark chocolate in between, with our afternoon tea and for dessert at night. My brother still walks the hundred feet from his house to the corner bakery to fetch freshly baked white bread for breakfast, lunch, and dinner. (That was supposed to have been my chore when we arrived in Paris over sixty-two years ago.) In June I gained five pounds, and my doctors were very pleased.

When we were first married, I told Fred, in bits and pieces, the saga of our escape from Angers and of the summer 1940 spent scrounging for food in Toulouse. Fred kidded me, "I hate to think what you would have done for a bar of chocolate." In fact we left just in time before temptation got the best of me.

I don't recall how long I stayed in Madame's school near Orléans, that first spring and summer of 1933. I remember the chestnut trees were in bloom in Paris before Mama put me on the train. Papa had taken me for free walks in the Luxembourg gardens (chairs to sit on cost a small fee), which were not too far from our miserable lodgings. Since I spent my days in the safe enclosure of Madame's schoolyard, I had no idea of the surrounding area. On Thursdays and Sundays (Saturday was a school day), we drove to Orléans to shop or admire the cathedral with its lovely smiling angel. Did Madame point out the Maid of Orléans, proudly seated in full armor on her fighting steed? Orléans was pretty much bombed to smithereens before the Occupation. The modern buildings surrounding the statue in the center of the square bear no resemblance to the city I had once barely known.

At school, during recess, my classmates added "school" to their repertory of classic games. I was their lone pupil, facing eight or ten "teachers" who each took turns making sure I knew the lesson of the day. "What's this?" and "What's that?" I was quizzed mercilessly on the parts of the body, articles of dress, parts of buildings. "Very good," one would smile; "non, non, non, non," another would exclaim, repeating the offending word until I got it just right.

At dinnertime, I was asked to pass the bread and told the names of the various dishes. This was a formidable task since I was unable to identify the vegetables, fowl, fish, or meat in their French-cooked condition. Some of them I had never seen before. Not heart, not brain, not kidney, certainly not snails. I was shown how to fold my napkin properly and return it to its napkin case, *pochette*. At the end of the meal, I was allowed to gather all of the napkins, each in its individual *pochette,* and return them to their assigned place in the top drawer of the buffet. Madame was very precise and very strict. She made me repeat every phrase until it was absolutely right. "What was that? I don't understand. Repeat it again. Like this . . ." ("Qu'est-ce-que tu dis? Je ne comprends pas. Répète . . .")

Once I almost cried. "Would you like to take off your cardigan?" "Non, Madame," I replied, having become very attached to it. "What do you mean, no. Take it off. This is an order. It is much too warm." I had come face to face with the use of the polite conditional, which with a no-nonsense kind of intonation means, "Do it, or else."

It was the end of spring, perhaps the middle of June. It was raining. After my chocolate sandwich, I dashed back next door to the empty class-room. Madame had given me a box of colored chalk, shown me how to erase the board, and pointed out the maps, posters, and pictures on the walls. I was in paradise. I had the whole classroom to myself. I could draw on the board to my heart's content and quiz invisible students as I used Madame's pointer to show them the cities on the map of France. I traced the rivers flowing north, east, south, and west, the natural borders of the "Hexagon," that is, the Channel, the Atlantic Ocean, the Pyrenees, the Mediterranean Sea, the Alps, the Rhine, leaving only the plains of Normandy exposed and open to the north, sharing an artificial border with Belgium.

I wrote arithmetic problems on the board and counted aloud, demonstrating addition, subtraction, multiplication, and yes, long division, all in the careful rhythmic singsong I had learned listening in class. I drew houses. I drew floor plans of houses, detailing each room. I drew furniture, each piece with its proper name, which was never capitalized, and most importantly, with its correct article.

I drew the moon, *la lune,* and the sun, *le soleil.* The moon smiled in French; she was a lady. The sun, a brutal master, was fierce. He burned the skin and fields in summer. They were not the same as the mean macho moon, cold and unfeeling, and the gentle lady sun who melted the snow, warmed the earth and made people happy in Berlin.

Carefully, I read and copied and reread the legends under each picture, illustrating poems the class had learned by heart and fairy tales I knew well.

School let out just before Bastille Day, the fourteenth of July, France's national holiday. I am not sure how long I stayed after that, perhaps a week or two. I recall having the classroom to myself all day, the schoolyard empty.

When Madame returned me to Paris, my little brown suitcase tightly packed, teddy bear under my arm, I ran to Mama's anxious outstretched arms and could only mumble, "Je parle français." "Elle parle français," Madame repeated as she shook Mama's hand. "Merci, Madame," Mama responded in her newly acquired Alliance Française French.

Thank you, Madame, for opening the door to a confused little girl who lost her language, for teaching her French and the love of France.

Family fortunes had improved somewhat. Mama had found lodgings in a decent sort of apartment house. Was it a room in an apartment with a shared bath? Was it an apartment building converted to a hotel? At any rate, it looked out on a wide avenue opposite the Bois de Vincennes, the large (by European standards) park at the eastern edge of Paris. Mama was "working." As refugees and stateless persons, we had no work permits. We had to have our temporary residence papers periodically reviewed and stamped at the police station. There were exceptions. Mama could treat Russian friends, but could not write prescriptions. She could "volunteer" for a token salary as a nurse's aide. My brother was lucky. He found interesting, legal, and remunerative employment in the circulation department of a German daily published in Paris, the *Pariser Tageblatt,* since it required his skills in German.

Papa was less fortunate. The occasional article published in the Russian daily paper brought a pittance. His speaking and writing talents, confined to Russian, were useless in getting work in Paris at the height of the depression. Papa was an expert at appreciating the finer things in life—good food, good wine, good cigarettes and cigars, elegantly tailored clothes, all of which required money, and a good deal of it. He spent his days, I gathered, making the rounds of Russian acquaintances, in ever-fading hopes of making the right business connections, though in what business was never clear to me. While he eventually learned to read and write French fluently, his spoken French could only be described as broken. Papa had no ear for music; he could not follow a tune, nor the proper cadence of a language foreign to him.

For the remainder of the summer, I was sent to camp in Belgium under the auspices of a progressive left-wing organization. I knew it was progressive because boys and girls, even ten to twelve years old, were mixed up together and slept in the same tent. I knew it was left-wing because we sang the same songs in French which I had learned in Germany. There was a socialist emblem on flags and lapel pins: three arrows signifying freedom, progress, and solidarity.

The camp, a huge tent city, housing perhaps a thousand children, was set up on the beach of Ostende near the Channel, not far from the French border to the south and Dunkerque to the north. I was used to camp and to camp discipline. When I was six, I had spent two weeks in ski camp in Germany. I had learned to hang up my socks on the lower rung of my bedside chair, to fold my clothes neatly over the back of the chair, and to put my shoes, carefully aligned, underneath the chair. I even ate the loathsome hot breakfast cereal, a sort of grits, without protest. (At home, Mama had to resort to endless stratagems, such as hiding a slice of orange, a delicacy then, at the bottom of the plate; or better yet, a piece of dark chocolate.) I did not understand why the other children cried. "They are homesick, they miss their Mutti, they do not like the food," explained the counselor. I thought it was fun. We played games, we made snowmen, we threw snowballs, and we put on skis, or rather the skis were painstakingly attached to our high-top shoes. Hours of practice in Montessori nursery school patiently lacing, tying, buttoning, and fastening hooks finally paid off as I was able to lace and tie my shoes, and get in and out of my heavy clothes, with a minimum of assistance. The slopes were dotted with Christmas trees; we sang "Silent Night" and "Tannenbaum." Of skiing, I only have one recollection: I made it down a gentle incline, a beginner's beginning slope, to land in a high pile of snow that almost buried me. I learned many things at that camp, but skiing was not one of them.

Ostende was different. There was a great deal of talk in small groups, in different languages. I was in a group that spoke French, though many of the boys and girls spoke another language or two as well. We were told about the battles of World War I and combed the beach for remnants of shrapnel, for pieces of metal. I recall field trips to military cemeteries, rows of white crosses as far as the eye could stretch. We sang songs around the campfire at night, songs about a bright future, about a world without war. ("Never shall we fight again. . . . Let the gentlemen fight their own battles.") There was a "wall journal," a canvas stretched between posts, on which the best stories were fastened with thumbtacks. We were encouraged to talk about our experiences. "Julia, what can you tell us about your last year in Berlin?" asked the camp director.

So I told him about the broken glass, the smashed windows, the blood on the sidewalk on my way to school. "You should write it down, and we will post it on our wall journal. You may write it in French or in German, as you wish." This was the opportunity of a lifetime to get started on a writing career. I tossed around all night, figuratively speaking, as I was snugly buttoned into my makeshift sleeping bag, a folded blanket, hastily sewn together (zippers came later). I was speaking French all day, but neither my basic vocabulary nor my minimal writing skills sufficed to render my traumatic experience in French. I panicked. I hadn't written a word of German since my unmailed letter to Dog. How could I write? It was to take me seven years of living in France, of classical French drama, of French literature, of weekly essays, of daily debates and conversation to feel confident enough to write in French, at which point we left for America.

As long as I spoke French, I was no longer the enemy. Germany, as in "Deutschland über Alles," the national anthem that used to bring tears to my eyes, was the enemy. The things I loved had turned flip-flop. Yes, I loved wieners, sausage, stuffed cabbage, red cabbage, and especially sauerkraut. I missed my daily portion of plain steamed potatoes. I missed hearty rye bread and dark pumpernickel. I missed the brisk walks in woods and fields, the sheer pleasure of walking on weekend outings, spring and summer breaks, when I was sent elsewhere to camp or to summer school, marching and singing old journeymen's songs, which inevitably ended on a note of "home sweet home" in the last verse. Home, the same Anglo-Saxon root as the German *Heim,* from which *Heimat* is derived, which means homeland; except that *Heimat* made me cry in the old sentimental way the French made fun of, and because I couldn't go back, and it never had been mine to begin with. In English, "homeland" to me is just a word.

I kept silent. I had a growing feeling that the words, once out of my mouth and in full view in print, could be misused, out of my control. I was wary, and for good reason.

Barely six months earlier, a friendly "good morning" in Berlin had been officially changed to "Heil Hitler." A simple car, the French-derived *Auto,* had been transformed into a 100 percent pure German "power vehicle." The "Horst Wessel Lied" had supplanted, or at least complemented, the national anthem. A powerfully heart-wrenching melody, its martial rhythm accenting the Nazi goose step, it filled every patriotic heart with pride and fearless arrogance.

"S.A. was on the march," there was no doubt about it. Yet all the while, in camp, we were singing "No more war, never, never shall we fight again," and "Left, left, forward pioneer!" (In the blue songbook of the Thaelmann Pioneers, the third verse reads, "Left, left, left, Lenin's party is with us, he's the leader [*Führer,* just like Hitler], he makes us free.") In

French, "left" has the connotation of "awkward." It didn't make much sense to me, put your awkward foot forward. Later, I was introduced to the confusing (morally speaking) political concepts of Left and Right, since according to our socialist group, only the Left was right. I thought of the Left Bank of Paris, where we were so miserably lodged, as the abode of the Parisian Left (read "liberals"), students, writers, and generally weird unconventional characters, whereas the Right Bank, with its teeming department stores and financial institutions, was obviously the precinct of the Parisian Right (read "conservatives"). This wasn't such a farfetched notion, but as I later learned, the Left and the Right Bank of the Seine River refer to their geographic location relative to the river's flow. The war of words was one I didn't want to get caught up in. Ever since I've had a phobia about joining any cause, putting my name on any petition.

On my return to Paris, I was briefly enrolled in a school not far from our lodgings. Mama arranged for me to have lunch with the family of the concierge, the fabled building manager, gatekeeper, and cleaning lady. This was an adventure, as we squeezed good-naturedly and with much aplomb around the dinner table of a two-room apartment the size of a modest motel room, with a kitchenette half the size of a motel bathroom, and the bathroom somewhere down the hall. Madame's husband, brother, and son, in burly work clothes, helped themselves to the four bottles of red table wine, which were emptied one after the other. There was a lot of talk, a lot of back slapping, fists pounding on the table. I was urged to partake of the grape, just a tablespoon—perhaps a bit more, it's good for you—in a glass of water. There were no looks across the table signifying "not in front of the young lady," no warning gestures indicating "watch your language." I was introduced to the heartiest of French five-letter words, which punctuated every sentence, and to the classic Parisian street argot, passed on from father to son. I was never able, and am not to this day, to let one word of it pass my lips in spite of my male students' pleading, my excuse being that slang is very difficult to learn and can get you in trouble when used on the wrong occasion. I nonetheless learned to appreciate its full impact.

Thus coached in the ways of a man's world, I was fully prepared to enter the French seventh grade, the last year before the dreaded exams which guaranteed access to the academic world by way of the lycée. Before World War II, only about 5 percent of the French school population succeeded beyond these cutoff exams, through the following three academic grades, and beyond to the last year of the lycée and the French baccalaureate. There were two of them, separated by an intensive year of the study of philosophy or math and science. The baccalaureate was the threshold to any professional career, the ticket to social aspirations, the universally acknowledged badge of the educated person. It has since been devalued, following the American model of equal opportunity misread as "passing grades for all," to the point that French university students are now protesting the crowded conditions, the lack of preparation, the failure of the university system to take care of the 80 percent of the student population labeled "educated."

Among members of the Group, whose rise to fame and misfortune as the Revolutionary Minority Party had been predicated on their disciplined scholarship, their study of political and economic theory, their thorough grounding in western philosophy, literature, and the arts, it was unthinkable that their progeny not pursue a professional career.

It must have been late fall, 1933. It was my fourth move, not counting summer camp in Belgium, since I left Berlin the last week of March, whispering German in my teddy bear's ear. Mama had found a sunny, spacious (even by today's French standards) two-bedroom apartment with a terrace and a tiny maid's room in a modern building at the foot of rue Jullien, across from the entrance of the parc of the Lycée Michelet, which accepted girls in the lower grades in an all boys' boarding school.

Our family's first priority had always been communication and information, which in the thirties meant a telephone, when most people had none, newspapers, and access to people "in the know." Accordingly, we sat in empty rooms by the telephone and read newspapers in Russian, German, and French. My brother read the French papers to Mama in Russian until her Alliance Française classes assured her sufficient French reading proficiency. Unfortunately, between running around, marketing, working, scrubbing and boiling sheets, there was never enough time left for French. People dropped in unannounced, each with a tale of woe, which I both did and did not want to hear. Eventually, Mama installed some sadly mismatched pieces of furniture retrieved from the flea market: a small desk on spindly legs, a horribly sturdy, squat armchair, a floor lamp with a shade askew, a couple of small rugs that didn't cover the floor. We slept on mattresses. Since my parents had separated, Papa roomed in a succession of hotels and private apartments. My brother slept in the living room, which doubled as Mama's prospective consultation room. I shared one bedroom with Mama, of which I recollect nothing. To help with the rent, Mama took in a small boarder, an eight-year-old boy named Benno, whose parents were busy putting their business and life in order after a hasty departure, not from Berlin. Benno had strict instructions to speak French at every opportunity, as did I, but every now and then he broke down and we spoke German.

The tiny maid's room adjoining the kitchen was rented out to Boris Nicolaevsky, patronymic Ivanovitch, whom I had known in Berlin as a friendly giant who refused to speak a word of German. Boris Ivanovitch now proceeded with equal determination to resist any attempt to learn French, instead concentrating his intellectual resources on daily debates with his best friend, Denicke, who was equally tall but only half as broad, and permanently sunburned. The debates took place in the kitchen. Boris Ivanovitch's curly unruly locks threatened to get tangled in Denicke's equally unruly strands of long red hair. (Denicke had no patronymic that I recall. Everyone referred to him as Denicke. Being tall, thin, and red-faced, he always reminded me of the quintessential man of the north, obviously a Dane.) Boris Ivanovitch's thick fingers stabbed into Denicke's concave chest to punctuate their argument as his voice rose into a series of menacing shouts. Mama's slight figure would appear, holding a teapot high in the air. With her best patient-commanding voice she would prepare a cup of tea in the nick of time, before Denicke was throttled by his best friend or Boris Ivanovitch had a fit of apoplexy. Mama carefully shoved forward two giant cups, acquired for just this occasion, poured tea, set sugar cubes and cherry marmalade on the table, and thus silenced the two protagonists. Sipping boiling hot tea was a ritual which required careful concentration. Flared tempers subsided. Denicke left with profuse and confused thank-yous; Boris Ivanovitch disappeared silently into his maid's room.

I was not the only foreign child to enter the French seventh grade a month or so after the start of the school year. With me was my best friend from grade school days in Berlin, a boy named Leo, now Léon, who had acquired a most enviable mastery of French slang in a short time, one advantage being that he could practice it at home to his heart's content since neither of his parents understood a word of it. (This reminds me of my grandson Réda in Casablanca. Réda was perhaps six and his little cousin Nadia four or five. Suddenly, for no apparent reason, Nadia burst into uncontrollable tears while Réda stood by with a most suspicious smile.

He had done nothing. He had not touched her. He was innocent of any wrongdoing. Tanya asked, "What did you say to make her cry?" and out came some awful words in Arabic which neither Réda nor Tanya understood, except that they had the power to make a little girl cry.)

There was another boy, an acquaintance from Berlin, stodgy and a bit slow, named Noah. On the third floor of our building, I found yet another long-lost friend: little Alexander, now eight, he of the red fire engine, turned into an accomplished pianist, a whiz at math, and a veritable Dennis the Menace, who had turned both his parents' hair permanently gray (his father having very little of it left). Alexander had violent tantrums, alternating with the most devastatingly charming cherubic smile that would melt any grown-up's heart.

In addition, we met newcomers whose parents were somehow befriended by the Group, including a girl named Zina and a pale asthmatic boy with a cleft palate named Marc. All of these children spoke Russian, German, and now French. We were all our parents' valued interpreters. Our job of mastering the French language without an accent was serious business. We corrected each other, forbade the use of German categorically (poor little Benno, who spoke only German, had a hard time of it), and met the challenge of the Lycée Michelet head on.

Since I had skipped a grade in Berlin and slid back a grade in Paris, I found myself exactly where I should be, with boys and girls the same age and, more importantly, the same height. I was already familiar with the subject matter covered in math, science, and geography. My months of diligent work at Madame's two-room school had prepared me for the French italic writing style. I was used to German declinations, conjugations, and grammatical analysis, compared to which French grammar was a cinch, once the idea of the unpronounced grammatical endings was grasped.

We had one period of French grammar and one period of French composition every day, all very neatly outlined and graphically explained, with hefty doses of sequential homework, so that I made predictable and satisfying progress. Of most help to me in vocabulary building were the daily lists of definitions to be learned by heart, the charts in geography, and especially flowers, bees, and the like, with all parts carefully pointed out and labeled on the board. There was a great deal of oral repetition, of recitation of poems, of memorization of paragraphs, and summaries of historical events. These had to be rendered word for word on our history tests and caused me grievous pain, not because I failed, but because I earned the almost unattainable mark of 20 without having understood a word of what I had correctly written!

I complained bitterly to Mama about this incomprehensible French teaching style but kept my tears carefully in check, mindful of big brother's punishing swats. Instead I consoled myself with chocolate pudding, one of the few desserts Mama knew how to prepare, with the help of Nestle's premixed powder in a small paper envelope. I ate all four portions of it, slice after slice of a magnificent chocolate jellied fish which I found cooling on a plate in the window box, a sort of outdoor pantry installed underneath the kitchen window sill which took the place of an icebox.

I had become a model latchkey kid. After several episodes of having to climb, I can't recall how, up to the terrace and through the French doors of the living room, a most unladylike procedure for a well-behaved ten-year-old schoolgirl in a neat baby blue checkered smock, Mama solved the problem by hanging the apartment key around my neck. I was also free to visit the Wittenbergs, Alexander's family. Their three-bedroom apartment in the rue Jullien was a far cry from their palatial quarters in Berlin. The floors were bare. Six plain chairs stood around an equally plain table. Gone were the fire engine, the tricycle, long outgrown, and the many other toys. Alexander consoled himself with Babar, chess, and the piano. A magnificent black grand was squeezed into these modest surroundings. When his older sister Sarah was not practicing, which she was an average of five hours a day, Alexander took over. He had an uncanny musical ear and could play some of the easier parts of Sarah's recital pieces with vim and vigor, if not with the same precision. He also practiced on his own, most of the easier classics, which he memorized after a few readings. And he improvised. Thus, I was treated to concerts every time I ran up to the third floor.

However, the highlight of the day was an invitation by Mr. Wittenberg to visit him in his maid's room on the seventh floor, which he had transformed into an office, the Paris headquarters of his Esperanto journal. Mr. Wittenberg, unlike the other members of the Group, was a do-it-yourselfer before his time, and prided himself on his handiwork. He had constructed a desk which left exactly enough space for him and his not inconsiderable Santa Claus belly to squeeze by and sit down behind it. With his crown of prematurely white curls, twinkling eyes, and ruddy jolly face, Mr. Wittenberg was a prime candidate for playing Santa Claus. Since he had built the desk inside the room, I wondered how he would get it through the door or out the window, which is the French way of moving furniture which cannot go up or down the stairs, if he ever had to move again.

I remember standing next to this most original carpentry work, then unstained and unfinished, with curious little shelves and holes built in, trays, small lidless boxes, larger lidless boxes, all cut to fit large and small envelopes, fat and thin pencils of all colors, stamps, thumbtacks, paper clips, glue. There were also several built-in inkwells for inks of different colors. His pride was a sliding shelf to support his typewriter which he had built in at exactly the right height to fit comfortably over his knees when he pulled it out. When not in use, which was very seldom, it disappeared underneath a flap in the desk top.

Mr. Wittenberg explained about Esperanto, and how it would help people who spoke different languages to communicate. He showed us envelopes with strangely beautiful stamps with tropical flowers, exotic birds, and writing I had never seen before: stamps from Africa, the Pacific Islands, China, Japan, India, the Middle East, North and South America, from every part of the globe. Was there a globe on his desk? A world map on the wall behind with little pins stuck in, representing his many correspondents around the world? Carefully he tore off the stamps and put them in the appropriate lidless box. The interview came to a satisfying end. I took Alexander to his apartment and returned to my own.

One afternoon after school, which let out at four o'clock (I believe I ate lunch at school even though we lived only five minutes away down the hill, which I took at a run), I found Boris Ivanovitch sipping tea in the kitchen. He seemed most distraught. Perhaps he and Denicke had another argument. He chided me for not speaking Russian, the most beautiful, harmonious language. I nodded my head in shame; I couldn't have agreed more. I couldn't bring out a single word, precisely because it was so beautiful and my tongue, used to German guttural sounds, broke the melody, grated over the rolling *r*s, and massacred the sound of it. Perhaps Boris Ivanovitch understood. Perhaps that was the real reason he refused to utter a word in German or French, because it sounded ugly to his ears.

He always kept his room locked. I had strict orders not to bother him. So I am not sure how I came to stand between his neatly made up cot and the stacks of cardboard boxes which filled the rest of the tiny space.

There was no other furniture. A few hooks on the back of the door held some clothes. It was eerie. I didn't solve the puzzle of the cardboard boxes until some forty years later.

I had always thought of Boris Ivanovitch as a friendly giant, huge but harmless, and, in spite of his threatening outbursts during arguments with Denicke, a thoroughly kind and genteel soul. So what was he hoarding under lock and key? Why was Mama adamant about my never, ever, opening the door to anyone when I was alone? It was disconcerting, to say the least, to cast him in the role of a modern-day Bluebeard, which was the obvious image that came to mind. Just the same, I never told any of my friends about the mysterious boxes; never did I venture beyond the kitchen to the forbidden door again.

Once, two gentlemen in somber black clothing rang the doorbell, their wooden looks the sort one associates with the FBI on duty, inquiring about Boris Ivanovitch's whereabouts. Mama sent them on their way, firmly standing her ground in the doorframe, acting her innocent best: she knew no such person. They went away, doffing their hats politely. The conversation was in Russian. In later years, there was mention of Mama's heroic stand against the dreaded NKVD agents (Soviet secret police), come to take away Boris Ivanovitch's precious boxes. Or a variant thereof: the NKVD offered Mama a handsome reward, which she refused, pretending not to know what they were talking about.

At any rate, Boris Ivanovitch's treasure escaped the hands of the NKVD and remained safe and sound in our diminutive maid's room. How they were eventually whisked out of Paris hours before the Germans occupied the city, how they reached America's safe haven, I do not know. We saw Boris Ivanovitch occasionally after our next move, in the fall of 1935, when he and Denicke came to tea in our two-room apartment (no subtenants), in the rue Jules Simon, a few blocks from the newly built, all pink girls' school, the Lycée Camille Sée.

The next time Boris Ivanovitch's name surfaced was in the late sixties. One of my star language students at Benjamin Franklin High School had accepted a full scholarship at Stanford University. She came to chat briefly during summer break. Yes, she was taking Russian from a Russian Russian teacher, a venerable old gentleman. His name was Boris Nicolaevsky.

A few years later, a book review caught my eye: *Culture in Exile: Russian Emigrés in Germany, 1881–1941.* I ordered the book. Sure enough, I found Boris Ivanovitch and Denicke on page 302. Boris Ivanovitch had obviously succeeded in "salvag[ing] his archives from the clutches of the police in Berlin," that is, all of the writings and correspondence relating to the Menshevik party. Some time after his arrival in the States, his papers found safe refuge in the Hoover Institute.

Fall 1933 to 1935 were the years of the Musketeers, of Napoleon's battles, of African expeditions, the latter an outgrowth of Dr. Doolittle's adventures assiduously played out since second grade in Berlin. We children spent many an afternoon acting out the books we read. The stairs lent themselves to daring duels. A wooden sword that a carpenter had fashioned for me in Mecklenburg was but a memory; never mind, we used sturdy twigs or waved our arms instead. There were hair-raising escapes. Marc, because of his asthma, was not to run, jump, or exert himself. He was our director, the expert in matters of wardrobe, our historian. He had memorized every date, every general's name, every battle of Napoleon's wars; and before them, every known utterance of the Sun King, his ministers, his generals, his consort, and his mistresses. He could recite entire pages verbatim from Dumas' *The Three Musketeers.* He distributed roles accordingly, with remarkable patience made each of us repeat our lines, and contributed pieces of his mother's wardrobe: hat, gloves, cape. He had us practice complicated reverences walking backwards, sweeping the floor with imaginary feathers stuck in our berets. Richelieu was the most majestic of his characters. Marc spared no effort to impart to the hapless actor the proper stance, the haughty smile, the careless gesture of dismissal. When he started coughing, Marc slowly climbed the stairs, a small undersized blond figure of a boy barely ten, whose powerful imagination and disciplined intellect made him the respected leader of our not-so-childish games. I suspect the other boys, whose French reading ability lagged far behind their vaunted mastery of French argot, had not actually read any of Dumas' novels, at least not at that time. Little Alexander was given roles, too. He played everybody's page and groom.

We stayed on at rue Jullien another year, even after I passed the lycée entrance exams and was enrolled in sixth grade at the Lycée Camille Sée, which was the absolute opposite of the Lycée Michelet to which I had become accustomed. I especially missed the graciously ascending avenue lined with venerable old chestnut trees, behind which lay the forbidden park, a sort of miniforest with real live rabbits and, who knows, perhaps deer and foxes. I always entered the school grounds by the gates at the bottom of the hill. Once on top, I faced an elegant eighteenth-century palace, which had a broad flight of stairs leading to a classic bank of French windows. I supposed that it had been appropriated by the French Republic at the time of the Revolution. Now it was a respected, highly ranked boys' boarding school. The boarders lived in another building, probably the old stables. Our classroom had traces of cherubic angels on the ceiling, intricate plasterwork, and a few spindly columns which impeded the view of the blackboard for those seated behind them.

Recently, in a conversation with my French friend Colette, I mentioned my one memorable year at the Lycée Michelet and Colette, a most reserved and private person, almost fell into my arms. She was raised on the grounds of the lycée; indeed she had had the run of that fairy-tale park, her father being the *intendant,* or manager of the whole affair. She was still living there in 1933, in what had been the caretaker's house in pre-Revolutionary days.

I was not quite the youngest, nor quite the smallest in this practically brand-new girls' school, featuring escalators inside that whisked girls from floor to floor, enormously wide hallways that doubled as recreation areas, and a flat roof that served as a gym in sunny weather. There were neat locker rooms in the basement. Each girl had a whole locker instead of a hook in the back of the classroom to hang up her coat, put her hat on a shelf, and her white gloves beside it. Hatless students were asked to wait in the office for a parent or maid to pick them up. Each girl, no matter how elegantly or, in my case, inelegantly attired, covered up demurely in the same regulation baby blue smock with a square-cut neckline trimmed in white, buttoned on one side. Ingenious pleats were held together by a same-cloth belt to accommodate blossoming figures. The smocks were not available in stores. The school thoughtfully provided a pattern for the family seamstress. I had to embroider my name on the left side two inches below the neckline in white embroidery thread. There was also a pattern for the regulation gym shorts, navy blue tailored midthigh shorts, very fashionable, and yet another pattern for knitting the white short-sleeved gym sweater. Mama made the shorts and I knitted the sweater. This was the first time I had a pattern coordinated with the appropriate weight yarn. The sweater turned out a perfect fit. Being partially ribbed lengthwise, with slightly puffed sleeves, and a bit long, it grew with me until I made a second one when I turned fourteen.

Our classrooms were large and airy, with continuous windows on one side facing the street and a glassy green chalkboard reaching from the windows to the door. There were a plethora of maps that could be pulled down from the top of the chalkboard: geological maps, geographical maps, political maps, historical maps. The two remaining walls were hung with prints representing statues from great antiquity and reproductions of famous works of art.

There was one entrance and one exit in the rotunda facing the Square Saint Lambert, jealously guarded against any possible unsavory characters, salespeople, nonstudents, and/or nonemployees. The safety and chastity of some two thousand girls aged eleven to eighteen were at stake. No one was allowed in without presenting proper identification. Students each flipped up an identification card as they passed the door, no slouching, no pouting, no giggling allowed. Poise was everything. Navy blue hat askew, dirty white gloves, or crumpled knee socks were rewarded with devastating looks, a bad mark against behavior, a discreet hand pointing to the restrooms to put matters right. Parents were called on the carpet and warned to see that their daughters arrived neatly dressed. Among the lower grades, or the first three grades of the lycée, I was the exception: I had a special written dispensation to leave school on my own, as Mama was otherwise occupied and we had no maid. Most of the girls, especially if they lived more than three or four blocks away, were not allowed alone on the street and had to wait for a responsible adult to pick them up. I had no money, no standing, no grandparents in the country, only a precarious refugee status, but out of necessity or possibly ignorance of the imagined and/or real dangers ever present in the streets of Paris, I was given the unheard-of privilege of going anywhere and everywhere by myself. This was downright shocking in the rarefied atmosphere of "good families." Parents were intent on preparing their daughters for a charmed life with the proper well-connected young or not-so-young gentleman of their—the parents'—choosing. Most of my classmates had never taken a long walk alone, taken the subway in second class, hung on for dear life on the back of a bus, or gone anywhere without the ever-present chaperone, often a maiden aunt whose unfounded fears put a damper on any natural exuberance.

This was a sharp contrast to the Group's children's outings. Unaccompanied, we rowed on the lagoons in the Bois de Boulogne; rode the bumper cars near the Porte de Versailles; went to watch the goings-on at the fair, with its shooting galleries, clowns, weight lifters, fat ladies and thin men, giants and dwarfs, small children out of school doing impossible tricks as their acrobat parents balanced them on the soles of their feet, sending them flying from one pair of fast pedaling feet to another. I sensed that any mention of these most unladylike pursuits, especially in the company of boys, exposed to their dreadful language, would not be welcome at school.

I started leading a carefully compartmentalized double life. The first year at the Lycée Camille Sée, when we were still living at the foot of the Michelet park in Vanves, a suburb south of Paris, I prolonged the transition from school to home by walking the three miles from the Square Saint Lambert instead of riding the bus. The many shops on the rue de Vaugirard, the longest in Paris, were a constant wonderland. There were old button shops, old toy soldier shops, old doll shops, old toy shops, old sword shops and armor shops, old jewelry shops, weird gilded and inlaid furniture shops, porcelain and pottery shops. There were stamp shops, coin shops, hat shops, and haute couture and pattern shops, as well as a magnificent Woolworth's store closer to the outskirts. There were fancy and not so fancy shoe stores, butchers and bakers and pastry makers; there were rabbits and pheasants hanging from hooks, whole pigs and halves of calves; there were pet stores with exotic birds. The variety was endless.

People behind the counters were delighted to impart a bit of their expert knowledge. See the shape of this hat pin? Ladies had a time keeping their hats on their hair, which was piled up high before they cut it short after the Great War. Look at this medal. A beauty. The inscription is Greek. It's over 2,000 years old.

It didn't occur to me that hat and gloves, knee socks pulled up tight, a respectable if well-worn leather briefcase, excruciatingly correct grammar, and a faultless accent announced to all concerned a young lady (all of eleven years old) of academic promise and future standing. I was treated respectfully and addressed formally as *Mademoiselle,* none of that "little girl" stuff.

Once past the Porte de Versailles, I started running, hat and gloves stuffed in my briefcase, knee socks crumpling down my skinny legs. I dashed all the way back to our apartment, where Boris Ivanovitch and Denicke were arguing in the kitchen and Mama was in shock on the telephone: "Not possible! How terrible! When did it happen? What are you saying?" My Russian was barely sufficient to catch the highlights of an unspeakable disaster. Thus I lived in an atmosphere of perpetual mystery.

I closed my ears, took refuge in my homework: neat Latin conjugations, safe and elegant geometric proofs, eloquent prose.

People came to see Mama, the doctor, for a splinter, a boil, a cracked finger, a torn nail, a sore throat, but mostly to cry, literally, on her shoulder. (She could treat Russian and ex-Russian friends, but since she was not allowed to write prescriptions, she would then send the patient to a naturalized French colleague.)

Mrs. Wittenberg was at her wits' end. Alexander had gone off on his new bicycle, she knew not where; he was uncontrollable; he yelled at her; he threw fits when his sister needed quiet and calm to practice. (My personal opinion, but I was not asked, was my brother's miracle remedy: a good spanking.) Little Benno had nightmares; he was homesick; his mother, a Junoesque, spectacularly handsome woman, came to visit him. After she had sung to him and safely tucked him in for the night, she said good-bye to Mama, tears streaming down her cheeks. "I cannot thank you enough for the good care you are taking of Benno. As soon as we are on our feet, I shall take him to live with us." She did, shortly before our move to rue Jules Simon. I saw Benno once again in Toulouse, in the summer of 1940. He had become a tall, tanned, self-assured, handsome young man. His parents had built up their business, whatever it was. They lost it again when France was occupied.

Some of our belongings—Mama's medical books, Papa's German and Russian classics, political and economic treatises—had finally caught up with us, together with the steamer trunk which Mama installed in the bathroom. I always thought "steamer" referred to the steam in the bathroom, which for some reason was the same size as the kitchen. The bathroom was exactly that, ample for a bath: a big tub on lion's feet, a wash basin, and in France the enigmatic bidet, which came in handy for soaking dirty socks and underwear. But a bathroom-sized room was ridiculously small for a kitchen. Since food was at the bottom of Mama's priorities, we ate in the kitchen. This was a tight squeeze. When Denicke and Boris Ivanovitch had tea, there was no room for anyone else. Mama maneuvered between the sink, the back of the chairs, and a gas burner set on top of a supposedly sturdy coffer. There was a high shelf for plates. Pots and pans dangled from hooks underneath the shelf.

There was no money for smoked salmon, pâté, steak of any kind, or any of the prepared delicacies at the corner *charcuterie*. Mama may have experimented with the cheaper horse meat. I know she boiled whole chickens and made, I thought, pretty good chicken soup, sometimes with leeks and carrots, sometimes with rice, sometimes with noodles. My favorite was rabbit stew, on rare occasions. More frequently Mama served what Germans call "pretend rabbit," which is meatloaf with every kind of leftover baked in.

Mama was pretty good with leftovers. She threw them in a pan, scrambled them with a couple of eggs, and called it mishmash. Boiled potatoes, vegetables in season, spinach (which I actually liked), small round meatballs, occasionally stuffed cabbage (when there was a guest). These pretty much exhausted Mama's repertory. My job was to grind the coffee.

Mama introduced us to grapefruit, which arrived mysteriously in a small crate once or twice a month, directly from Palestine. She made yogurt in little pots sitting on the window sill, which she then ate regularly with great relish, and which I refused to eat as well as the ever-present sour cream or any kind of cheese.

Standard dessert for special occasions, besides fresh fruit in season, was a paper-thin crêpe the diameter of a dinner plate, spread with large gobs of cherry preserve, carefully rolled up, and dusted with powdered sugar. My other favorite was a jelly made with red currants, which Mama called *kissel*. It took a lot of expertise, as the juice had to be strained through a muslin cloth in which the berries were crushed, and the whole mess cooled on the window sill in winter or in a tub of cold water in summer. Since my fingers were permanently ink-stained from the new fountain pens, I wisely stayed away from *kissel*-making and the ever-present danger of splashes of red juice.

Mama trusted me implicitly, having impressed upon me the menace of microbes. She looked askance at the French custom of kissing friends on each cheek, of relatives' more fervent embraces, of couples' passionate enlacing in subway trains, on park benches, or behind columns and trees, all of which could and did lead to the spread of dreadful diseases painfully illustrated in minute detail in her medical books.

I was very careful to wear gloves: thick woolen ones in winter, thinner cotton ones in spring and autumn, wispy lace ones in summer, especially when riding the Métro or bus. It was convenient to keep ready change inside the glove, on the palm of the hand, and it was reassuring to shake unknown hands with gloves on, though that was not the polite thing to do. Handshaking was definitely not a healthy custom. Mama had once saved the arm of the young daughter of a good friend in Berlin who had neglected to take care of a minor scratch on her left middle finger which she had incurred during a fast-paced volleyball game. The scratch got infected, the young lady developed a high fever, and her doctor recommended amputation of the arm at the shoulder as a life-saving measure. Mama persuaded both parents and the doctor to amputate only the guilty digit; if that didn't bring down the fever, the arm could always follow. As it turned out, the young lady recovered nicely, minus a middle finger, able to pursue her passion for volleyball. So when I ventured out with the children of the Group, sharing bicycle rides, roller skating on borrowed skates, tossing a ball around, or playing a game of tag which we called "Cowboys and Indians" (Gary Cooper was speaking French, as were all of the other cowboy stars in the nearby movie theater), I was ever mindful of skinned hands and knees. It slowed me down considerably.

I always remembered my one scary experience with blood gushing forth from my own small knee. I was five. My brother had come down with scarlet fever. Mutti rushed me to a colleague for a painful shot in my thigh, then home by taxi, always a forewarning of unknown catastrophes, to pack my little brown suitcase. I was sent off the same afternoon with our maid whose family lived in a village somewhere in Mecklenburg, a couple of hours away by train.

For a small city child, this was truly a voyage of discovery. Our maid's family lived in a stolid nondescript house with an acre of vegetable garden sloping down behind the house to a small brook. There were brothers, as well as parents and grandparents, so one small child more or less did not matter. For once I was positively encouraged to dig in the dirt, real black dirt, loose black soil, which yielded clumps of potatoes. I was fascinated by the potatoes which were washed down under the garden pump, then peeled by the pailful for the midday meal. I contentedly munched on a washed-down raw carrot and wandered among stalks of green beans clambering up stakes three times my height. There were strawberry beds, raspberry bushes, gooseberries, and rhubarb. I had never seen those things grow up all by themselves like flowers and trees.

Emma, my maid, was also my interpreter, as her family spoke a kind of German I had never heard before. She took me down the main street in the front of the house to stop by the butcher's and talk to the baker. She left me sitting on a stone step looking down into a sort of barn where cabinet makers were making tables and chairs. The floor was covered with sawdust; there was the constant buzzing of saws, the smell of wood; rows and rows of table legs lined up on shelves, in various stages of completion. Emma had indulged my taste for chocolate. I was sucking chocolate milk from a baby bottle, very much aware that this was a pretty ridiculous sight, yet I thoroughly enjoyed both the milk and the bottle. To their credit, the apprentice cabinet makers did not make fun of me and rather enjoyed their unaccustomed and appreciative audience. I was rewarded with a beautifully silky smooth, sanded wooden sword, custom made for my size. Thus armed, I became the envy of a blond, crew cut boy named Kurt who had previously ignored me, being at six and a half almost twice my size. I had been vaguely aware of Kurt's presence, as he vaulted over rows of tomatoes, whipping off the heads of plants with a long stick.

We were pretty much given the run of the garden, which featured temptation at either end: a small skiff with oars anchored in the shallow waters of the brook, and an old carriage house which was next to, or possibly attached to, the family's sturdy residence. My sword booked me passage in the boat, from which Kurt and I threw handfuls of pebbles into the swift waters. The art of gracefully throwing a polished flat stone to skim the surface, causing ever-widening circles of rippling waves, was a skill I didn't acquire until later. Tired of cruising, Kurt led the way to a more enticing means of transportation behind the barn door, which had been left ajar. Nimbly he clambered up and into an imposing, worn black leather coach; seizing imaginary reins in one hand, my sword in the other, he urged on impatient, nonexistent steeds to run at full gallop. Huge, steel-rimmed wooden wheels loomed above my head; two precarious steps hung loosely from the floor of the carriage, which was as high as my chest. "Come on, you can climb up in here." I tried, but my best was not good enough. I slipped, hit my knee on the steel rim of a wheel, and fell to the floor. When Kurt saw the blood, he scrambled down and ran out the door. The cut was razor sharp, three centimeters wide, and bone deep. I do not recall any pain. I only panicked when I saw the blood. So did Emma. She scooped me up, washed away my tears, cleaned the wound with soap and water, and stopped the flow with a wadded-up handkerchief. I was not taken to the doctor; the doctor came to the house and stitched up the wound. Kurt got the spanking of his life.

That weekend, Papa came to visit. We walked down the garden path to the brook. Papa sat me down on a bench? a stone embankment? He was sad. He was serious. Mutti couldn't come because Max was very, very sick. She was in the hospital with him. I had to be brave, be a good girl, and mind Emma. I was no longer a baby. Papa had brought my favorite chocolates, cats' tongues. I could take one from the box.

He told me about his mother, my grandmother, who was in heaven, and his father, my grandfather, who had remarried and was now very, very old. Papa was only a few years older than Max when his mother went to heaven and he never saw her again. Papa cried. "Is Max going to heaven?" I asked. "We must look up at the sky and hope," he told me. This I proceeded to do fervently, seeking fluttering departed relatives behind every cloud. I knew my brother to be no angel—slamming doors in my face, making fun of my whining ways, dragging me to nursery school at a run. I recalled our rare looking-at-stamp sessions with a mixture of awe and dread. I well understood these were my brother's treasures and would promise anything for the privilege of having a carefully supervised peek at them, seated on his lap. I tried to keep my hands folded, but the urge to rip a pretty stamp from the page was beyond me. Every time my hand went out to touch a particularly enticing miniature of a bearded gentleman, it got slapped. I had no trouble keeping my brother out of heaven. When Papa next came to visit, he seemed relieved. Max had survived a risky operation against all odds; he was very weak; he would stay in the hospital with a big bandage around his neck until he was strong enough to come home.

In the meantime, I could be working on a special gift, a napkin holder pouch embroidered in cross-stitch with my brother's name on it. Papa had thoughtfully provided the pouch, already sewn up, with a cross-stitch canvas on the upper flap, and white and red embroidery thread as well as a dull-tipped embroidery needle.

He knew that I had helped Mama with a blue and white cross-stitch embroidered tablecloth the previous summer, spent at the beach; what he didn't know was the first thing about early child development and embroidery. The crosses on Mama's cloth were white on blue, easily visible, a quarter of an inch square, and clustered together in a pattern requiring no more than a dozen stitches. The napkin holder flap was to be covered solid in white-on-white stitches a sixteenth of an inch square with the letters *M*, *A*, and *X* faintly traced in a corner to be dealt with later in red. I could barely count to five. The rows of stitches went on and on in disorderly array, crossing over in the opposite direction, all most unpleasing to the eye. It was an exquisite exercise in frustration. To her credit, Emma packed away the offending needlework, let me dig up potatoes to my heart's content, and continued to provide chocolate milk in a baby bottle with my midmorning snack.

Max recovered, as Papa promised. On my return early in the fall, I found him whispering with a big bandage around his neck, building complex vehicles with his erector set, a set of flat metal rods which could be assembled by means of screws and bolts into enticing shapes which I was not to touch; tending to his stamp collection, which I was not to touch; receiving friends behind hermetically sealed doors. After a while the bandages came off, revealing ugly red welts from ear to collarbone on either side of his neck. (They later faded to a rosy pink but never completely disappeared.) He recovered his voice, which turned barely two years later to a vibrant baritone, unmistakable at the end of the phone line in post–World War II years as we kept in touch, infrequently but firmly, across seas and continents.

Eventually I finished that napkin holder, having learned to count up to and past ten, and I presented it to a nonplussed big brother on his thirteenth birthday, the following summer of 1929.

I doubt that Mama knew what I was doing after school during spring 1934 in Paris five years later. Most of the time we children played in the immediate neighborhood in a block of brand-new apartment buildings which featured basement garage facilities for tenants, electric ranges, built-in closets, and several electric outlets in each room, at a time when "modern" in Paris meant indoor plumbing with running water.

Each day found us inching a bit farther beyond this safe and well-bred enclave, mainly to watch the bumper cars near the Porte de Versailles, one of the major access roads to the city within the ring of outer boulevards. A brisk two-hour walk would lead us straight to the center, to Notre Dame Cathedral on its own island in the Seine between the Left and Right Banks. Taking the opposite direction, a bicyclist would reach the Palace of Versailles in three or four hours of energetic pedaling.

For the moment, we did neither. We followed the curve of the ring boulevard going west, four or five youngsters with three bicycles to take turns on, until we reached a most inviting sand and gravel lot, several hundred feet across. There were some sort of hangars in the background. Enormous pieces of abandoned pipe thirty inches in diameter begged to be crawled through. Scattered mounds of dirt dotted the eerie landscape. Bits of barbed wire, rusty cans, parts of abandoned machinery left us in no doubt: we had found the ideal battlefield. The cavalry, that is the bicycle brigade, promptly assaulted one hill after another, while foot soldiers took shelter in the pipes. Since Marc, our historian, was safely resting at home, there was no reality check to unbridled imagination. Traces of ditches quickly filled with the enemy in foxholes, to be routed with volleys of pebbles. When the battle was won, wild animals took over the field, now become a jungle, as we merrily rode up and down each forlorn sandy peak. "We" is not exact. The boys rode, and I watched. Finally, someone took pity on me and very generously lent me his bicycle, too big for me and unwieldy, with my pleated skirt. I could only pedal standing up, which I did vigorously, flying over a hill and gracefully somersaulting over the handlebars. I was escorted home with much sympathy mixed with fear, a limping, wounded veteran, knees and hands bandaged in an assortment of handkerchiefs, an ugly blue bump on my forehead. Once home, I submitted to the painful cleansing of my torn skin and to the burning iodine, mindful as I was of the host of microbes hidden in the dirty sand and gravel that had gotten under my skin. These war wounds did not keep me from further explorations of our "battleground," but I resolved to campaign for the right of girls to wear trousers when I grew up.

In the summer of 1984, I took advantage of a cheap study trip to Rome, Paris, London, Amsterdam, and points in between. In Paris we were to be lodged in a hotel "near the Eiffel Tower." In fact, the hotel turned out to be a good distance away, on one of the outer boulevards. Something about the view from my window looked faintly familiar, a helicopter landing field a few hundred feet square. I decided to walk southwest along a nondescript, boring avenue lined with new high-rises, bars, coffee shops, and service stations. A twenty-minute walk led to the new Parc des Expositions, just before the Porte de Versailles. The distance was right! I marched back to the helicopter field and booked a sightseeing flight of Paris and its surrounding palaces, the best money ever spent on a whim. I had found our playing field. My pilot confirmed it; it had once been an abandoned landing strip.

Some time after the fall of Saigon, I met two Vietnamese children, a young boy and a girl, who lived in Vanves and were students at, respectively, the Lycée Michelet and the Lycée Camille Sée. They took me by the hand and walked with me along the streets of my French childhood, all the while telling me about their schooldays, their teachers, the games they played. I felt right at home! Over a year of lunch breaks in the teachers' lounge at school, I had been "initiated" into the horrors of the Vietnam War (conveyed in fluent academic French, a legacy of French colonial days) by their uncle, an ex-officer in the South Vietnamese army, who felt fortunate to have been hired as a substitute math teacher, since math made minimal demands on his rudimentary knowledge of the English language. What I retain from our talks is a vision of unforgiving self-discipline—physical, mental, spiritual—instilled in early childhood, which my Vietnamese colleague credited for his survival. He recalled his father, also an army man, taking him for walks in the jungle when he was five years old, teaching him silence and absolute obedience. He was to follow in his father's footfalls without making the slightest noise, no sound of surprise, no slapping insects from his face, watching his father's movements and sparse gestures for direction. He knew he would be lost if he fell behind. His father never turned around, knowing the boy was following. During a long march in the Vietnam War, wounded, without medication for a thyroid condition, on a diet of wild fruit, he willed himself to keep walking, breathing, sparing every superfluous gesture, not moving his lips to talk. "There was a young woman nursing her baby. We had no food for her. We made a circle of space around her, so she could walk unimpeded, avoid every stray movement, concentrate on setting one foot in front of the other; we created a circle of silence around her, so she would not have to utter a sound, preserving energy." Both survived. It reminded me of a story of enforced silence with a less happy ending. A young family fleeing the Holocaust had found refuge in a genteel gentile's attic. When the authorities knocked on the door, the young mother stifled her baby's wails by holding her hand over its face, terrified that her infant's cries would give them away and jeopardize their host's safety. The police left, satisfied that no unauthorized persons were on the premises. The baby was dead.

The example of the young Vietnamese mother in that long march has taught me how to build a wall of silence whenever unpredictable waves of weakness threaten to push me beyond consciousness. Eyes closed, I block out every sound, every image, a response to which, even if involuntary, would impede the effort to breathe. My nurse at the clinic concurs heartily, in less poetic terms: "Shut up, close your eyes, try to take deep breaths." After a while, when the weakness subsides as mysteriously as it has come, I can turn my head, look about, and listen to my friends without fear that movement will rob me of my breath. I have rejoined the living; I am here. It has been a long road since I last hiked half a mile down a small canyon and fought my way up with labored breath. I've learned to husband every gesture since, count my steps, rejoice in sunlit days (a rare treasure in New Orleans, an almost daily bounty in Santa Barbara) and hold on to their memory when life-saving, drug-induced doom and gloom fog the spirits, throw mind and body into slow motion. Suddenly, after five or six days, the fog lifts, the mind clears, fingers grasp a fork without dropping it, I step without fear of slipping, am able to indulge in idle talk, in pleasant greetings, in healing laughter—all of the extraneous gestures, banned from my wall of silence, which spell welcome to life, here and now. I didn't know that as a child, always seeking my home elsewhere.

At the end of the school year, as I prepared for my trip overseas, my Vietnamese colleague asked me to visit his wife's sister's family in Paris, which I did. After six months' residence in a country estate graciously offered by a French connection, they had been able to purchase a three-story private residence in Vanves, near the Lycée Michelet. I was greeted by an elderly woman in traditional dress whose embarrassed smiles did little to overcome a categorical language barrier, until the family heir, perhaps eight years old, came to the rescue in fluent French. "This is my grandmother. My parents and sister will be home for lunch shortly." I could not help but marvel at the exquisitely carved furnishings. "I arranged to have our belongings shipped from Saigon to Paris via Moscow, a railway carriage load," explained my host, priding himself on his foresight to leave Saigon well before the fall. "Moscow was very beautiful," he added. We sat down to an elegant meal in a formal dining room, served on gold plates, a far cry from the crowded kitchen in a modest shotgun house on the West Bank in New Orleans where the ex-officer turned math teacher helped his wife feed their six children.

Family Israel on the Baltic, shortly after our arrival in Berlin in July 1923.
Left to right: Max, Mama, Nanny holding infant me, Papa.

*Jeffim Israel and daughter, 1926.
I remember the silk dress, white,
with green trimming, little mother-
of-pearl buttons in the middle of
each green stripe. This is my favorite
photo of Papa. He was then
almost forty.*

*The old gentleman is Pavel Axelrod,
a patriarch of the Mensheviks. I
know I didn't feel comfortable
sitting in his lap. 1926.*

Berlin, 1928. I loved my tricycle.

Going away, elsewhere, with my very own brown suitcase.
A park in Berlin, 1927.

*Six years old and ready for school, 1929.
The traditional Zuckertüte, or sugarcone,
was filled with candies and chocolates to ease
a child's fears when starting school.*

*Second-grade class picture, Christmas 1930. I'm seated in the second row, second
from right. Our teacher, the World War I veteran, is at the far left. As a rule the
boys sat on one side of the room, the girls on the other. We were crunched together in about half the space to squeeze into the picture. There were steam ra-
diators on the right, beneath the window. We could dry our caps and mittens on
them, and sometimes "bake" our second-breakfast apples.*

Sexta (fifth grade), Fürstin-Bismarck Gymnasium, early 1933. I'm in the back row. Second from right. Most of the other girls were ten, some eleven years old. I was the only nine-year-old.

Lev Israel, my paternal grandfather, a biblical scholar. 1926.

*Ida Chaifetz (Mama), Misha Israel (my uncle), and a
friend (seated), Tiflis (now Tbilisi), 1907.*

Childhood's End
Paris, 1935–1940

The move to rue Jules Simon in 1935 pretty much marked the end of childhood. I became adept at hopping back and forth across the invisible line separating school and family; the one in French, securely scheduled and predictable, the other multilingual, teetering in the shadow of world events which sent shivers of fear throughout the refugee community.

1935. Stalin's purges continue in earnest, following the assassination of Kirov, one of his top aides. We heard of executions without trials, arbitrary denunciations. As news of the Gulag filtered back, Papa stormed helplessly against the fiend of fiends, Stalin, whose second five-year plan had plunged the Soviets into abysmal economic chaos.

1935. Hitler's ominous demand for Danzig becomes ever more threatening. A major port on the Baltic, the capital of west Prussia until 1919, Danzig was a free city united with Poland by a customs union under the supervision of the League of Nations. The Nazi Party campaigns vigorously for its unconditional return to the Fatherland.

1936. Hitler begins the remilitarization of the Rhineland and starts building the Siegfried line.

1936. Franco's insurgent army plunges Spain into civil war. Spain is left in ruins after three years of fighting. The Generalissimo seizes absolute power, and maintains Spain's neutrality during the war.

1938. Hitler orchestrates a triumphant entry to Vienna. The annexation of Austria is consummated on March 15.

1938. In September, Daladier and Chamberlain travel to Munich to sign the Munich Pact, convinced that with the return of the Sudetenland, the German-speaking borderland of Czechoslovakia, Hitler will be appeased and war averted, buying "peace in our time."

1939. In March, threatened with the destruction of Prague, part of Czechoslovakia joins the Reich.

1939. Hitler and Stalin conclude a nonaggression pact in August.

1939. September 1. Hitler attacks Poland. France and England declare war two days later.

The fall term of 1935 at the Lycée Camille Sée renewed my resolve to be a proper schoolgirl, minding my manners as well as my grammar. No more wrestling with the boys of the Group, no more pillow fights. I left them to their games of playing "chicken" on their bicycles and soccer in the streets. We still got together occasionally, huddled around that new marvel of scientific progress, a shortwave radio set. American jazz came to us live on mysterious airwaves. For the first time we heard English, at least the American variety, which did not sound at all like the English in my classes at the Lycée Camille Sée. About that time, I was introduced to a young girl who lived on the third floor of an adjoining wing of our apartment building, a leisurely fifteen-minute walk from the lycée. She was a year older, a grade ahead of me, and very mature for her age. I was forewarned not to believe everything Vivi said (Vivi was short for Victoria, not for Viviane), as she had a reputation for wild tales. I was to walk to school with her every morning. Since I got up at the last possible minute, swallowing my bowl of hot chocolate milk with one arm in a blazer sleeve and one arm out, our walk was a brisk one and did not allow for any stray roaming. Just the same, Vivi treated me to daily hair-raising adventures. It started with Dumas' novels, which I was reading diligently at the rate of one or two a week and which accounted for my bleary-eyed awakenings. They were page-turners, one and all, even though, as Vivi carefully instructed me, I had missed the whole significance of the Musketeers coming to the rescue of "true love," a rare commodity. Ah! Love! Vivi had met a young man who had looked at her in that certain way; there was no doubt about his ardor; yet her parents would not let her out of their sight. The description of the young man in question changed from day to day, but the scenario was always the same: he would take her away to live blissfully on an exotic isle, or in a fairy tale castle, away from the oppressive atmosphere of her parents' apartment, the whispering, the crying, the fearfulness.

Vivi's uncle had fled to Mexico. Did I know where that was? Very vaguely, on the other side of the earth. His life was in constant danger from enemies who wanted him dead, the same enemies who had tried to kidnap her older brother in broad daylight, in front of a café on the Boul' Mich in the Latin Quarter. That's why her parents didn't let her go anywhere by herself. It was not fair. Vivi was born in Paris, but spoke Russian at home. Her parents had seen to it that she learned to read and write in Russian as well, because they would all return to Russia one day. Vivi's

Russian was vibrant, resonant; she could recite pages of Pushkin to bring tears to the eyes. She was a born dramatist.

She let her ash blond hair float down in Lady Godiva fashion, rolled her big blue eyes, and with a wave of the hand, a pout of the lips, transformed the most innocent remarks into coded phrases, laden with hidden meaning. As she gazed at the blank walls of buildings, they seemed to hide a retinue of spies.

Vivi shared a room with me the following summer in a cottage Mama had rented in Brittany on the Atlantic coast. There were perhaps half a dozen other boarders, all children of the Group. We were free to walk to the beach a couple of blocks away to gather mussels and play ball. To swim? Only when the sun warmed the water well above freezing, in the early afternoon, and then within reach of bulky terry cloth robes. A frantic rubdown followed by a warm-up sprint kept circulation and spirits high.

One afternoon, returning from the beach for our hot chocolate and crusty white bread warm from the bakery oven, spread with butter and homemade jam, we found the cottage in an uproar. Mama was flitting about giving orders to the cook, to the one tearful adult—I can't remember whose mother it was—to comb the beach. All of us were grounded, confined to the backyard. We silently plucked snails from the hedges for dinner, afraid to speculate on what disaster had befallen us. Mama manned the telephone, choosing her words carefully in French, more voluble in Russian and German. She called us in, sat us down, and took us into her confidence: Vivi had disappeared. Who had seen her last? Had we seen her talking to anyone? Had anyone been hovering in the background? Had she mentioned going anywhere? Vaguely I seemed to recall a receding figure, long blond hair waving in the wind, heading north along the shoreline. Was it Vivi?

Vivi had confided in me. A school year of early morning walks had yielded countless romances, real and imagined, mostly imagined, in which Vivi always surfaced as the irresistible heroine who drove men to distraction and commanded them to obey her every whim. To cast her in the role of a wayward, misguided teenager, barely thirteen years old, went against the grain. Besides, anyone who could recite and discuss pages of classic poetry and reveal the inner secrets of Hugo's *Les Misérables* was deserving of admiration and respect. Such a person would not be foolhardy.

Just the same, I was scared. Not as scared as Mama, though, who had been entrusted with Vivi's safety.

The next morning Vivi reappeared, not exactly glowing with her latest adventure, about which she kept wisely mum. Apparently a very good-looking gentleman had invited her to walk along the beach. What happened later in the next village, we were never told. The police, who had been promptly alerted by Mama, found her and brought her back. Vivi's mother came the same day to take her daughter home. Shortly thereafter, it was time to pack my little brown suitcase for my first solo train ride to Paris, where Papa would pick me up and arrange for the boat trip to England in Uncle Rudi's company. I was growing up.

When I returned from England in the fall, Mama sat me down and reminded me of the rules of the house. I was to let no one in at the front gate. I was not to talk to any stranger, especially if he was nice-looking. I knew that. I had a hard enough time talking to gentlemen I was properly introduced to, so ignoring someone I didn't know came very naturally. Returning home from school one afternoon, just such a nice young gentleman deliberately stood next to me while I opened the gate with my key and asked me politely to let him in. I gingerly slipped past him through the gate and slammed it in his astounded face.

"Do you know what Lulu did today?" Mama later asked rhetorically of the assembled dinner guests hunched most uncomfortably around our kitchen table, elbows alternately digging into each other's ribs. "She slammed the gate in Lev Lvovich's face, Trotsky's son, come to visit his uncle." She turned to me: "Vivi's cousin. Her father, Mr. Bronstein, is Trotsky's brother!"

I knew Mr. Bronstein as a mild-mannered, graying gentleman, whose wife, Vivi's mother, towered a head above him, her blond hair in unruly waves, with deep-set eyes that trusted no one. She was a troubled lady, as the mother of Vivi had every right to be. In spite of my well-intentioned faux pas regarding her politically notable cousin, I continued to be entrusted with Vivi's safe arrival at the lycée on school mornings. Barely sobered by her summer escapade, Vivi continued to instruct me in the ways of the heart. More importantly and more relevant to my education, she introduced me to Balzac and Zola, having exhausted the main works of Dumas and son, and a heavy dozen of Hugo's major novels. When the subject of summer vacation and a safe haven for Vivi next came up, we girls cooked up the perfect solution: we would both spend the summer with my British host family in their railroad station house near Cambridge.

Vivi was a quick study. She took mastery of the English language seriously. Mrs. Ducky set down firm rules, how far away and for how long we could explore the surrounding countryside, including visits to Cambridge. She kept us busy clipping hedges, picking plums, setting the table, ironing, waxing furniture, folding linen. Joyce, her daughter, took care of a pet rabbit and several cages of white mice intended for intriguing experiments in her biology class, which had something to do with different diets. We actually practiced speaking English even when we were alone together.

On a particularly mild and sunny day spent in Cambridge, we decided to walk back following a major thoroughfare that ran vaguely parallel to the railway lines. Dressed in neat walking shorts, cardigans slung over our shoulders, we started marching the fifteen or so miles to our destination, a three-or-four-hour pleasant hike (or so we thought) along fields of wheat, oats, potatoes, and assorted vegetables. The four hours had run out. Sheepishly we had to admit that we had no idea where we were; we had miscalculated the distance, forgetting that miles were a lot longer than kilometers. We would have hitched a ride, but the road was deserted; it was past suppertime and no car came along. Then we saw the tracks. It was getting dark, past ten in the evening. We decided to walk along the tracks, which would eventually take us to a railroad station—hopefully ours. They led not to our station, but to a small rural station just like it. Frantically, we knocked on the closed doors, yelled up to the windows, until someone heard us. Did the stationmaster come down, a robe hastily thrown over his pajamas? Did he come down hastily dressed in his uniform, buttoning his jacket? At any rate, he appraised the situation quickly and accurately. One phone call to Mr. Mousy's station to apprise him of our safe arrival, another to arrange for the next express train to make an emergency stop at his station. A quick cup of tea later, and the express train came huffing and puffing to a stop. We were helped up into the locomotive, next to the engineer. It was an exhilarating ride: a clear, starry night sky, silvery tracks piercing the darkness ahead of us. Did we get to pull the warning bell at crossings? Ten minutes at incredible speed—fifty miles an hour or more—and we were slowing down in front of our station. Mr. Mousy and Mrs. Ducky were too relieved to see us to give us a well-deserved scolding. They correctly concluded that we had been scared enough and would not soon undertake another similar escapade. Thankful, we fell into bed without a word.

To Mrs. Ducky, I owe a peaceful and orderly interlude in a disorderly way of life, fraught with the unexpected at every turn, at least outside school hours. Obviously a lady of genteel breeding, Mrs. Ducky faced adversity with spunk and muscle, laboring from dawn to dusk to keep her three-bedroom apartment above the station spotless. This was no small task, considering the smoke and coal dust floating in as trains seemingly thundered through the house.

Mondays, she scrubbed four pairs of linen sheets, pillow slips, towels, tablecloths, napkins, and her husband's dress shirts on a washboard in a big tub in the yard when the sun shone, and in the bathtub when it rained. The sheets were wrung out into heavy, twisted rolls, shaken loose, and then expertly hung out to dry, billowing in the wind. There was an art to folding the sheets as they were taken off the line, which required two pairs of hands, one at either end. The trick was to pull the sheet taut after each fold in a series of sharp shakes in rhythm with one's partner at the other end, and without letting go of it. The folding did not preclude ironing but made that task considerably easier. Monday, therefore, was a day of sandwiches, fruit, warmed-up soup, and leftovers.

There was no electricity in the house and no heating that I was aware of besides the open fireplaces. Mornings were chilly and damp. Mrs. Ducky complained of rheumatism, lit a fire in the dining room, and proceeded to hang all of the ironed sheets and towels on racks in front of the fire to warm them. Tuesday was ironing day. It took fifteen minutes to iron one dress shirt, and four small flatirons heated in turn over a minuscule petroleum cooker: a week's supply of shirts meant an hour and a half bent over an ironing board. Joyce's school blouses (French summer vacation was twice as long as the English break), Mrs. Ducky's frilly summer shirts, sheets and tablecloths, plus two or three dresses, made ironing a strenuous all-day exercise, with ample weightlifting built in. One false move and the iron slipped from one's hand to leave either an ugly brown spot on a favorite embroidered guest towel or, worse, a permanent brand on one's exposed knee as the iron crashed to the floor.

Mrs. Ducky did her own professional dry cleaning of Mr. Mousy's stationmaster uniforms, removed spots from skirts and blazers, cleaned windows every week, dusted daily, polished and waxed furniture and floors. In between, she made jam from plums and cherries from the small orchard, several kinds of puddings, and fancy cakes for the weekend. She used a small tin oven set on two petroleum cookers. I thought we ate very well, although Vivi missed the finer touches of French cuisine.

Back in Paris for the *rentrée,* the start of the school year in the first week of October, my double life took off in earnest. Much of it was devoted to "hiding Margot."

Margot appeared one day courtesy of my big brother, with a change of clothes, worn-out shoes, a cheerful smile, and no papers. She did not speak a single word of French and moved in deliberate, long Teutonic strides, her every movement betraying her foreign origin. There was no alternative. Margot moved in with us. The risk of being picked up by the French police—of being sent back to Germany to camp and to certain death—was very real. (Margot was afraid of the French police because of her illegal residence, illegal employment, and heaven knows what political connections. On those grounds, she would be subject to immediate deportation back to Germany, where political persecution had already started.) She was perhaps eighteen years old. In 1934, in Berlin, when she was a sixteen-year-old school girl, she had fallen madly in love with an older man, a university student and a radical who fled to Amsterdam. Her family, good solid German citizens of Jewish ancestry, refused to see the writing on the wall and could not conceive of leaving their business behind. Since they refused to consider exile, Margot took matters into her own hands. One night, she climbed out of her bedroom window, which looked out on the inner courtyard of her apartment building, slid down a twisted bedsheet rope, and started walking. She made her way to Amsterdam by hitching rides. I can imagine her convincing tales of a sick aunt in the next village, a dying grandmother in the next, her beguiling innocent smiles, her ready laughter, joining in carefree song, charming one and all. It is a mystery how she cleared the Dutch border, how she found her friend. Her hands were red, calloused, and scarred, her nails nibbled to the quick. Someone had found her a job sewing furs; she was strictly on the lam. Sewing ten, twelve hours a day, she made good money, even on the black labor market, enough to feed and clothe herself. But then the civil war in Spain beckoned. Her friend decided to organize and join the loyalist forces. He went off to Spain. Margot tried to follow him. She got as far as Paris; how she crossed the border remains another mystery. She met my brother, and he took her home. Home was half of a narrow armoire, half the space on my study table, a cot with a mattress, the top of my bookshelf. I was sworn to silence. No such person lived with us, as Margot entertained us night after night with stories of police raids on the fur-sewing sweatshop where she worked, a kind furrier, the friend of a friend of a friend having risked his license to employ her. Margot got pretty good at disappearing, usually into the w.c., whenever she heard French voices and a knock at the door. While we spoke German out of necessity, I made some halfhearted attempts to teach Margot French, but we were both too tired at bedtime for real progress.

The day came when Margot had to present herself at the police station to regularize her status as a refugee of German nationality and obtain a temporary residence permit, which would have to be renewed every three months. A work permit was out of the question. She took off a couple of hours from sewing furs, but my brother could not accompany her. "Don't worry," he told her. "If you don't understand, just smile sweetly." Dutifully, she handed the officer on the other side of the counter the precious and irreplaceable document attesting to her identity. He gravely perused this, looked up, and asked her something to which she responded with the requisite smile. Waving the document in his hand, the officer led the way out of the station and to his car, by which time Margot came to her senses, screamed, grabbed the paper, and ran. What you don't understand can hurt you, and smiling can definitely send the wrong signal. Henceforth, we devoted ten to twenty minutes every night to the serious study of French.

The years 1935 and 1936 brought the worst of the Stalinist purges. News trickled in slowly, via news correspondent friends. Mama was worried sick. She had had no news of her family in Leningrad, now St. Petersburg again. A curt letter of the type, "We are well. You sister Luba went away. Will keep you informed," cut short any attempt at correspondence. Read: "Don't write to us. Luba was arrested."

I was used to strange characters knocking at our door, mostly courtesy of my brother, who as circulation manager of the *Pariser Tageblatt* rescued any number of down-and-out German-speaking political refugees, whom he recommended to Mama's care. Young men appeared with hacking coughs and hollow eyes, often hiding bare chests under a smart suit coat for lack of a decent shirt, dizzy with malnutrition and cigarette deprivation, seething with anger as they saw promising careers cut short, unable to cope with the language barrier, the maddening red tape, unwilling to compromise their status by doing humdrum, meaningless, back-breaking work, instead idle and unemployed. They were prime candidates for heroin—vaguely I heard the dreaded word tossed about—anything to relieve the pain of being stripped of one's identity, of the feeling of impotence to make a difference on alien soil. Mama was not allowed to write prescriptions, nor did she keep drugs in the house. She took away their cigarettes, fed them chicken soup and yogurt, listened to their anger and desperation, and sent them on their way with vitamins. The Spanish civil war came in the nick of time to lend new meaning to their lives. Many of them enlisted enthusiastically to fight fascism in Spain.

Horst, another of my big brother's friends, was a lucky fellow. He had a small girlfriend who stayed home all day sewing up simple dresses for a word-of-mouth clientele. Home was a ten-by-six-foot hotel room with a hot plate and shared shower bath down the hall. It was a good thing that Mäuschen ("little mouse") was small, because Horst was very tall. As a professional athlete, a runner, he needed to eat healthy meals to keep in shape. Mäuschen faded into the background, with her pale skin, limp blond hair, and gray eyes. They were deeply in love. Mäuschen's face would light up whenever Horst looked at her. Horst would recite Mäuschen's domestic virtues to all who would listen; he spent hours spinning fairy tales about an impossible future in the European equivalent of a rose-covered cottage where Mäuschen would reign supreme dressed in a dirndl and a white starched apron. It was unclear to me what university activities had led to Horst's arrest. What stands out in my memory is his sprint to freedom.

He ran. He jumped from the train headed to a concentration camp and started running. Being a professional runner, he outran the guards pursuing him. He outran the police the guards had alerted. He dodged bullets. He ran. He ran through fields and woods, shed his clothing and ran in his shorts, jumped into a creek, and melted into the countryside. Did Mäuschen's family take him in? Did Mäuschen hide the young man with the brash smile in the barn? Bring him food? They ended up crossing the French border, both political refugees, clinging to each other in an alien land.

Horst, more than Mäuschen, who was chained to her sewing machine, was a frequent guest at our house, where the cramped kitchen offered solace in the form of simple foods, which we would call health food today:

Russian buckwheat, yogurt, cottage cheese, stuffed cabbage, chicken soup, grapefruit, every other fruit in season, and lots of vitamins. Hot tea was brewed at every hour of the day.

Besides food, the kitchen was a headquarters for networking and for letting down one's hair in a safe and friendly place, which guests did with great abandon—so much so that I preferred to stay out of it, claiming a much-needed trip to the local branch library. There was entirely too much fist-shaking at very real, but absent, enemies; too much weeping, bemoaning the unknown fate of families left behind, of friends snatched away in the middle of the night, their whereabouts unknown.

One day, my brother talked to me sternly: "I am bringing a German author to tea. Do not stare at him. He has been badly disfigured in a concentration camp. He is very ill." I do not recall the gentleman's name. I was prepared to feel pity and sympathy. I was not prepared for the stream of venomous hate that poured forth from the toothless mouth, the mad gleam from the solitary eye.

"I live but for one day, the day I shall catch my torturer and kill him with my bare hands, slowly, just so." His knuckles turned white as he grabbed an imaginary neck in midair. "I shall do to him everything that was done to me and more. I won't let him fall into unconsciousness. That would be too easy. I want him to suffer every agony." He went on, in slowly deliberate and bloodcurdling detail, to describe exactly and anatomically what he would do. I was shocked.

I had come face to face with evil, not the evil that had been done to the man's face and body, but the evil that had destroyed his humanity.

That same year I met an extraordinary human being, an escapee from the Gulag who had survived ten years of solitary confinement. His sparse gray hair, his scraggly unshaven face belied his age. He looked a stooped, well-worn sixty-plus. In fact, he was barely forty. He had kept his sanity by learning and mastering the French language from pages in a French grammar book. Unfortunately, he had never heard it spoken. When he stepped off the train in Paris, he realized his errors in pronunciation; he understood no word of the French spoken to him, nor could a Frenchman understand what he said. It had taken him two years to make his way across Stalin's Mother Russia, all of which he was putting into a book because "no one would believe me." For some reason, he felt at ease confiding in me because I was not a grown-up. We took walks together, armed with pen and paper, on which he would write out in deliberate, grammatically precise French what I did not understand in Russian. Perhaps he was simply using the occasion to practice pronouncing the French he could write so beautifully. He was not a good student. His spoken French, mispronounced for hours, for days, for years in his solitary cell to keep alive the human spirit, defied correction.

I asked him what was the worst and best of his experiences. "To face death. Once you know that you are going to die, you are no longer afraid. Each day, I was blindfolded in the prison yard, facing a firing squad, waiting for the bullets, eight days, ten days, thinking I was dead. Wishing they would make an end of it. Scared to hope. But they didn't kill me. They put me back in my cell, where I could hear others fall under the bullets." He was transported to Siberia and survived. He had been strong once. He lived through hunger, frostbite, and disease. He recited poetry. He conjugated French verbs. He concentrated on riddles and mathematical puzzles. He kept track of time. Time was of the essence. It was hard to know when days ended and days began. He scratched a tiny mark on the door for each day. People thought him mad.

He didn't know of anyone else who had escaped and stayed alive, but he had nothing to lose. It wasn't at all clear to me how he got away. I imagined him walking through fields of snow, keeping alive by drinking melted snow, following railroad lines, maybe hopping rides. He was a writer, a good talker, I had been told, both in Russian and in his native language, which was Romanian. He could entertain and charm with words; he could make people forget their miseries, make them happy in the glow of a fairy-tale future, transform a slab of gray bread into a satisfying meal even without vodka. He lived on trust. Trust was perhaps the rarest and most precious commodity in Soviet Russia. No wonder his friends thought him mad.

One day when he was too weak to get up out of the snow, he fell asleep and would have frozen to death. Someone found him, dragged him to their log cabin, thawed out his clothes and his feet, nursed him back to life. That was the best of it. He was going to put it all into his book, which he was writing in French. He could write French, he just couldn't pronounce it. But first he needed to get home and find his family in Romania.

We didn't see this strange scarecrow of a man for quite a while; he had stopped coming by for tea and news. One evening I found Mama and several assorted guests huddled around the radio, newspapers in assorted languages fluttering over the backs of chairs, shrieks of despair, of disbelief, moans bewailing the latest disaster: "Noted Romanian writer and journalist assassinated!" Amidst all this confusion the doorbell almost went unnoticed. I opened the door to be greeted by the same Romanian writer, grinning from ear to ear, in a new hat and overcoat. "You can't be . . .You're dead," Mama brought out matter-of-factly. "I know," he replied, waving his own copy of *Paris Soir,* "but here I am."

Under these circumstances, it was difficult to muster any enthusiasm at school in the basement locker room for the latest styles in hairdos, the exact and proper length of shoelaces, the finely embroidered edging of a lace collar which peeked out from the sternly square neckline of a baby blue uniform smock. Teachers and supervisors, the staff hired exclusively to supervise students in the halls during recess, in the dining room, in the locker basement, used the formal form of address and called us *mademoiselle.* Even our favorite teachers, who called us by our given names, never departed from the formal *vous.* Young ladies (and I use the term advisedly) all around me were being introduced to society in earnest as they approached their midteens, barely out of the giggling stage. They went to dancing lessons, accompanied female relatives to tea, helped their mothers and grandmothers "receive" on "their day," pored for hours over fashion magazines, stood still for their seamstresses as they were fitted for fall, winter, spring, and summer suits. They vied with each other to wrangle invitations to dances via friends' brothers and cousins. I, too, had a big brother, though the few schoolmates privileged to glimpse a sight of him had a hard time convincing me of his irresistible charm. Besides, there was Margot, about whom the word was mum; and besides that, we were exiles without a country; and worse, much, much worse, we were exiles without any money. The invisible barrier was insurmountable.

Almost all of Mama's clothes and mine were recycled. Mama ripped suits and skirts donated to her apart at the seams, had the fabric dyed (unfortunately in colors most becoming to her fair skin but not to mine), and resewed them to fit. "Resewing them to fit," meant that I stood without moving seemingly for hours while Mama fitted and carefully basted the pieces of fabric together. Sewing was Mama's great solace and pastime. She went at it mathematically, constructing a three-dimensional costume out of two-dimensional pieces, cutting into fabric without the help of a model, a pattern, or even a fashion magazine. She got her ideas from window shopping: that is, by walking slowly past the few ready-to-wear dress

shops on the rue de la Convention, the rue de Vaugirard, and, much farther away, the rue de Grenelle. Once home, she made sketches of the details she wished to incorporate into future projects.

It helped that we were both small, Mama at five feet being just two
inches shorter than I. This meant that there was enough leeway to cut
away the telltale seam traces from the pieces of recycled fabric, and that
Mama could produce a fashionable midcalf-length skirt from a taller lady's
just-below-the-knee, no-longer-stylish one. Blouses were cut from used
men's shirts, though it was harder and harder to come by those. Most gentlemen of our acquaintance were unabashedly reduced to wearing shirts
with frayed collars and cuffs, which someone like Mäuschen turned so
skillfully that no one noticed. From our Paris years, I remember perhaps
six dresses that Mama made from new, that is, store-bought fabric, which
she bought only when it was on sale, using at least half a yard less than
any pattern would suggest.

Fitting the pieces together so no one noticed presented Mama with
her greatest mathematical sewing challenge. Luckily, summers spent on
the seashore in Brittany saw me through with two pairs of shorts, Mama-
made; a couple of square cotton bandannas which, skillfully tied around
one's bosom, became a stylish halter top in warm weather; a couple of
shirts; and two hand-knit (by me) sweaters. I became an expert at recycling wool. Unraveling a much worn donated hand-knit garment, as machine knits were usually too fine, especially if it had belonged to a normal-sized German refugee lady, for example, would yield enough wool
for an acceptable sweater or cardigan. The yarn was dipped in warm water,
then left to dry, then wound up fairly tightly around a bit of cardboard. It
was best to knit in a small pattern to hide any unevenness.

Shoes and socks were a serious problem. I walked an average of five
to ten miles a day, not counting stairways in apartment buildings and
kilometers of tunnels and stairs in the Métro, rain or shine (it seemed
mostly rain, which turned into alternately frozen or melted slush in winter). I owned two pairs of shoes, one good, one bad. When the bad pair
had to be resoled, the good one was in jeopardy of a similar fate, and since
it was not a model suitable for everyday school days, it risked being un-
usable both for special occasions and for everyday running about. Socks
got torn, so much so that I ended up darning holes already darned. I had
learned darning in second grade in Berlin and prided myself on a neat
job. I could even darn holes in trouser knees with strands of fabric pulled

from the inseam so that the repair was barely visible. Hose, mostly knee socks, were expensive. A mistake in the right shade of mending thread was catastrophic. Many of my classmates had grandmothers who knitted wool slips and wool knee socks as well as gloves, scarves, and cardigans. I had no knitting grandmother, so I started knitting my own things. I still have my first pair of French steel knitting needles which Mama bought for me in fall of 1933.

In the morning, Vivi's serial soap operas continued to provide welcome romantic relief and a smooth transition from my frantic home life to the predictable world of math, Latin, French grammar, French literature, English, history, biology, geology, geography, and more, all in neat separate compartments. Facing home after school proved more difficult. There was no way to bridge the gap between home and inexplicable fun and giggles, a merciful hilarity which punctuated an otherwise rigid schedule. I was unable to translate jokes for Mama, assuming that I had understood them in the first place. Everything that had been fun dissolved into meaninglessness. I gave up trying to explain my school days at home, just as I was unable to mention to my classmates any of the calamities that regularly befell guests and friends of our household. Nor did I mention my social life, which consisted of some leisurely wanderings, solo or in the company of some of the Group's children, now teenage boys and girls, to the Latin Quarter, to the Bois de Boulogne, on occasion to Montmartre with sidelong glances at the goings-on in the Place Pigalle. I hated the crowded Métro with a passion and often walked miles rather than risk the pinching and inevitable pursuits down long corridors. None of my classmates were allowed to venture out alone. When they took the Métro, which even then was far safer and quicker than any other mode of transportation, it was under the watchful eye of a chaperone and always in first class. They were not allowed to read daily newspapers, lest they catch glimpses of cabaret shows, gleefully advertised with nothing left to the imagination.

Our book list of forbidden books was longer than the one of recommended readings and included almost every nineteenth and early twentieth century author of note. Heading the list were Zola, Flaubert, and Baudelaire, to name a few, which, of course, prodded on by Vivi's enthusiasm, sent me straight to the neighborhood branch of the public library. This led to a fateful collision. My bent head, hatless and disheveled by wind and rain, made contact with the chest of a tall, elegantly clad lady, our principal, Madame la Directrice. "Julia, you should be ashamed of yourself, running in the street, and without hat and gloves! A young lady shouldn't be about on her own at this hour! Where were you?" (It was close to seven in the evening and I was running to catch a last loaf of bread at the corner bakery for dinner.) I didn't have to answer. Zola's *Nana*, Baudelaire's *Fleurs du Mal*, and Flaubert's *Education Sentimentale*, among others, were cascading to the pavement. "I want you to return those books at the first opportunity. Please remember to comb your hair and walk like a young lady." Her admonition, couched in overly polite irony, was glacial. Literally translated, "You will please reward me with the pleasure of . . ." and "I beg of you to carefully consider . . ." I am ashamed to admit that I did nothing of the sort. I slunk home, stashed the books on my shelf, and continued reading them one after another, late at night, under my blanket with a tiny pocket light so I wouldn't disturb Margot's sleep. I was getting a first-class education.

In France, studying was translated as work. Teenagers who worked, preparing themselves for the rarefied atmosphere of higher education, were spared every mundane chore, whether they were surrounded by servants or relegated to the dining room couch in a walk-up, no-water flat. The dining room, because the kitchen was usually too small to eat in, was where family meals, the guts of family life, were taken. The formal parlor or salon, both referring to the genteel art of conversation, was a luxury and a sign of relative affluence.

One of my classmates, a willowy blonde with long straight hair framing her pale oval freckled features, lived in just such a flat. I felt very privileged to be invited for tea after school. We trudged up the four flights of stairs, an exercise which, together with tummy-tucking corsets, was one of the secrets of the vaunted Parisian silhouette. We had tea, not hot chocolate, because her parents had left Russia before the Revolution, and tea was de rigueur, as was Russian, which my classmate, I was chagrined to admit, spoke fluently and I did not.

Tea was served on the side of the table not occupied by Madame's sewing paraphernalia (she was an expert corset and brassiere maker), after my friend had galloped down the stairs with an empty pail to refresh the family's water supply from a pump in the courtyard, this being her only chore. Her father was the proverbial Russian émigré taxi driver. Both parents cheerfully invested ten-hour workdays to provide the necessary leisure for their only child to work and thus eventually to succeed in a professional career. I was politely excused after tea to make room at the table for my friend to work, while Madame cleared the dishes, washed up, and started the preliminaries of dinner.

About this time or perhaps a bit earlier, I recall a fun theme for our weekly French composition: our dream room. My classmates' concerns about color schemes, choice of furniture styles and wallpaper motifs were to me unbelievable and unattainable. The whole idea of a room of one's own was pure wishful thinking. Just the same, I managed to cram into "my room" what I held most dear: a view. In Paris, my only view was the brick wall facing the back courtyard. In this instance, I wrote about a view of the ocean, of the Atlantic, ten-foot breakers engulfing the mussel-covered rocks in a cascade of foaming surf off the coast of Brittany. My room had a wall of windows for the view, with bookshelves up to the window sill, books covering the adjoining long walls, and books above the couch on the opposite wall. The couch was covered with a tasseled paisley shawl, specifically the shawl Papa had brought back from Turkey before World War I and which Mama kept in the steamer trunk in our bathroom. The floor of my dream room was covered with thick Persian rugs. There were lots of pillows on the couch to pick up the hues of the rugs and of the shawl. I forgot about the drapes or curtains; after all, what was the point of covering up the view?

I found my room thirty years later in Metairie, Louisiana. Double windows were facing a jungle garden in full bloom, not the ocean; there were shelves built around the windows, and lots of wall space for additional bookshelves. I bought the house on the spot, or rather I bought the garden view. The room became my study, the heart of the house. I filled it with books. I threw thick colorful rugs from the Atlas Mountains on the floor, on the couch, and hung them on the remaining wall. I had forgotten my old assignment, which the teacher had marked "incomplete," but it had not forgotten me.

Soon after I entered the Lycée Camille Sée, I had made friends with my alphabetically seated neighbor, a chubby, snub-nosed, twinkle-eyed girl named Maud, an English name, she explained, after some English ancestor on her mother's side. Maud introduced me to Simone, and the three of us became fast friends until World War II broke out. That is, we were inseparable in school; after school, we went our separate ways. For two years we giggled; something about my lost-in-the-clouds look never failed to amuse Maud, who would alert Simone with a knowing wink. Their good-natured laughter was infectious.

About Maud, I only knew that she was the only child of aged parents. Her father was a four-star general in the French army, close to retirement, and her mother a rosy pink, curly-haired lady of partially British extraction, alternately proud and put out by her young daughter's mischievousness.

Simone, too, was an only child. There was talk of a pharmacy. Simone would eventually study chemistry. In the meantime, she was enrolled in the "literary" track at school, as being more suitable for a young lady's proper upbringing.

The three of us stumbled through Cicero's wars together, recited Ovid's poems, dissected Molière's characters, analyzed text after text of French literature. I was careful to read my favorite authors before they fell victim to our teacher's merciless *explication de texte,* which robbed the writing of its soul, gnawing it to the bare bones. We memorized English vocabulary lists; reproductive cycles of ants and bees, of frogs and higher creatures; the French centralized railroad system and network of canals; the capital and major products of each of the eighty-nine French *départements,* each of the historical provinces of France having been subdivided into smaller sections with suitable geographic designations for each; and how to get from one *département* to the other. I recall one particularly trying geography test for which, having spent half the night reading one of Madame la Directrice's forbidden books, I was ill prepared. In desperation, I invented a canal that logically ought to connect two southern cities, since otherwise the trip by train would involve riding all the way back to Paris from City A, changing railroad stations in Paris, and returning from Paris to City B. I felt like a cheat when the papers were returned. It appeared I was the only student who had remembered the newest canal, recently put into operation, and thus earned an above passing grade on an otherwise weak exam.

As we grew older, we tried to fill in the gaps between the artificial compartments of learning created by the French school authorities, and groped for the "meaning of life." We were careful not to bring our families into it. Instead we discussed what we saw and heard on the newly audible silver screen and tried to project our future from there. Our model was America, as interpreted by Hollywood, its brash blonde heroines unafraid to break into a man's world, to marry for love, or not to marry, to write, to explore, to fly, to photograph, to do their own bidding. Yet it was a French classic which sealed our friendship and provided the common framework for otherwise diverse lifestyles.

I was not much of a moviegoer. Detective plots lost me. Romances bored me. French comic repartee went past me. I could not relate to horses cavorting on the black and white plains of the far west. But there was one movie, as interpreted by my friends, which was more to the point. In *Un Carnet de Bal*, a young girl had danced the night away at a debutante ball and had kept her *carnet de bal*, her dance card, in which were inscribed the names of the young gentlemen with whom she had agreed to dance. She decided to find out what had happened to them fifteen or twenty years later, with some predictable and some not so predictable outcomes.

Maud, Simone, and I decided on a slight variation: we would each pursue our individual destinies, then meet together fifteen years later at the ripe old age of thirty to compare notes.

Maud divulged her secret plan. She would enjoy life to its fullest, meaning a series of romantic liaisons, safely excluding marriage. She would be wined and dined, and then, say at age thirty, she would settle down in the lap of luxury with an older gentleman who would provide her with the family name, the security, the respect of society; the relationship would be a business arrangement whereby husband and wife would host parties together, while they each continued to be active in their chosen careers and pursued their private affairs.

Simone pledged loyalty to the pharmacy she was to inherit and decided then and there that she was not to share it with any man.

I confided that the purpose of marriage eluded me. Those of our acquaintances who had married for love, had fallen out of it. They ended up living with other people, while maintaining amicable relationships with their spouse-in-name-only, which made introductions at some parties a nightmare. None of this I dared to admit to my French friends. It would go something like this: "Meet Sasha and Olga. Oh, Olga's husband, Misha, is over there with Helen. Did you know Helen's husband? He and Maria are very happy." Since, in Russian, women as well as men were referred to by their patronymic (the person's given name followed by her or his father's given name, with the ending indicating "son" or "daughter" of), the husband's family name was left out of the sequence and was anyone's guess. It was most confusing.

While Papa applauded my voracious reading (I spent every penny of a scant allowance on acquiring the beginnings of a solid classic library) and my not inconsiderable output of knitted garments, both he and Mama in their separate ways were concerned about my lack of, or rather resistance to, the "social graces," which was evident in my deliberate disregard of meaningless polite phrases, refusal to spend even one extra minute on combing recalcitrant lanky strands of hopelessly straight hair, unwillingness to smile when there was nothing to smile about.

Papa took matters into his own hands and introduced me to a Russian émigré family from pre–World War I Tsarist Russia, who lived on the other side of the rue LeCourbe, a short walk from our apartment on rue Jules Simon. "They are hard-working people. Their daughter, Diane, is a year or so older than you. She will introduce you to her Girl Scout troop."

Diane's mother, a small plump cheerful forty, received me graciously in her minuscule parlor perhaps eight by eight feet square, which was strewn with decorative little pillows, and furnished with a brocade-covered settee and a couple of similarly upholstered chairs that defied anyone to sit on them. "This is where I measure my clients," she explained, leading the way down the narrow hall, made narrower by a series of heavily laden bookshelves, to a tiny dining room the exact size of the parlor. "This is my daughter, Diane. I shall make some tea while you two get acquainted. Diane, why don't you take Julia for a walk later and explain the Girl Scout program to her." We sat down—it was a tight fit—at the dining table where pieces of a lady's suit lay ready to be assembled.

Diane was the embodiment, not of the proverbial, but of a very genuine, sweet sixteen. She glowed with pleasure and good will and made me feel at ease. Her pale oval face, framed by black locks parted in the middle, Victorian style, and small red lips (none of us wore makeup) did not match her powerful, a bit pudgy, build—her special blessing, I was to discover, and the source of a chillingly moving singing voice.

Her father, a tall gentleman with a russet beard, was a professional singer, a cantor at temple services, weddings, and receptions. "My parents work so hard," Diane told me, "and they insist I continue my education. I could have helped with Mama's sewing, done the marketing and the cooking, but they wouldn't hear of it. The big exams are coming up in a year, and I need to concentrate on serious study in addition to singing practice." Although she was enrolled in the same school, our paths never crossed there.

I was duly inducted into Diane's Girl Scout patrol, which met at the other end of Paris in the rue de Naples, in an elegant neighborhood of wide boulevards near the Parc Monceau. While I contributed to the building of the girls' characters by being the subject of their charity in the form of donated parts of a costly, tailor-made all-wool uniform and of careful instructions regarding the Scouts' code of behavior, I felt like a minor asset and came to question the whole concept of authority. The best part was the singing.

Diane introduced us to the haunting melody of "Swing Low, Sweet Chariot," which was to stay with me, the only tangible link to an America I knew nothing about, and a far cry from Hollywood's romanticized interpretations of life in the United States. The New World always came last in history and geography, with the most cursory and frantic review to include it, if at all, just before the year-end examinations. We never, ever reached World War I; most of our efforts were concentrated on French sovereigns and their mistresses, and the heads that fell under the guillotine. I filled in as best I could by reading *All Quiet on the Western Front,* Jules Romains' series *Men of Good Will,* and by watching Jean Renoir's *The Great Illusion.*

Diane's singing repertory was an eye-opener. I took the voices of the past to heart, starting with Roland and his horn, words set to a seventh-century melody. As we sang verse after verse, following Diane's sweet-tempered lead, we entered into lively dialogue with the folk figures of French history. Many of the songs were ballads, with antagonists speaking to each other, the chorus providing both the refrain and the moral at the end. There was the beggar, the jilted suitor, the unjustly condemned prisoner, the returning soldier thought dead and buried; the lovelorn maiden sent to the convent or, worse, jumping into the well; sailors lost at sea, children starved and frozen, cheated husbands poisoning their wives. No wonder most of the songs were sung in a minor key!

This vale of tears was the backbone of France's glory, which royalty ignored at its peril. Merrily we girls acted out the saga of Lorraine, echoes of the Maiden of Orléans, born in Domrémy. An older, poignantly moving fifteenth-century version featured Anne of Brittany, who married the king of France "in her wooden shoes." "France gained a province, while

Bretons were left to weep in pain." As we tramped in a circle in Anne's
heavy footsteps, repeating all twelve stanzas of the song, we became
wretchedly conscious of the mud clinging to our shoes, the blessed earth
which had always provided for France's well-being. Earth was a woman.
Justice, freedom, and the French Republic are personified as women on
stamps and coins. Of all my Girl Scout gear, only the belt made it to the
New World. I can see it now, with my name and our den's address, "rue de
Naples, Paris 8e" printed in ink on the inside. It was made of thick solid
brown leather with metal clips on each side to hold a tin cup, a compass,
a Swiss pocket knife, and, if necessary, a small canteen filled with drinking
water. (Water on trains and in public restrooms was not drinkable.) Although my waist expanded from nineteen to twenty-five inches with the
birth of two children, and beyond that with advancing age, I faithfully
kept that belt hanging in a long series of closets until my last move.

At the end of World War II, my brother brought me a small paper-
back edition of *Roland, Chansons Populaires,* which doubled as a collection of Scout songs. It got pretty worn out as I used it almost daily in
French class. After twenty or so years, I had it recovered in a fancy leather
and gold embossed binding in Rabat, Morocco, which in turn is showing serious signs of wear.

The worst part for me of French Girl Scouting was the cooking. Not
that the food was bad, it was delicious. However, we spent an enormous
amount of time discussing menus. "We" does not include me, as I prudently stayed in the background—so much so that my totem animal by
unanimous consent was a rare sort of little fish that disappeared, unnoticed, in the deep.

Our weekend outings consisted of practicing cooking al fresco,
equipped with restaurant- sized kettles, frying pans to match, and bags
of raw vegetables to be peeled. All of this activity, beyond carrying my
share of the equipment, my tin plate and tin fork and spoon, was totally
beyond my ken. I am sorry to report that I was content to eat the result-
ing stew without the slightest idea of what went into it. However, I became quite expert at cleaning-up detail.

All of this activity surrounding meals precluded any sort of marching
through the woods. The word "scout" in German translates as
"pathfinder." That's what I thought scouting was about. Not so in French.
It meant eating well even under the most primitive conditions. We did
build beautiful campfires, which seemed to explain the French term for

Girl Scouts, *éclaireuses,* meaning "lamplighters." Seated cross-legged in a circle, holding hands, swaying in rhythm to song after song, praising the flames lapping at the moonlit sky, we felt a wondrous surge of unity and peace.

Mama's well-meant attempt at socialization rather backfired, though it was to provide a rare *aperçu* on a lifestyle totally alien to ours, a fact I am sure Mama was unaware of. A couple of summers previously she had rescued a young lady she had found wandering stark naked in the woods of Compiègne, either comatose from a drug overdose or lying in a pool of blood with slashed wrists. I was inclined to believe the latter from her deathly pallor. Mama wrapped her in her jacket and nursed her back to life. That is, she shot the girl full of vitamins and fed her liver pâté and chicken soup, while lending a willing ear to her hour-long bemoaning of a useless life. This occurred during a summer vacation spent at a camp for underprivileged youth. Mama was in charge of the infirmary and minor pains and ills; she also, I am afraid, supervised the dietary regimen. The untypically healthy food was spurned by a vocal majority of the camp's inmates—growing French adolescents whose lust for life centered around the dinner table and when unsatisfied was displaced further afield. Distracted by the spectacle of nubile girls in tight black swimsuits merrily diving into the nearby lake, the boys showed off their diving skills and dove in after them. This was the cause of untold disasters, disasters not repeated within earshot of Mama, whose black-dyed hair would have turned white if it hadn't already done so. Her stern puritanical standards, which extended liberty, equality, and fraternity to women as well as to men on an equal footing, were no match against the prevailing double standard which ruled French society. A coed camp for adolescents was unthinkable, except to the farthest Left, and then with the predictable consequences.

In the fall, the young lady who had been rescued—tall and skinny, the perfect fashion figure for the new long, clinging, and wasp-waisted look—continued her weekly visits. She was German. I believe her name was Gisela, and she was punctiliously addressed as Fräulein, in the formal German fashion. Mama had taken it upon herself to contact Gisela's lover, a gentleman named Pierre. A French gentleman was of noble origin, with a *de* particle before his name, a family inheritance to look forward to, and a château in the country.

Apparently, Gisela's despair was caused by the realization that Pierre was not destined to marry her, that her life made his impossible, that his family, for centuries on guard against the German "enemy," winced at her German accent. She did not want to be the cause of Pierre's misfortune. Nor, to her credit, was she willing to settle for being his plaything. Her resistance took the form of refusing all financial help, and surviving the winter of 1937 in one threadbare (but becoming) green wool suit, unlined fashionable black leather gloves, and lots of expertly applied makeup and perfume, traditional gifts she could not refuse and which hid her anemic pallor.

Monsieur Pierre came to the house as Gisela's significant other and potential provider to receive Mama's advice on a suitable blood-building diet and other strategies to build up the young lady's strength and self-esteem. It turned out that Monsieur Pierre had a younger sister. He had offered his sister's last season's coat to Gisela, who refused to wear it, it being just a trifle short and not the right shade or tailoring to complement her fashion-model figure. She actually preferred freezing to wearing Pierre's sister's coat.

The upshot of Monsieur Pierre's visit was twofold: I was invited to meet his sister, Paulette, and I inherited a goodly portion of Paulette's past season's wardrobe, which in due time underwent the usual transformations, thanks to Mama's tailoring skills, until no item of clothing bore the slightest resemblance to its high-class origins.

Paulette impressed me as a lifeless effigy of what a young lady should be. Every impulsive gesture had been bred out of her. Ordinary conversation turned into an exercise in elocution, with proper breathing and expansion of the lungs; whereas I stumbled all over my sentences, didn't compose my speech in advance, repeated the same thing several times, jumped from one topic to another without apparent rhyme or reason, and worst of all, got excited when an idea got hold of me. Her measured steps matched her measured speech. It was no small achievement to walk in even steps, shod in pointed, high-heeled shoes, on uneven sidewalks, with a carefully understated swaying of the hips showing off her trim, tall figure to advantage. It reminded me of "walking lessons" in Berlin, in my introductory dance class. I strode at her side, unladylike, in my shabby worn oxfords, my shapeless school attire, interrupting Paulette at every turn.

It seemed that Paulette's family trusted me in spite of my obvious lack of polished manners. Paulette was allowed, in my company and at the ripe old marriageable age of nineteen, to venture out to the Tuileries Gardens, do a bit of window shopping on the Champs Elysées, perhaps have an "ice" (cream is not part of French ice cream, which used to have the consistency of sherbet, or of the ice that floated down the Seine on cold winter days, so it was called just "ice") in an elegant tea house, as pastry was too fattening. This arrangement, according to Paulette, was a big step forward and infinitely preferable to the company of her maiden aunt, her aged grandmother, or other equally well-meaning but unsuitably old-fashioned relatives. Paulette had successfully passed the two parts of the French baccalaureate, but was not encouraged to pursue her very sound formal education any further. She was not quite engaged, despite some serious *pourparlers,* or negotiations, with two or three possible suitors' families involving business matters, which Paulette thought of little interest. I had the distinct feeling that Paulette, being no dupe, was bored by the young gentlemen's perfunctory attentions, which only reflected their own barely disguised disinterest. I felt utterly helpless to cheer Paulette up under the burden of her fate, nor could I muster any enthusiasm for the serious business of proper dressing, which, besides a small family fortune, entailed countless hours spent over fashion magazines, and even more countless hours being fitted. The results—stunning in their simplicity, fluidity of line, harmony of shades, quality of fabrics—belied the efforts of a team of seamstresses and the expertise passed down through generations in matters of deservedly acclaimed French taste.

I continued to accompany Paulette on occasional outings. Paulette even introduced me to literary gatherings in private homes, the so-called *causeries,* which I enjoyed tremendously, unaware of the privilege of meeting well-known authors eye to eye, in elegant surroundings, being a mere schoolgirl.

Eventually, Paulette got caught up in pre-engagement activities—receptions, teas, soirées—and faded from my social scene. Gisela in turn was swept off her feet by Pierre, who took her along on an extended holiday. (I'm not exactly sure what Pierre actually did, if anything. He seemed to enjoy a life of leisure.) I was to see Gisela once more, in Paris, in the first week of September 1939, after Hitler marched into Poland. This was no time for polite greetings. Gisela arrived breathless, in the same green tailored suit, her face flushed, her hair in disarray, to thank Mama and say good-bye. Pierre's family had come through for him. They would shelter Gisela in one of their country estates while Pierre answered the call to arms. There was no time to lose; she had to run before she was rounded up by the immigration authorities and sent to camp as an enemy alien.

I can't remember where, when, or how I met Pierrot, an unfortunate name, as it designated the traditional folk figure of the clown in puppet shows and classic theater. Possibly at an informal get-together of socialist youths. Pierrot, having had to quit school at thirteen to help his father in his tailoring business, was in awe of my grammar. He was a thoroughly nice, hard-working young man, and the first person I knew raised in an Orthodox Jewish household, his parents having fled what used to be Poland before World War I to escape recurring pogroms. He lived in a no-water walk-up flat somewhere in the garment district.

Curiosity has always been my downfall, so when Pierrot insisted that I meet his parents, I went along, knowing full well it was not the prudent thing to do, since I had no intention of letting a casual acquaintanceship progress even the slightest bit further. I had miscalculated.

This must have been 1937, the year of *Le Carnet de Bal* and the World's Fair. Hammer and sickle were facing the swastika on the banks of the Seine across from the Eiffel Tower. The familiar red brick Trocadero Theater had been dismantled for the occasion, and replaced by the resplendently modern and streamlined *Musée de l'Homme,* its wings embracing a series of playful waterfalls cascading down to the river's edge. There were those Parisian purists who had proposed dismantling the Eiffel Tower instead, a perennial eyesore in their view, but to no avail.

I had free tickets to the fair courtesy of my big brother, who worked as an official interpreter, judiciously stationed between the two buildings on which those two monolithic symbols, were displayed, alternately directing visitors from the competing evil empires to appropriate rest facilities. My brother, the soul of discretion, never divulged the names or the business of any of the personages that crossed his way. He was a born charmer; he kept his ears open and his mouth shut. This was to be a major asset in a career which depended on people confiding in him. He also appreciated his little sister's penchant for poetic license, and made it a fast rule not to talk to me. Being a young man of few words in each of several languages, he opted for the draft as a private in the French army rather than suffer the agonies of exams at the Sorbonne. "Opted" may be misleading, as a man without a country was subject to the draft of whatever country he resided in.

Papa was incensed. The two literally never spoke to each other. His son a private! Throwing away every chance at a decent life! Father and son had not been on speaking terms for a long time, since before we left Germany. Now the break was definitive. Since the arguments proceeded in Russian, I was spared the worst of it (part of the reason I had spurned my mother tongue in the first place), but I could not help gathering some of the gist of it, which had to do with Margot, of whose friends Papa heartily disapproved. "Cavorting with Trotskyites and Communists" was his ultimate insult.

It was true that Margot enjoyed a good time, such as dancing until the wee hours on Saturday nights with a group of young people whom she referred to as the Egyptians. The Egyptians were indeed from Egypt, then a British protectorate. They spoke English, a language Margot was more familiar with than French, after five years of high school study. The Egyptians had joined a group of Palestinian Jews who were just as intent on wresting Palestine away from the British to create the state of Israel as the Egyptians were on kicking the British out of their country. I had a hard time picturing the British Empire as an enemy to be toppled by a handful of Arab and Jewish students whom Margot described as divine dancers.

When our Girl Scout patrol had successfully mastered the art of French cuisine in the wilds of the Forêt de Fontainebleau and other nearby public parks, we ventured out on a two-week tenting trip in the Jura Mountains of Alsace.

I borrowed a small sturdy knapsack. The secret of packing consisted of anchoring major belongings on the outside of it: sturdy high-top hiking shoes stuffed with heavy wool socks, a blanket roll, and a share of the cooking equipment in the shape of a big pot, assorted ladles, and a box or two of foodstuffs. Ladles and shoes beat a merry tattoo on my back as we marched the ten miles or so from the railroad station to our rented bit of grassland, in an idyllic valley on the banks of a fast running brook. We shared the valley with a herd of friendly Alsatian cows. Each morning we woke up to the tinkling of their bells, to their gentle lowing, to roosters crowing in the barnyard a few hundred feet downstream, to dogs barking. If we insisted on ignoring this pastoral reveille, a cow would obligingly lift the flap of the tent just above our heads and lick our faces.

Those daring souls among us who were brave enough to risk an assault of fluttering hens and yapping dogs around a forbidding hillock of rich manure were dispatched for the morning's ration of thick, warm milk. It took two girls to transport each of two heavy wooden pails. We were invited to milk the cows ourselves, but wisely begged off after witnessing the acrobatics required to keep one's precarious balance on a small three-legged stool, while aiming the stream of liquid into the pail.

While personal acquaintance with the cows was pretty good insurance against catching any milk-carried diseases, we did not drink the milk. It was boiled in two huge kettles set on stones gathered in the creek, with a merit-badge assembly of twigs and dried wood in between, and transformed into hot chocolate.

The farmer's wife also supplied warm eggs, which we snatched up while the hen responsible was momentarily called away, freshly churned butter, homemade marmalade, bacon, lard and sausage, salad greens, and fresh vegetables from her garden.

I thought I detected a strong German accent, overheard snatches of Alsatian dialect, but did not let on I spoke German. It was obvious that our hosts considered French a foreign language, since they had spent their youth as Germans before World War I.

Our tenting skills were sorely tested when a rainstorm tore the tarpaulin flaps from their roped mooring; we were left shivering in the night, blankets and straw-filled gunnysacks a soggy mess. Our two young chieftains struggled mightily to build a roaring fire in the waning drizzle, while we frantically jumped up and down and around in a hastily improvised version of a sun dance. It took a day of sunshine and welcome breeze to whip the blankets dry. We trudged to the barn to stuff our ration of straw into clean gunnysacks for our bedding. None of these endeavors were gentle to the skin. Many of the girls devoted what was left of the day to damage control, huddled inside a dried-out tent, with little pots of cream mysteriously produced and passed around.

When our chieftain announced a day's hike, eight of us volunteered—anything to escape the rugged housekeeping chores of daily life in the meadow. We set out after a hearty breakfast of hot chocolate and thick slabs of rye bread generously spread with butter and marmalade. Traveling, or rather stepping light, was of the essence. For once, no provision was made for an haute cuisine midday repast. We each carried a canteen filled with fresh water from the creek, which we drank from cupped hands—it tasted better that way—and which supplied our cooking and washing needs. The canteen was clipped to the belt, along with a knife and an individual drinking cup. Our chieftain packed emergency rations of biscuits, jam, chocolate bars, a roll of surgical tape, gauze, and iodine in a small knapsack, which we took turns toting on our backs. Gaily we clambered up a fairly steep path to reach our marching destination: the top of a range, where I do not recall, with a heavenly view of a valley to our left and a ripple of receding ranges to our right, reaching somewhere into Germany beyond the Rhine. This was the closest to the clouds I had ever come before flying. We hit our stride, to the rhythm of every marching song we knew: strings of lost battles set to sprightly tunes in memory of the faithful drummer boy, the loyal soldier killed on foreign soil, the widow left behind. We stopped for a breather every five kilometers or so, or about three miles, which, according to our chieftain's map, would get us to our destination well before nightfall.

When the sun was high overhead, we peeled off sweaters and tied them around our waists; unwound the kerchiefs artfully tied around our necks and wore them on our heads; bravely marched on, to the tune of Napoleon's five hundred men silenced one by one as they fell on the battlefield. This was a catchy melody which ensured one's keeping in step, as each verse had the end syllable chopped off until there were no soldiers left, only the echoes of their footfalls.

By four in the afternoon, chocolate bars and biscuits notwithstanding, we were a sorry sight of collapsed bodies on the side of the road. To our chieftain's credit, she put a stop to our theatricals by taking us into her confidence, describing the real dangers facing us. It was too late in the day to turn back. We could not stop and overnight by the side of the road: clouds were gathering, and there might be wild animals about. We had run out of water and food.

Bravely we marched on, a subdued lot, saving our breath. Sadly, we intoned the slow rhythmic beat of the saga of Jeanette: "Don't cry, Jeanette, we'll get you married yet, to the son of a prince." "I don't want a prince, I want my friend Pierre, the one who sits in prison!" "Tra, la, la, la, la," ends the song. "See them dangle, dingle, dangle, at the end of a rope." I could relate to sitting in prison as an honorable occupation. Papa had spent the best years of his life thus sitting.

A few more miles, then a few more. To the east, mountains receded into shadows; to the west, a blanket of clouds lay over the valley, ominous. Suspended between heaven and earth, we followed a road to nowhere. I could have marched through the night, happily elsewhere. I was at home.

Separation between things German and French had become so categorical in my mind that I had developed a sort of double vision, a visceral geography of my own, which put all things German safely east of the Rhine. One cannot sing the German national anthem on solemn occasions with tears in one's eyes for ten of one's most impressionable years without visualizing the German fatherland stretching from the Rhine to the river Elbe. I took the Rhine border literally. According to this logic, Elsass-Lothringen, being incontestably German, was located east of the Rhine. It was to take me over thirty years to adjust my sight to realize that Elsass-Lothringen and the French Alsace-Lorraine of my Girl Scout camping days were one and the same thing, located west of the Rhine. Crisscrossing the Rhineland in 1969 in my Volkswagen bug, I was taken aback as I approached Aachen. Unconsciously, I had positioned Aachen, the headquarters of Karl der Grosse in the eighth century, a goodly hundred miles east of Aix-la-Chapelle; yet the road sign clearly proclaimed, "Aachen, Aix-la-Chapelle." Charlemagne, the kindly, fatherly figure of French legend, was none other than the Kaiser, head of the Holy Roman Empire. Aachen was the French city of Aix.

Brought to a halt by distant lights, we verified our position on the map. We had walked forty kilometers, a respectable distance of twenty-five miles; one more mile downhill would see us to a village, food, and lodging. Alas! Only a tavern remained open. Reluctantly, the innkeeper's wife showed us to a hay-filled granary. Our chieftain negotiated a round loaf of rye bread, a slab of cheese, and a jug of drinking water. I went hungry rather than eat the cheese.

We tried to sleep in the hay, fully dressed, aware of the stomping and raucous singing below, as villagers made merry without any inhibitions. Bleary-eyed, we plucked hay from our clothes as best we could in the morning. People around us did not speak French. Neither did they speak German, though I caught the drift of their meaning here and there. I had the distinct feeling that we were not welcome. We caught an early morning bus, which dropped us off a mile or so from our rented meadow, in time for a midmorning snack of hot chocolate and bread with marmalade.

Our camp, with all the inconveniences of roughing it, was a heavenly refuge of civilized orderliness. Merrily we pitched in, plumping up our gunnysack mattresses, hanging blankets to air outside, scouring pots and pans, cleaning vegetables, and attending to other mundane chores.

By contrast, I spent the summer of 1938 in the lap of luxury, accompanying a well-to-do couple on their honeymoon. As I understood the situation, I was to entertain Monsieur's young son, about six years old, when Monsieur and his newlywed wife, not the boy's mother, went out for their afternoon walk. Neither Monsieur nor Madame was French, though they spoke the language with elegance. Neither were they Russian. As they each spoke a different Eastern European tongue, they had adopted French as their common ground, French being the language of love. The boy, Andreas, also spoke German, his mother's first language, which his father refused to acknowledge. I had strict instructions to carry out my conversation in French only, and I took my job very seriously.

We embarked in a new, richly upholstered brown Peugeot for a tour of the Côte d'Azur, Switzerland, and the French Alps, Monsieur in the driver's seat, Madame seated next to him, and the boy and I in the back. We took our meals in elegant restaurants. To Monsieur's credit, we ate *en famille*, Monsieur, Madame, his son, and the babysitter. To Madame's credit, as she was a wise and gentle soul, decisions about Andreas' behavior and activities were left to his father. To Andreas' credit, he obeyed his father's every wish.

It was a most agreeable journey, leisurely driving south through the lovely French countryside. At that time, few Parisians owned cars, which were a distinct sign of wealth. Country roads were two-lane, shoulderless affairs, with evenly spaced, carefully trimmed trees running along each side. In fact, when I first went to Cambridge, after I started speaking English, I told Mrs. Ducky that French trees grew in rectangles. It hadn't occurred to me that this was not the trees' doing, that they were coaxed into this most untreelike shape by vigorous and artistic yearly pruning.

Andreas was an alert and eager child, with his father's soft black eyes, matte coloring, and curly locks. We played guessing games, identified car models, spelled out road signs. At night, in our shared hotel room, we told stories, played cards, and read the exotic adventures of Babar the elephant.

This trip, while a welcome interlude of normalcy, was for me a reminder of earlier family vacations spent in the Harz Mountains in Germany. There I had struggled mightily with huge white napkins and heavy silver in a cavernous dining hall, staffed by as many servers in prettily starched white lace aprons as there were dinner guests to serve. This trip was tame by comparison. Andreas and I dutifully played on the beach along the azure coast, strolled along the famous boardwalk of Nice, held our breath as Monsieur manfully negotiated the hair-raising hairpin curves of the Corniche. I was to make the same trip by car many times, thirty years, forty years, fifty years later. It was not crowded that first time; the palatial whitewashed villas perched on cliffs and draped in cascades of bougainvillea spoke of true opulence.

As we continued on, to take in the sights of a picture-perfect Switzerland, the dreamlike trip was undercut by an uneasy feeling of unreality. Margot's friends had joined the Loyalists in the Spanish civil war; my brother was in basic training in Cherbourg; Mama had had no news from family in Moscow and Leningrad; Hitler had annexed Austria; every new recruit to Mama's kitchen and/or consulting room confirmed the worst rumors about concentration camps. Mussolini had made war in Abyssinia; the Japanese were fighting the Chinese. I knew because a journalist friend had returned from China and described some of the horrors there. (I have never been able to repeat what he said. It was too abominable. I recall reading a book about China in the 1930s. It was true. I also checked when I was in China.)

I have been accused of being too gullible by family, friends, and students. Yet on the few occasions that I refused to believe, I was wrong. There was a girl in our class who constantly raised her hand, and when the teacher called on her, she forgot why. One day when she raised her hand, the teacher ignored her. She raised her hand again and asked to be excused. "You will wait until the bell rings in ten minutes, with the rest of the class." The next day, the girl was absent. She had died of a perforated appendix. In memory of that girl, I preferred to believe whatever my students told me.

When I first started teaching German at Benjamin Franklin High School in the early seventies, I wasn't quick enough. I was still struggling to suppress the negative connotations of the German language inherited from the war years, while facing a class of mostly tall blond teenagers, many of German ancestry, who delighted in mock Nazi salutes and similar shenanigans. We were watching an excellent sequence of a film on loan from the German consulate, which succeeded in impressing upon my class the irregular forms of the verb "to shoot," with unforgettable bangs directed at wooden ducks in a shooting gallery. *Er schiesst, er hat geschossen* (he shoots, he shot) was repeated enthusiastically with impeccable intonation just before the bell rang. A hand was raised hesitantly in the back row. "Morgen schiesse ich, ist das richtig, Frau Schueler?" ("Tomorrow I'll shoot, is that correct, Mrs. Schueler?") "Ja," I answered. What a weird question, I thought, as thirty young men rushed out the door. Who was it? I tried to reach the boy but was caught in the rush of the next class coming in. The next day I was interrupted by a messenger who handed me a slip of paper as I was just about to call the roll. "Richard (not his name) was found dead this morning. He shot himself."

Our heady motor sight-seeing trip ended in a peaceful valley in the Haute-Savoie, home to the Savoyards, known for their fierce spirit of independence, hardiness, and mountain climbing abilities. The shepherds of our host farm family had escorted their cows up the mountain for the summer; their sleeping quarters had been transformed into a summer rental. I suspect that my chamber under the eaves, with just enough room for a narrow bed and a chair, belonged to the farmer's sixteen-year-old daughter, who had cheerfully taken up residence in the big common room where we were served our meals from the hearth.

Andreas took to the gently sloping meadow with gleeful shouts and somersaults, and disappeared into the outstretched arms of a handsome blond woman of majestic proportions who laughed with tears in her eyes, while her companion, a string bean of a balding gentleman, stood by without expression. Later, Andreas was not present at the midday meal. I was informed that he had left with his mother, and that I could henceforth dispose of my time as I wished, bound only by mealtimes.

That is when I discovered my total ineptitude for things of the soil. I shook hands with Marie-Thérèse, a strapping curly-haired brunette, a head taller and a year older than I, with a peaches and cream complexion and lashes that would have been the envy of my beauty-conscious Girl Scout troop. Together, we ran down the meadow to a field of what looked like tall grass where her father and uncles were swinging their scythes in graceful arcs, a pastoral composition worthy of Millet. I watched as Marie-Thérèse picked up her scythe and started swinging in slow, seemingly effortless, rhythmic motions. "May I?" "Sure," she replied and lay the scythe down. It was too heavy for me to lift.

"I never shook hands with a young lady before. Could we shake hands again?"

"Of course," I answered.

"So soft." Marie-Thérèse was crying as she stroked my clasped right hand with her left. "Look at mine." She held out her hands, palms up. I had never seen such rough, scarred, and thickly calloused skin. Shamefully, I became aware of my own unsullied hands.

When Marie-Thérèse wasn't wielding a scythe, she carried her seven-year-old sister around on her back, fetched pails of water, peeled vegetables, and scrubbed piles of dingy, muddy clothes on a stone in the brook alongside the field.

"Have you ever thought of leaving the valley?" What I actually said was, "Don't you want to see the other side of the mountain?" Marie-Thérèse gave me an uncomprehending stare. "No. How could I? My little sister had polio. She can't walk, and I have to take care of her."

"Well, if you could, what would you most like to do?"

"Work for a nice family in the city, decent people. Be a chambermaid with a black dress and a white apron." I left Marie-Thérèse to her unattainable dream and scampered off to the village library some five miles downstream.

1938 was a year of gloom and doom.

In school, our ranks had been seriously depleted: a third of the girls had failed their third-year exams, the cutoff point for any advanced academic study. Those who were left labored in the shadows of the dreaded baccalaureate, struggling with math, physics, and chemistry as well as heavy reading in Latin, French, and English classics. (I read the latter in German translation.) To this was added a belated effort to keep me literate in German, starting with rows of handsome volumes of Heine, Goethe, and Schiller, which I discovered at the bottom of Mama's bookshelves, together with a complete set of Shakespeare's plays in German. Their puzzling provenance was only recently explained to me by my brother, together with the source of now rare stamps from Manchuria, which he parlayed into a twenty-thousand-plus stamp collection. In Berlin, Papa had been editing books in Russian for a renowned German publisher, Manchuria being one of the targeted Russian-speaking territories outside the Soviet Union, with ensuing correspondence. The German classics remained on Mama's bookshelves, much to the delight, I am sure, of the German officer who took over our apartment during World War II. My brother's stamps had remained in Berlin.

A year or so earlier, Mama had befriended a downcast German professor of Latin and Greek, a would-be writer well into middle age at forty-two. While grateful to have escaped with his life and fully cognizant of the liberating atmosphere of a vibrant artistic and literary scene in Paris, he despaired of ever writing again, torn from his German roots.

He was not alone. Writers, that is, novelists and poets, were particularly hard hit in exile, not only because they had lost their audience and would-be publishers, but because their native tongue was deprived of nourishment on foreign soil. Herr Professor Weimar (he used some alias or other) was persuaded to devote two hours every school-free Thursday afternoon to instill in us some grammatical discipline and respect for the German language. "Us" meant four or five of the Group's children, whose German language proficiency was in danger of becoming a casualty of our Parisian exile.

What I recall are lackluster sessions of paragraph writing until the day our Herr Professor broke every rule of appropriate conduct and announced that he was in love. He was positively radiant; his precisely enunciated speech gave way to overtones of Berliner dialect as he described the object of his affections, a Hungarian lady he was to meet that evening at the Gare de L'Est, arriving from Budapest. If we worked hard, we would share in his happiness and have the distinct privilege of meeting the lady. We did both. She was, if possible, more lovely than expected, petite, in a simple well-cut suit, her deep-set blue eyes laughing up at her friend towering above her. We were treated to a public embrace deserving of Hollywood, and shocked that love was not only for the young.

About the same time, I was introduced to Hannah, who was in dire need of learning French in a hurry. Rain or shine, on Thursday mornings we took in the street scene around her neighborhood (rue de la Convention, rue de Vaugirard) as an infallible stimulus to French conversation. Hannah was a twelve-year-old German bean pole, rigorously scrubbed, straight hair neatly, if not becomingly, pinned back. She bristled at the disordered traffic, the uneven sidewalks, the clumps of pedestrians impeding her even stride. Her mother had married (or maybe not married) an older, small, rotund, and silver-haired gentleman and followed him into exile with his library.

Alexander Stein, I was told, was a writer and journalist, editor of the Berlin socialist daily *Vorwärts*. How he appeared in Paris with his life and library intact, I do not know. On Hannah's and my return from our French conversation stroll, he would invite me, speaking German, to have a look at his books. I was entrusted with Thomas Mann one week, Feuchtwanger the next. "So what did you think about that book?" Herr Stein would inquire when I brought a volume back. I was most happy to oblige, struggling to compose my thoughts in articulate formal speech. "Try Kafka," he would urge me. "Try Nietzsche." And thus he kept my love for the German language alive.

At school, our French and Latin teacher, Mademoiselle Jehan, risked her career by introducing us to modern writers not part of the prescribed curriculum. I recall her enthusiasm for Marcel Pagnol, Roger Martin du Gard, Jules Romains. She encouraged lively discussions, a teaching method then alien to the French academic style. Her motto when class enthusiasm got out of hand was, "*Réfléchissez!*" ("Stop and think!") A bachelor lady, well into her thirties, of no great looks and with a pronounced limp due to a dislocated hip, she stunned us one day by announcing her forthcoming marriage. We had spent three hours of every school day with Mademoiselle Jehan for the past five years—one hour of Latin and two of French—entranced by her unfailing wit, her incisive criticism, her masterful literary analysis. It was unthinkable that she should share her devotion to her class with another. We called her Madame and felt sheepishly betrayed.

For Easter 1954, Fred gave me a birthday present of Paris. He would babysit Carl in Rome while I spent ten days or so with Tanya, whom we called Ruthie then, in Paris, showing our daughter the city I had learned to love. We were received by a white-haired Madame la Générale Hillairet, Maud's mother, who did nothing to conceal her grief, nor her sixty-plus years, and wasted no time in pleasant small talk. Madame spoke English and greeted Ruthie in that language, then gave me the facts curtly in French. Mademoiselle Jehan had been transferred to Lyon after the outbreak of the war in 1939. Her husband joined the Resistance in June of 1940, and she herself became active in the Resistance movement. Together with a long list of suspects, she was denounced by Madame la Directrice of our Lycée Camille Sée to the authorities (the Vichy government? the German occupying forces?) and duly executed for treason by the same. On that list as well was Madame's own daughter's name, since Maud also chose to help the Resistance (as did her husband, the general). Maud was arrested at the end of 1940 and spent four years in solitary confinement. Madame showed us small hardened clumps of bread which Maud had fashioned into a semblance of chess pieces to while away the time and exercise her mind while in prison. Madame then showed us a recent photo of a smiling, slimmed-down Maud, the result of four years of prison diet, disciplined daily exercise to keep fit, and recent forays into the world of ballet while teaching French in Tehran. The general had passed away. I did not inquire under what circumstances. Madame la Directrice had been tried, found guilty of collaboration, and executed after the end of the war.

"I am glad you left Paris when the war broke out, Julia. Your name was on the list."

I can't remember which came first, gas masks or my Aunt Mirrha. Gas masks were predicated on the assumption that Hitler would prefer to wage a "clean war," that is, poison the civilian population rather than reduce Parisian monuments to rubble. Possibly this was wishful thinking. There was not a French family who had not been touched by the devastation of World War I as depicted in the films *All Quiet on the Western Front* and *The Grand Illusion*. A graying veteran, one sleeve neatly pinned to the shoulder, was seated next to the entrance of every museum exhibit, surveying visitors and ready to give directions. Since my sense of direction, or rather lack of it, is legendary, I had to deal with the one-armed gentlemen on a regular basis every time I got hopelessly lost visiting the Louvre. Veterans with one leg were employed in the Métro, where they sat all day on a stool, punching tickets and guarding access to the trains. Their infirmity was not readily apparent until they got up, one trouser leg neatly folded and pinned up high above the missing knee, their crutches within reach. French women of my mother's generation wore black. It was simpler and cheaper. Once mourning clothes had been bought, or coat, suit, and dress had been dyed black, it was easier to accessorize with a discreet lavender scarf, a light gray blouse, a hand-knit gray cardigan.

Every one of my French acquaintances had a grandfather, an uncle, a cousin who had died in the trenches, been grievously wounded, been taken prisoner, or been gassed. One of my classmates invited me for hot chocolate after school. "My dad looks all right, but he is a grand invalid. He was gassed." "Looks all right" referred to the gentleman's not missing any limbs. My classmate's father was pale, emaciated, weak, a caricature of a man in his prime, and infinitely sad.

Two of my uncles, my mother's brothers who served in the Tsarist army in World War I, had been taken prisoner on the eastern front. One of them, Misha, died of his wounds. Isaac, who later named his firstborn Misha in memory of his brother, lost his son, a pilot, in World War II. Misha's plane was shot down.

The use of poison gas caught the imagination. It was cheap, it could be delivered by air, and it could paralyze a city. To counteract this threat, we were issued gas masks, each in a fashionably trim shoulder bag, and invited to practice the wearing thereof. This led to much hilarity at school, as we faced each other pig-snouted in the locker basement. Looking back, that gas mask episode provided much comic relief and eased the ever-present tension of the possibility of war. I am not sure we took the masks seriously. However, we could not avoid periodic shelter drills, which intruded into everyone's privacy. This was not to be a trench war. We would be facing the menace from the air; we would have to train ourselves to take immediate action to preserve our lives.

The accent here is on immediate. At the ear-piercing sound of the wailing sirens, we were to leave everything in midsentence, in midparagraph, in midbrioche and walk to the nearest shelter. If at home, it meant walking down the stairs to the basement. On the street, posters marked *abri* (shelter) directed pedestrians to the nearest basement. The entire Métro system was a ready-made shelter. There was a young German couple living in the apartment building on rue Jullien, across from the Lycée Michelet, with two children I knew, a boy and a girl. When the sirens wailed once during actual wartime, the children, then seven and nine, followed their school drill, ran out the apartment door, and slid down two flights of stairs on the bannister. They made it to the basement shelter, the boy with a broken leg. The building took a direct hit. Their parents, who had stopped to grab documents and money, never made it out the door and were found dead under the rubble. Mama told me the story on June 15, 1940, when she arrived in Angers on the last train out of Paris. German planes had dropped a few bombs before Paris was declared an open city.

When a friend proposed an Easter escapade which involved hitchhiking to the city of Tours on the Loire, about two hundred kilometers west of Paris, and tenting on the grounds of a youth hostel, I jumped at the chance to get away. We were fifteen; hitchhiking was an accepted mode of travel for the young and impecunious. Moreover, a boy and a girl traveling together inspired more confidence among drivers. My friend was very tall and mature looking, well, maybe sixteen. Just the same, we didn't hop into just any old vehicle. No! We carefully picked and chose "big" trucks (French trucks were exactly half the length of their American counterparts) and snazzy foreign cars. That is how I met my first American, at the wheel of an incredible dreamboat: a black, shiny, six-seater Cadillac, one and a half times as wide and long as the standard Peugeot. I know, because all three of us sat comfortably, very comfortably, in the soft leather seat in front.

The driver was a pleasant, middle-aged lady, maybe in her late thirties, who greeted us in school-taught French and informed us she was "on sabbatical" on a discovery tour of France. She had had her car shipped over, and intended to see every nook and cranny of the countryside. Yet she was no American millionaire. The car was a gift from her parents, and she had worked hard and saved for twenty years for this trip. If ever I made it to America, that is what I would do, I decided then and there. And I did.

I remember the days in Tours as a blur of soaking March showers (in German as in English they are called April showers, but spring arrives earlier in France); of intense encounters, whirlwind dances, young men and women from Scandinavia, the Middle East, and Africa. We met French foreign legionnaires, Jewish and Arab Palestinians, Englishmen, Swedes, and Italians. And exactly one American. We crowded around him, a young six-footer on a shiny new ten-speed bicycle. I think the bicycle was the greater attraction.

The American had a happy grin but spoke no French, so I was deputized to address him in English. "They want to know about your bicycle." He gave a technical description which, luckily for me, was accompanied by self-evident demonstrations. Yes, he had had it checked as baggage on the Atlantic boat crossing. It was cheaper that way to tour France and England. Why was he going to England? To go to medical school. He explained that his parents in New Jersey were too poor to pay medical school tuition in the States, that he had worked his way through college and saved money for the crossing and hoped to make it through medical school in England, where tuition was minimal. My world reeled. Here was this obviously rich young man on a racing bicycle worth a year's salary, and he was poor!

These two Americans, the teacher and the student, took the future for granted and acted as if they were masters of their destiny. I had a glimpse of what it meant to have a right to exist. Back in Paris, the city was cloaked in a mood of indescribable doom, as even French acquaintances acknowledged that the Nazi threat put a cap on the future. There simply wasn't any, and our discussions became centered on the most exotic biological, chemical, and explosive war scenarios, as our imaginations fed on science fiction.

I despaired of ever growing up. As stateless persons and political refugees, my family had been granted a temporary residence permit in France. This had to be renewed periodically and did not entitle us to the right to work. Should I ever attain the privileged status of resident alien, law and medicine and all civil service occupations, including teaching, would still be off limits. Wistfully, I stood in line at the corner bakery. I asked the baker's wife, a buxom black-clad lady in a black smock, if she ever had a vacation. She gave me an uncomprehending stare. "Do you go on a little trip sometimes?" I ventured. "To the country?" "Me, go on a trip? My husband is up at 4 A.M. stoking the ovens. We work from 7 A.M. to 7 P.M. When we retire, we will go back to the country."

Across the street was a laundry. I could see a dozen women through the half-basement windows, ironing shirts and sheets at long padded tables. I knew how to iron, but this was exhausting, numbing hard labor, requiring strong arms and a strong back. I had neither.

I met an artist, a girl perhaps sixteen, unusually fat ("chubby" by American standards), who had dropped out of society. She invited me to her garret. We sat on a mattress without sheets and ate unpeeled boiled potatoes, which she had proudly cooked on a minuscule one-burner gas plate. She explained that an older friend had discovered her unusual talent and persuaded her to devote her life to the arts. There were easels and squashed tubes of paint strewn around, piles of canvases smeared with oil, each one more garish than the next. I was well acquainted with the Old Masters from frequent visits to the Louvre; I had viewed original works by Chagall, Dali, and Picasso and was able to appreciate them as works of art, although I was not particularly fond of them. (When my brother visited us in our barracks apartment in Finkbine Park in 1950, he handed me a sketch of a deformed nude on a horse, which I hastily stuck away "in a safe place." "Did you ever find that Picasso I gave you?" has been a question to haunt me ever since.) My friend in her garret was no Picasso, but a misguided soul suffering from delusions of grandeur. I had enough sense to express my genuine thanks for the heartfelt gift of boiled potatoes and to flee down the seven flights of stairs and out into the fresh air of Montparnasse.

My foray into the arts had an unexpectedly happy ending. Two years later, in Toulouse, in the summer of 1940, Margot told me: "You remember that crazy fat girl who thought she was an artist? Guess what. I met her in camp. We were on the same shift. She slaved as a nurse's aide. I mean, she really sweated, and of course, she lost all that weight and had no time to think about herself. She was really devoted to those poor devils and became quite normal."

I then recalled Papa warning me a couple of years earlier about just such foolish behavior, dropping out, like that girl had done. I had seldom seen him so distraught. "A terrible thing has happened to a dear friend of mine. His daughter, Dina, has run away from home. He and his wife are heartbroken!" Papa's French was by that time no better than his miserable German, as he tried to articulate the tragedy in both languages. However, he was wrong. Dina is the only person of the Group to have become both truly rich and famous. I remembered her as a forceful teenager with a golden voice, a born orator, who could inspire a group of forlorn youngsters to do the impossible. She had run away to be the new model of the sculptor Aristide Maillol. Cast in bronze, a teenage Dina adorned the approaches of the Louvre in a variety of reckless poses until the new glass pyramid in the courtyard of the Louvre moved her over to the Tuileries. Upon the sculptor's death, Dina parlayed her inheritance into a fortune and dedicated her life to the memory of Maillol and his times. Her dream has come true: a privately endowed Musée Maillol, housing her private collection, opened in March 1995 on the rue de Grenelle next to her Paris residence.

Sometime in early spring (the Anschluss, or annexation of Austria, took place on March 15) we were awakened by the doorbell at two in the morning to find a disheveled Mirrha and a sleepy-eyed, nine-year-old Joshi standing at the door. Joshi was hastily bedded down on the floor of my room, and we repaired to the kitchen to partake of Mirrha's saga over steaming tea. I would have said "bewail the saga," as Mama was prone to cast a deep shadow over every happening, but Mirrha managed to lend her escape on foot over the Alpine border from Austria to Switzerland an aura of romance, praising her small son for his pluck and endurance. The only vivid image of Vienna I retain from her story is that of elderly Jewish people rousted from their beds and forced to scrub the sidewalks with lye that ate into their hands. Mirrha didn't say what was on the sidewalks. Blood? Vomit? Spilled garbage? While Uncle Karl had been active in his trade union, his family shared a three-room apartment with his aging parents. Mirrha was teaching in Anna Freud's nursery school, and although her German had improved "tremendously," which was one of her favorite expressions, there was no escaping her suspiciously foreign and gypsy looks. Karl sent his family across the border, destination Zurich, where they spent some time, perhaps a week or two, recuperating at the house of a generous friend. Joshi spent happy hours playing chess and reading history books alternately with comic books. He arrived in Paris, a blond, rosy-cheeked lad with a knapsack full of his own cartoons and a chessboard, his head crammed with the dates of Napoleon's battles and not a word of French.

Joshi was at the puzzle and riddle stage, made more endearing, but not easier, by his broad Viennese accent. Mirrha hustled him off to school and set out to find work, which she did fairly promptly, in a home for displaced children, whose traumas were thoroughly discussed during dinner, together with Freud's and Jung's theories. I found the references on Mama's shelves.

Most of Mirrha's new charges were children whose parents had disappeared. Camps were no longer a secret, and the names Buchenwald, Dachau, Oranienburg crept into the conversation. How these children had been rescued, I don't know. They had been terrorized and abandoned, surviving on garbage and living in attics. They spoke, if they spoke at all, in different languages: Polish, Yiddish, German, Czech, Hungarian, and dozens of dialects of each, as well as baby talk. Mirrha, who could barely carry a tune, reached out to them in the common language of music and dance and had the little ones clapping and skipping in unison to her irresistible beat, releasing tensions and frustration in the sheer glory of rhythmic movement.

Arms akimbo, Mirrha could give a convincing version of the Cossack dance; clicking her heels in a tight circle, she could be a flamenco dancer even without the castanets; she knew or improvised any number of folk dances, and managed to convey by sheer mimicry meanings that words could not express.

Eventually, Karl joined his family with a heavy suitcase. When he - wasn't following hopeless leads to land a job without working papers and without French, he spent his time in the kitchen with a French paper and a German-French dictionary, determined to master the language correctly and grammatically, revved up by cups of coffee so thick it had to be spooned up. Mama took up residence on my bed, I slept on the floor, and Karl and Mirrha slept on the wide sofa in Mama's consulting room, until Mirrha's dream of a place of her own came true: a maid's room on the seventh floor, accessed by walk-up servants' stairs only. For a maid's room, it was truly palatial, twelve by twelve feet square, with a private sink, hot and cold running water, a normal-sized window, and a sunny view. (Toilet and shower down the hall.) Mirrha put a two-burner gas plate on a box, a few pillows on a couch, hung photos on the wall, and managed to give her home a cozy, lived-in look. Joshi moved up to live with his parents, and I trudged up the seven flights of stairs willingly to visit with my aunt.

During those days when I wasn't visiting, I was reading or knitting. I later found a photo of Margot wearing one of my masterpieces, a dark yellow cardigan with a complicated cable stitch and fancy buttons. It was the same model worn by the actress portraying Anne Frank in the movie and on the book cover of *The Diary of Anne Frank*.

Mirrha did not approve of my reading. Mama did not approve of my knitting. Papa approved heartily of both, but wished I were more of a young lady. "If I had money, you would be taking riding lessons and dancing lessons, going out to parties and having fun. Someday we will go to America. You will have a house with a garden and a car." I didn't believe Papa. It was the wildest fantasizing.

Later, in 1954, after we returned from Italy and after his first bout with sickness, a gallstone operation, Papa came to visit us in our little yellow house in Coralville, on the outskirts of Iowa City. "Little" meant a 40' x 25' prefabricated Gunnison house made entirely of plywood panels on a concrete slab covered with linoleum tiles, sporting maroon shutters on lemon yellow walls, with a brick chimney jutting out in front. A two-year-old black Buick in the driveway, rows of corn and strawberries in the garden behind the house, and a struggling lawn in front completed Papa's prophecy: a house, a garden, and a car. It had taken us five years of living in married student and junior faculty housing to save $500 to buy the lot, and another $900 for the down payment on the $9,000 house.

Carl was two when we moved, just in time for Christmas. He kept running back and forth the whole length of the house, all forty feet of it, starting at one end of the living room and continuing down the hall to the end of the children's bedroom. He had never had more than four feet of space to move around in before. He loved it. He loved running out of it. There was no fence, and he and a newly acquired puppy, aptly named Puddles, chased each other around the house, spraying the pristine yellow walls with mud when the snow melted and before grass had had a chance to grow.

When Carl was a young man and I didn't hear from him for months at a time, he once phoned with just one question: "Where was our little yellow house? I am in Coralville, and I can't find it." On another day, a gentleman phoned. "This is Nick. I'm at the airport. Do you remember me? (I didn't.) I bought your little yellow house in Coralville." "How nice. How is it?" "Well, it's not yellow any more, I painted it barn red." More recently, I found the address of the house on the back of a photo and put it in a safe place for Carl.

In 1938, at school in Paris, we were no longer giggling. One year away from the big exams, study had become serious business. Maud and I were stars in English. Our teacher, Miss Duncan, was a gentle old soul, going hopelessly deaf. She made no pretense of hiding her infirmity and used her hearing aid, a sort of little trumpet, as a menacing prop. The class continued to mispronounce English as French, since most abstract concepts such as "revolution," "independence," "justice," and "joy" were identical in both languages; I chose to mispronounce English as German, since most of the concrete objects had Anglo-Saxon antecedents, many of them identical to their German counterparts. (My internal language barriers continued to be so strong that twenty years later I found myself standing in front of my German class holding up a finger, a finger with a capital *F* in German, unable to think of the word in English.) Maud and I took turns dictating answers to the class during tests. I am not sure that it did much good, unprepared students often being unable to process correct information. At any rate, Miss Duncan, ever the lady, did not raise an eyebrow, assuming she was aware of our stratagem: do I recall her deliberately setting aside the hearing aid, while pretending to listen to recitals of Wordsworth, Shelley, and Keats?

When I was in England, Mrs. Ducky's daughter, Joyce, had insisted on hours of laborious corrective speech sessions in front of the mirror, counting by threes and thirties, repeating words like "thrilling" and "circumstance" and "incomprehension," all to no avail. I never could pronounce the *r*s in my children's names. When Carl was three, he asked me why I called him "Cow." "Ruthie" was the ultimate challenge, combining both of the two sounds, *r* and *th*, that eluded me. When I taught fractions at Ursuline Academy in 1958, the class repeated in unison "One eighth, *t*, *h*, plus two eighths, *t*, *h*, equal three eighths, *t*, *h*." It was too confusing to explain that the letters *t* and *h* were not part of the fraction.

There was, however, some compensation in having poor pronunciation. In the sixties, after I started traveling regularly overseas, I went to see the vice president of my bank in charge of foreign exchange. "Just give me a call when you're in Paris and we'll transfer the funds you need. I'll recognize your voice." I've never dared complain of my accent since then.

One day in Paris, back in 1938, we received a surprise visit from an elegantly turned out young man who looked strangely familiar. Wavy black locks, matte complexion, high cheekbones, oriental eyes: the family characteristics were unmistakable. Papa had told me precious little of his family. Was this a long lost son of a previous marriage? Eventually, I understood him to be my uncle, the youngest of six children of my grandfather's second marriage, and at twenty-eight some twenty-five years my father's junior. Papa's hometown, Nesvizh, was in Russia when he was born and in Poland when he grew up, unless it was the other way around. Actually, Nesvizh stayed in one place. It was the borders that kept hopping back and forth. But Uncle Israel had his future very well laid out. The only hope for his people, our people, was a homeland in Palestine. Accordingly, he had prepared himself by studying English, Hebrew, and agronomy at the University of Warsaw, and was stopping in Paris on his way to Tel Aviv. I had met my first Zionist face to face. It was very hard to imagine this refined, city-bred young man in farmer's clothes, making the desert bloom, but such is the power of dreams that it did. Bloom, that is.

A week before Christmas, I had a phone call. We had a phone everywhere ever since I can remember. The phone was the first thing sitting on the bare floor when we moved in and the last object to leave the bare floor when we moved out, but the idea that it was to be used for conversation was outlandish. Appointments and emergencies only. This was a happy emergency. Could I be ready in twenty-four hours to join a ski group at the Gare de Lyon? For a ten-day skiing trip in the French Alps? We would be staying in a ski lodge (not what you think of in America, but an unheated, thatched roof, stone shelter with a huge fireplace at one end and two wooden sleep platforms at the other, one for girls and one for boys). I could rent the skis on location, but would need ski boots, a suit, ski underwear, mittens, a warm cap, and a modest sum of money, plus student train fare. (I do not think any Frenchman pays for a regular train fare. The menu of discounts is mind-boggling: children, students, veterans, regular commuters, seniors, families, state employees; for down-and-outers, the risk of riding without a ticket was at least worth a try.)

Papa came up with the money. Any trip was worth borrowing for, and I ran from one acquaintance's place to the next, up and down stairs, until I felt fairly fit and was properly equipped with an outmoded ski suit over one arm, and a pair of high-top shoes two sizes too large, dangling from their laces, over the other. Margot and Mirrha joined the hunt. Misshapen mittens, a striped woolly snug-fitting cap, several pairs of wool socks, and the necessary wool underwear were ready to be packed into my knapsack. Never mind that my first and last attempt at skiing had ended in disaster—more precisely, in a mound of snow that swallowed me up on a baby slope when I was six years old in the Riesengebirge, the Giant Mountains near the Czech border, home of the giant Rübenzahl, who played tricks on unwary travelers by causing avalanches. I was going elsewhere. Away from the miserable slush of melted snow, of gray winter skies and doomsday clouds of war.

It was, however, no use. We were greeted by a fairyland of white on white, studded with Christmas trees. We snuggled around a roaring fire in our lodge, sang brave songs, and tried to envision a world without war. Spain lay in rubble, not at all a figure of speech as I was to witness on my way to America. Mussolini had clobbered Abyssinia (Ethiopia), Hitler's armies were marching according to his master plan. First the Rhineland, then Austria, now Czech lands were to enjoy the bounty of the Fatherland. Our group leader, a Zionist from Palestine, was caught in the paradox of facing service in the British military while fighting for independence for Palestine. For the first time, I perceived the cracks in the British

Empire. Thirty-five years later, in a Goethe Institute seminar in Berlin, I met a group of Egyptian teachers of German and puzzled at their interest in and mastery of the German language. "Germans have always been good to us. I remember them during the war."

That last day of 1938, we celebrated New Year's Eve by skiing cross-country in Indian file, gliding in unison through the blanketed silence, Japanese lanterns weaving a string of lights as we swung ski poles gently up and down. "Sky and earth will perish, music alone shall prevail," we sang with an eerie feeling of unreality, suspended as we were between layers of glistening snow and a starlit sky.

Daladier and Chamberlain had brought an extension of peace, but no one knew for how long. My brother came home on furlough spouting such outrageous five-letter words (five in French, four in English) that he had to give up speaking French altogether in our presence. That gutter slang was to save his life. Confronted by a group of peasants as he was negotiating a bumpy cross-field ride on his motorcycle behind the Maginot line, in spring 1940, he promptly recited his credentials: motorcycle messenger, rank, and unit. His accent was unmistakable. "We caught us a German spy!" the men yelled, fetching up their pitchforks. "Let's get him!" My brother let go a stream of barracks French that stopped them in their tracks. "Hey, he's a French soldier. No German could learn to speak like that!"

Meanwhile, Vivi's morning fantasies were threatening to become an idée fixe: she had met the most charming, enchanting, handsome young man who was passionately in love with her. He was Spanish. He had a castle in Spain (in French, as in English, "a castle in Spain" means "a pipe dream"). He had a title. He had a fortune. He drove a white coupe. I listened piously, afraid to drive the poor girl over the edge, but her story never varied. His name and whereabouts were secret. Her parents were not to know.

Pierrot, on the other hand, was no knight in shining armor, but he had an uncanny sense of where to find me—at meetings, at Métro exits, at bus stops. Casually, he would walk by my side for a block or two. At eighteen, Pierrot was no teenager. He had read few books; there was no time. His world was simple and straightforward: in two years, he would be a master tailor. He would work hard. He would make a living. There was no elsewhere for Pierrot. His city pallor betrayed him. No summers at the beach, no skiing in winter. His sole escapes from drudgery were workouts at the gym in his neighborhood. His vision of the future was firmly anchored in the here and now, and I wanted no part of it.

Mirrha, ever the prodigal aunt, decided to tear me away from my books by blowing a whole dollar—it sounded like a lot more in French francs—on a movie at Place de la Convention with a treat at a café opposite the theater afterwards. I sat mesmerized, watching some futuristic mayhem, sirens wailing, as people scurried like ants from buildings blown to smithereens. It had been daylight when we went in; it was pitch dark when we came out, and the sirens were still wailing. People were running about. For a moment, I thought myself in a time warp, back in the movie. "What happened?" we asked. "It's the end of the alert drill." We skipped the treat and went home. There was no escape.

The boys of the Group were fantasizing, too. Childhood safaris à la Dr. Doolittle gave way to precisely planned elephant hunts for white ivory, to oil explorations in the Far West, to gold digging in South Africa, or simply to playing the stock market ensconced in an easy chair. But first they had to get to America, where everything was possible. I was not so sure. America was for the ambitious and enterprising. I was neither.

Mama became concerned about my chemistry. This was something she knew about, but could not explain in French. To flunk chemistry would be a serious setback. Worse, how could I face tomorrow's world without an understanding of experimental science? Simple. By marrying a chemist. Five years later, Mama and Fred understood each other perfectly as they discussed the central nervous system and the effects of chemicals thereon. In the meantime, Mama sent me to the depths of the Latin Quarter to a quaint medieval street with the unlikely name of la rue du Chat qui Pêche (the street of the fishing cat), where a young acquaintance versed in the sciences tried to help me to unravel the mysteries of chemical reactions. Like cooking, they remained a mystery. Shamefully, I relied on a photographic memory to fix pages of text in my mind just long enough to write a barely passing paper without understanding a word of it.

Then tragedy struck. A motorcycle with a sidecar landed on my brother's back. He was riding in a military convoy when a horse-drawn carriage suddenly appeared from the right, crossing the road in front of him. Crossing military convoys was against the law, but the horses didn't know that. My brother veered to the left and was thrown into a ditch.

The soft earth saved his life as his body was crushed under the weight of the machine.

My mother flew to his side. That is, she threw stuff in a bag, grabbed a cab, and took the train to Cherbourg. My indestructible brother came out of a three-day coma, and after two weeks he could move his toes. Condemned to a body cast for three months, he knew he would walk again. No wonder. He knew no fear. After the war he told me that he never dodged bullets; he drove across fields at night with bombs exploding close by. Later, when he was finally hit while escorting his commanding officer to a post behind the lines, he was sent south on an ambulance train a few days before Paris was occupied. He was the only one of his patrol to survive.

The school year drew to a close. I was pretty blasé about the annual *distribution des prix*, the awards ceremony where heavy volumes in gold-embossed bindings for first and second prize in each subject were given out. Over the past five years, I had accumulated quite an enviable library in this fashion. This year was no exception. Math, English, French, biology, art, history, physics: my pile of books reached to my chin. I almost dropped them when I saw a white coupe standing in front of the lycée, a young man in dazzling tennis whites opening the door to a radiant Vivi. Her prince was for real!

Mama had returned from Cherbourg, satisfied that Max was on the mend. She arranged for a summer rental in a small village on the Channel south of Boulogne. I had invited an English exchange student to spend the summer, courtesy of my English teacher friend in Cambridge. Beryl arrived, bespectacled with double thick glasses, frightfully shy and home-sick from the start. She made no attempt at using the little French she knew. I was happy to oblige in English. She was a good swimmer and not afraid of the cold; the sea was her solace. There was a family on the beach whom Mama knew, or at least there was the female component of the family: mother, aunts, cousins, all busily embroidering napkins, towels, and pillow slips with the monogram of a betrothed pair. The young lady in question, a ravishing brunette, was leading her friends in fun and frolic, six or seven young men competing for her attention as she dashed about in the sand. Her fiancé, in officers' training school, was conspicuously absent. "She's only eighteen," her mother explained. "Let her have some fun before she is married." I thought this a bit strange, but then any distraction was a good one. The spectacle of this family preparing for an elaborate wedding, discussing the guest list, the catering, a thousand and one details, was a reassuring sign of normalcy.

Beryl and I decided to go off on a bike ride some ten kilometers north toward Boulogne. We noticed a clump of vacationers standing in front of a bar, listening intently, straining to understand a stream of invective from the shortwave radio set near the open door. There was something wrong. It wasn't French, and it wasn't English, and I knew that voice. "What's he saying?"

"Sh! Let me listen. . . . It's Hitler. He is marching into the Polish corridor. He is calling German men to arms. He is fighting for the glory of the Fatherland, for the right of all people of German ancestry, *Volksdeutsche,* in Bohemia, in western Poland, in the Rhineland, to be part of the German Reich. His tanks are ready, his air force is ready, it will be a quick strike. He will not be stopped. This is war."

The speech was a long one. I retained only the bare essentials: Poland and war. The small crowd dispersed, eying me with suspicion. Beryl only had one question. "When is the next ship leaving for Dover?" We raced back to the cottage with the news, had a catch-as-catch-can supper, and packed our bags. I took Beryl to Boulogne early in the morning. Mama and I closed out the cottage and returned to Paris in the afternoon, September 1, 1939.

In Boulogne the mood had changed to one of palpable sadness. At every doorstep, at every storefront, every bar, the same despondent scene of parting. Women wept, children cried, and men sobbed openly. This was general mobilization: all men aged twenty-one to forty were to report to their units. There was nothing selective about military service in France. Able-bodied men served two years in the military. Everywhere, groups of men trudged stolidly toward the nearest bus stop and train station to report to their units. My brother, who had been on convalescent leave, recovered his strength just in time to be declared fit to serve, and returned to his motorcycle unit in Normandy. In Paris, we found Margot gravely ill, unable to report to the Commissariat de Police to have her temporary papers renewed; worse, all enemy aliens were to report within three days to a central stadium for safe internment in the south. This included all German and Austrian refugees, those vociferously anti-Nazi escapees from Hitler's prisons and camps who were only too eager to serve in the Allied forces. No such chance. Margot left as soon as she was able to stand up. Mama had mounted a veritable campaign to procure the necessary affidavits from French licensed doctors certifying to Margot's illness, thereby obtaining a postponement for the police paperwork. Internment in France was infinitely preferable to internment in Germany. Uncle Karl was in an impotent rage. He wanted to fight, and he could do nothing. He too reported for transportation to internment camp. His younger brother Rudi was interned in England. In Vienna, his brother Willi was drafted into the German army.

We took out our gas masks and made sure we knew how to put them on in a hurry. Rumors were flying. The enemy—that was the polite word, as epithets of the grossest vulgarity were invading everyday speech—the enemy was capable of every deception, poisoning wells, blanketing cities in clouds of gas, sending over swarms of bacteria, bombing houses into the ground.

We were advised by my lycée that students wishing to leave the city should report to the Lycée Joachim du Bellay in Angers, on the Loire River, two-thirds of the way to Brittany and the Atlantic coast. Mirrha took Joshi with her to an abandoned castle south of Lyon, where she continued to tend to her charges under the most austere conditions until she was able to join us in America early in 1942.

War was officially declared on September 3. On September 7, Mama and I found seats on the train to Angers, no small feat amid the general confusion and the crowds, as thousands of Parisians just back from their August vacations decided to rejoin their relatives in the country, while foreign tourists were frantically seeking transportation home.

I don't know what grapevine supplied Mama with the address of a genteel family who would take us in as boarders, nor how it happened that several of my friends from the Group were also in Angers.

I can see us sitting at the dinner table—Monsieur, Madame, her elderly mother, a maiden or widowed aunt—straining to maintain polite, discreet, and noncommittal conversation. Knitting saved the day, or rather the nights. After fruit, cheese (not consumed by me), and coffee, the ladies fetched their handiwork. This was no idle pastime; this was serious business, keeping French soldiers warm. In the three weeks before the opening of school, we produced regulation scarves, socks, gloves, all in the same shade of gray to match the gray-blue uniforms, wondering what their prospective wearers would do with them when the war was over in three months. A fast knitter knits by touch, especially scarves; it is most relaxing and conducive to conversation. When the conversation stopped and all eyes were on my needle-flinging hands, I became aware of an embarrassing difference. The yarn was looped over my left index finger, not my right; I was holding my needles in a distinctive German knitting style. Henceforth, I adopted the French—and, to me, more cumbersome—method when in public.

Mama requested an interview with the directrice of the lycée, or should I say "audition," since it was held in the *auditoire* of the original monastery before it was turned into a young ladies' boarding school with only minimal alterations. It took on the name of a Renaissance poet, Joachim du Bellay, which had an alluring romantic ring. The directrice, a lady in her late fifties, straight as a ramrod in severe black and no makeup, had "no nonsense" written all over her. She had none of the mitigating charm of Madame la Directrice of the Lycée Camille Sée in Paris. All directrices were addressed as Madame, even when they were not married, but in Angers this lady introduced herself as Mademoiselle, thus reflecting her linguistically, if not socially, correct status.

No Frenchman at that time arrived at middle age and beyond without vague complaints of a medical nature, usually concentrated around the liver. Things have changed since then, and improbable as it seems in retrospect, the French imbibe tomato juice, orange juice, and even milk. Mama was prodigal with free medical advice. The free advice and more often the free remedy, consisting of simple adjustments in diet and lifestyle, were highly appreciated by our suffering hosts who recommended me to a relative of Madame as a boarder for the 1939–40 school year, or until the war was over, whichever came first.

Nothing had happened in the following three weeks. Paris stood unscathed, Hitler having concentrated his troops on a rapid takeover of Poland after being assured of a free hand by a nonaggression pact with Stalin, which confirmed Papa's most dire forebodings and propelled every card-carrying member of the French Communist Party into a wrenching identity crisis. Some stabbed their cards and some stabbed themselves.

In this hiatus, Mama decided to return to Paris after settling me in with the Aguilé family in a solidly built three-story townhouse, 33 Square Jeanne D'Arc, a couple of hundred feet from the main railroad line.

It took me a while to realize why the parlor was off limits. The sofa was occupied by the young man of the house, Albert, whose comfortable quarters under the eaves had been rented out to me. I especially relished an antique French provincial armoire and matching table-desk. Best of all was an unimpeded view of the square and the railroad tracks beyond from my mansard window facing east.

Juliette, Albert's sister, suffered from a delicate condition and was being constantly warned not to run, lest she break a bone. No taller than I, she held herself confidently erect with a great deal of poise, her shoulder-length ash blond hair caught by a ribbon on top of her head, à la Alice in Wonderland, which was my secret name for her.

I was given instructions on how to descend the stairs, which, like every piece of furniture in the house, shone with weekly applications of paste wax buffed to a silken finish. The family moved to a precise rhythm without any words being exchanged, each arising at a fixed time, each taking their assigned seat around the dining room table at unalterable intervals for breakfast, lunch, and dinner. More often than not, I crashed into this peaceful scene two minutes late, less than immaculately groomed, having lost my footing on the polished stairs as a result of heavy concentration on the test ahead and possibly the beginnings of a severe astigmatism of which I remained unaware for the next twenty years. Trying to balance coat, scarf, and briefcase while buttoning a cardigan on the way down was no help, either.

Feeding a family of seven—Monsieur, Madame, Madame's elderly mother, Madame's mentally challenged sister (a sweet, middle-aged maiden lady blessed with the manners of a five-year-old), Albert, Juliette, and now me—took the concerted efforts of the competent ladies, plus whatever small tasks the maiden aunt could reasonably be expected to accomplish. All three women disappeared into the kitchen the better part of the day, their wonders to perform.

I say "wonders" because sometime during the phony war, which the French thought ludicrous and facetiously referred to as funny (*la drôle de guerre*), rationing was instituted. I became keenly aware of the scarcity of sugar; supplies of coffee, meat, and butter were seriously affected. It is to Madame's credit that I never noticed the lack of these ingredients. Every meal was a feast, as dishes earned the unqualified endorsement of Monsieur Aguilé, *père,* and Monsieur Aguilé, *fils,* with a knowledgeable recital of every herb, spice, and condiment found therein. This is what is referred to as a trained palate. Mine is blind, as a result of which I enjoy foods that look pretty colorwise, have no taste, and are pleasant to the touch.

Life settled into a routine of daily living punctuated by Monsieur Aguilé's gold watch, which he extricated from his waistcoat pocket not to confirm the time, but to verify if the noon train was on schedule. He never altered his wonted route to the office where, as a civil servant in the tax department, people stood in awe of him; he had only to put his hand on said pocket for Albert to start closing the shutters at dinnertime following strict blackout protocol.

Albert was a pleasant youth, or rather a young man pleased with himself. He was a head taller than his father. I think he sported sideburns. He always excused himself after dinner to "study with the boys." I groped my way upstairs to read until bedtime. (Habits die hard. Only a near concussion in the dark, banging my forehead on the edge of an open door when I returned to Paris on sabbatical in 1969, convinced me to start turning on the light at night. Being a slow learner, I suffered a second collision four years ago in my own house in Metairie.)

It took us, Juliette and me, forty minutes to walk to the lycée, a bracing walk when the sun shone and bone-chilling when it rained. However, I felt sorry for the boarders, the *pensionnaires,* who stayed in the lycée at night. Unless their families came to fetch them on the weekend, they were not allowed outside, even at age seventeen. They slept in the erstwhile monks' dormitories, ate in the monks' dining hall, promenaded around the colonnaded walkway which encircled a bit of formal garden, and spun endless fantasies à la Vivi.

Except for a charmingly timid young teacher of French language, French literature, and Latin who bravely smiled when she wanted to cry, being separated from her newlywed husband (who was in the service, whereabouts unknown), I remember nothing of my classes at the lycée.

Juliette was laid low by colds and flu. I fought periodic attacks of nausea and vague stomach aches. The non-news from the front lulled us into a sense of false security barely shaken by posters imploring silence lest spies be listening. It was a well-calculated war of nerves. There was nothing funny about it.

My brother appeared on furlough in full uniform to take me to Paris for Christmas vacation. I was perfectly capable of making the five or so hour train ride by myself, but I knew better than to ask Max any questions. We were approaching Paris when Max turned to me: "Do you know where you are going tomorrow?" "No, where?" "To the hospital. You are going to have your appendix out."

I remembered my bout with stomach cramps that had had me doubled over and vomiting nonstop through the night soon after our arrival in Angers. Mama had suspected my appendix all along but couldn't be sure. The classic symptoms of an acute attack left no doubt. Since I had a history of feeling sick to my stomach the way other girls complained of headaches, I was not surprised by my brother's news.

Back at the apartment on rue Jules-Simon, Papa and Mama were shouting the way that had made me not want to learn Russian. As always, however, when I heard *ona* (she, meaning me), I pricked up my ears, straining to understand. "She is not going to the Hôtel Dieu, a charity hospital for beggars!" Papa screamed.

Mama shouted back, "She is not going to the clinic. You know what happened to Mr. Bronstein's nephew, Trotsky's son. He died on the operating table."

The implication was that it was no accident. Mama had been at the same private clinic for minor surgery and knew the staff. The full impact of that argument did not hit me until some forty years later, when I chanced upon a documentary about Trotsky's son at the Prytania Theater in New Orleans. I recognized Dina Vierny filling the screen. She introduced the film, which made a pretty explicit case for murder at the clinic. On the other hand, the charity hospital of Paris, Hôtel Dieu, was on the Ile de la Cité next to the Commissariat de Police, which I knew well. In addition, one of the young ladies of the Group, Lia Abramovitch, was interning there. In the morning, I took the Métro to Hôtel Dieu, carrying my trusty brown suitcase.

Blackout in Angers had been barely noticeable. The town was hermetically shuttered shut at nightfall in any event. Few people ventured out at night, so there was no night life to speak of. Not so in Paris. To see the "city of light" plunged into total darkness was shocking. It was dangerous besides, since headlights were not allowed. I spent my entire Christmas vacation in the hospital, where post-op recovery meant two weeks in bed, under observation. Therefore, I saw nothing of Paris at all, but I could hear it. The rush of traffic along the Seine, the bells of Notre Dame Cathedral, the constant tinkling of police cars and ambulances, and periodically drowning out all else, the wailing sirens of an air alert.

Still weak and wobbly from two weeks' enforced bed rest, I gratefully returned to the routine of school and piles of homework in Angers.

In April, I received an unheard-of gift for my seventeenth birthday: half a pound of sugar cubes in a blue cardboard box. It had come in the mail, wrapped in layers of brown paper. I always assumed that Mama posted these; only now, as I write, does it seem to me that Papa would have been the more likely candidate, sympathizing as he did with my penchant for sweets. They were meant as a precious condiment for coffee or tea. For several days the blue container remained untouched on my writing desk, the object of devout contemplation, until, stymied by a particularly recalcitrant Latin phrase, I consoled myself with one little cube. Then another. And another. When the Latin assignment was completed, the box was empty. I could not hide the consequences from Juliette as I stumbled down the stairs in haste, with a well-earned case of indigestion. The sugar binge cured me of any further desire for unobtainable sweets, a most sobering experience as I faced the uncertainties of the phony war and an inscrutable future.

On balmy spring days I enjoyed walking along the Loire River, absorbed in earnest conversation with one or the other of two new friends, desperately reaching out for a vision of normalcy. Denise in particular left an indelible impression. At eighteen, she was faced with the dilemma of accepting the offer of a substantial dowry from her grandmother, whose dying wish was to see her married to a well-established, no-longer-young gentleman, or to continue solo with dreams of university studies and a career of her own, unbeholden to any man. Denise felt herself caught in a web of family obligations worthy of a classic seventeenth-century drama. She impressed me as mature, eminently well balanced; a handsome young lady projecting a sense of serenity, of spiritual well-being. Her revelations caught me by surprise. Due precisely to her generous nature, knowing how much it meant to her aging grandmother to see her only grandchild safely established in matrimony, she considered it her duty to oblige. Yet, at eighteen, she shied away from a lifelong commitment which excluded the advent of true love.

I never saw Denise again. Perhaps the fortunes of war gave her resolve. Perhaps she joined the Resistance in the south. I liked to think that helping her grandmother with the household accounts, meeting the daily challenge of shortages head on, gave her the confidence to face the future on her own terms, freed from the burden of her family's expectations.

Escape from Angers, 1940
Reaching the Golden Shores

Unlike Denise, I was spared any decision between planning a career or a wise marriage. In the last week of May, three hundred thousand Allied troops were evacuated from Dunkirk as the German army invaded France from the north, cutting off the defenses behind the Maginot line. When Paris was occupied on June 15, my options were reduced to the single-minded objective of survival, aware that under German occupation my family would face certain death.

Italy declared war on France on June 10, while the Soviet Union, under the terms of the nonaggression pact, pursued a hands-off policy which undercut the Allied war effort.

On June 22, France's capitulation was sealed in the same railway carriage in the forest of Compiègne where Germany had surrendered on November 11, 1918. The southern half below the demarcation line was turned over to the puppet government of Vichy.

I grew up at 1:00 P.M. on Saturday, June 15, 1940.

The phony war was over. The Germans had marched into the Rhineland. They had marched through the Netherlands, through Belgium, and into the northern provinces of France. The French army was in retreat. For weeks we were glued to the radio at every meal. When we heard planes, we counted until we heard the bombs explode, which gave us an idea of the distance—usually safely on the periphery of the city.

Ambulance trains loaded with wounded soldiers from the front passed the main railroad station without stopping. For three days in June the town was overrun by a goodly portion of ten million Frenchmen, the great exodus, seeking safety in the south. They came by car, by motorbike, by wagon, truck, or cart, by bicycle, on foot. They bought the town clean. Gas pumps were empty, shelves were bare. The lycée closed because refugees were bedded down in the gym. When I first met my friend Jacqueline in Orange, in the summer of 1968, I explained I had fled Angers on June 16, 1940. She stared at me. "You know, we stopped in Angers on our way south from Alsace. We slept in the gym at the lycée."

We fell into each other's arms like long lost friends, having been caught up in the memory of the same dramatic events at the same point in time.

June 14, 1940. I saw a woman carrying a dead child in her arms and another woman crying over a broken porcelain cup. The town of Angers was closed; shutters fastened tight, metal blinds pulled down, streets empty. Paris was to be occupied the next day. Angers was soon to follow.

Mama arrived in the afternoon. There was no time for explanations. She had caught one of the last trains out of Paris. Papa was on a train headed south toward Toulouse. She brought one suitcase; documents, papers, and a little money were carefully folded in a square of oilcloth.

June 15, 1940. I took Mama for a walk through eerily deserted streets. At the police station we presented our temporary residence papers for official permission to travel to Toulouse and were met with uncomprehending stares. "We have no such official stamp."

We kept an eye open for bicycles, since neither of us knew how to drive a car. There were none in sight. Stores and repair shops were closed and shuttered with steel blinds. At the post office we checked general delivery, and were handed a scribbled, barely legible postcard: "Wounded, heading south on hospital train. Love, Max." We cried and we laughed. I tugged at Mama's arm and hurried the pace back to the Aguilés'.

Distractedly, we sat down to lunch. We had just started dessert when the doorbell rang. It was 1:00 P.M.

"There's a young man for you at the door; he looks terrible."

Indeed he did. It was a white-faced, sweat-streaked Pierrot on a bicycle. "I've come to take you south. You can't stay here. The woods near Paris are on fire. They've bombed the highways. They've shot into the crowds. They're going to round up all the Jews. I'm joining the Resistance. We have to leave right away, you can ride on my handlebar."

"I can't."

"What will you do? Where will you go?"

"I'm going to America."

Pierrot pedaled off, tears mingling with the sweat. He had been on the road for three and a half days. I never saw him again.

Mama and I spent the afternoon going over papers, for it was clear we could not stay. It was not clear how we could leave. Passenger trains and buses had stopped running. Like everything else, life as we knew it had come to a complete standstill. Mama gave me my Nansen pass, an affidavit of identity in lieu of a passport. I assembled my documents: residence paper, student identification, library card, rationing card, a French translation of my birth registration. Mama sewed something into the hem of a vest. I doubt that it was jewelry, as she had none save her big amber teardrop and a brooch which she used to wear pinned to her shirt collar. We counted money. Mama gave me two hundred francs, which was a tidy sum, perhaps equivalent to $40.

We then packed a "big" suitcase (the size of a weekender) with the things Mama had brought with her from Paris. I remember our family photo album, her medical degrees, references, a small Mannekatz oil portrait of Max as a little boy, a portrait of me which my piano teacher's son, I think his name was Marc or Michel, then fourteen, had hastily sketched in rust pastels on the back of a gray shoe box when I was twelve (it appears as the frontispiece of this book). We carried the suitcase down to the cellar and joined the Aguilés for dinner.

Dinner was glum. On the radio, the fiendish enemy had been transformed into civilized occupying authorities, as Paris had been handed over to the Germans to spare the city. The Mayor of Angers was pleading for cooperation. The German army was expected at 4 A.M. Citizens were to keep their shutters closed and stay inside until further notice.

We were in the middle of the meal when the sirens wailed. Mama stopped her fork in midair and got up while six Aguilés stared in disbelief at this breach of etiquette. Worse, "Everyone down the cellar steps!" Mama yelled, leading the way down the hall. (When I returned to Angers in 1967, teenage son and married daughter by my side, Madame Aguilé told us that Madame le Docteur, referring to Mama, had saved their lives. "How?" "She pushed us down the cellar steps.")

We had just sat down on the cellar floor when the house and the earth underneath shook and we thought we were dead. "Deaf" was more like it. When the all-clear sounded, we gingerly climbed back up the steps and pushed open the door to the entrance hall. The walls were standing; only windows had been blown out. The floor was littered with glass all the way up the stairs to our room.

"I'm not going up there," I told Mama. There had been a skylight just above the stairwell. I was sure the remains would shower down on us.

Outside it was drizzling, but even I could smell the smoke. There were fires all along the railroad tracks where the bombs had hit. There were fires smoldering in the square. "Let's go," I told Mama. "Let's find some bicycles." I meant *find*. Like a bicycle propped up next to a tree, or against a wall. We would take them and ride off.

"I haven't bicycled in fifteen years," said Mama. "That's okay. It's like swimming. You never forget." We had to skirt around a big crater in the square. There was a small plane circling above, diving repeatedly down close to earth. I could see the pilot.

I led the way down the street on the other side of the square. It was getting dark. I heard voices ahead of us, women's voices. "We can't go. You should see his feet. He walked from the Maginot line, three hundred miles. They're a bleeding mess." The voices came from a carriageway to our right.

"Pardon, Madame, where is it that you cannot go?" I asked one of the women.

"South to Bordeaux. A milk delivery van is stopping by at half past two in the morning."

"Can we take your place?"

"Sure. Just be here. I'll tell the driver."

On the way back to the house, we concentrated on not stumbling on the uneven sidewalk in the dark. Madame Aguilé had swept up the worst of the broken glass. We said our good-byes and packed. My small suitcase held some underwear, a spare skirt, two blouses. I added my prize Latin dictionary, a concession to seven years of academic endeavor which had defined me as a student, and my braided leather girl scout belt: we were prepared. Mama set the alarm for 2 A.M. We lay down fully clothed.

It was raining on the stairs when we got up. I grabbed our umbrellas, and we left silently, two small figures ambling down the street in the middle of the night, each holding a suitcase in the left hand and an opened umbrella in the right.

A voice greeted us from the carriageway. "I'll give him the money and tell him we're friends. He'll leave you at the railroad station in Bordeaux." Mama handed the woman some franc notes. "Don't say anything, or they'll notice your accent and ask questions," I told Mama as an open pickup truck drove up. It was already full of people, perhaps seven couples, wedged in like sardines, with their backs to the side panels and their legs stretched out toward the middle. We climbed on board over the back panel and squeezed in. It was raining hard by now; we shared our umbrellas with the people next to us. It was half past two.

About half an hour later, the van stopped. A massive square stone tower loomed against the night sky to our right. We heard men's voices, and faintly distinguished uniforms with hats unlike any I had seen. Our driver spoke to one of the men, then revved up the engine and sped across the bridge, the bridge over the Loire River. "It's okay. They're going to wait for us to get across before blowing up the bridge. Anything to slow down the Germans."

A few hundred feet on the other side of the bridge and the sky lit up. We watched spellbound as pieces of the bridge were flung into the air in slow motion, the guard tower spewing flames. Our motley group of passengers clapped and cheered, cried and laughed. We were safe, driving south. We had the road to ourselves; the last of the exodus had passed two days earlier. Smoldering carcasses of cars, ditched cars, abandoned cars lined the road on either side.

(In the seventies, a Polish Holocaust survivor who was a recent immigrant to the United States, one of my students' parents, gave a gripping account of his escape to my class. He mentioned joining Polish volunteers in France in 1940, working on a demolition squad. I gave him an account of the bridge explosion. There was no doubt in his mind that the unfamiliar hats belonged to Polish volunteers.)

In the back of the pickup truck, our legs were numb and we were drenched. We dozed off and slept, to wake up to incredible sunshine and blue skies in a city famous for its red-tiled roofs. It was a scene untouched by war—until our truck delivered us to the railroad station.

People were squatting on the platforms almost as tightly packed as we had been in the back of the diminutive truck. Loudspeakers were blaring: "Do not board the trains! The trains are full! Do not board the trains!" I made sure I knew which direction was south and told Mama we would board the next train that stopped.

That is when Mama told me about the trains in Russia—much like they would be shown in the film *Doctor Zhivago.* "I'm not getting on any train! People got trampled. Babies were thrown out the window. People vomited, urinated, and worse. They clung to the windows, to the doors, lost their footing, and were crushed under the wheels!"

"We can't stay here. We've got to get to Toulouse. It's only a two- or three-hour train trip."

"There are no more trains heading south! Do not board the trains!" the loudspeaker bleated as a train came chugging to a stop. "Come on!" I shouted to Mama. "We're going!" We stepped over legs, swinging our bags and umbrellas. As we approached the train, we were pushed from behind, up the steps onto the rear platform of a coach. The train was packed exactly as in Mama's nightmare. People were hanging out the windows; they were crowded into the restrooms; an eight-person compartment held a dozen or two dozen people, with children stuffed into the baggage nets above the seats. The corridor was impassable. I found a toehold, literally—I stood on one toe with two hefty backs holding me up. "I got to go!" a fat woman yelled as the train pulled out of the station. "So what!" someone yelled back. "Let it go!" People laughed. They joked. They made fun of their ridiculous plight. The crush was worth it. They were going south, far south of the probable demarcation line that was to divide France into occupied and unoccupied zones. We popped out of the train at the railroad station in Toulouse, a bedraggled pair. Mama had some addresses; some of the Group had preceded us.

We were hungry. We were to remain hungry. For the three months we stayed in Toulouse, we got up hungry in the morning and went hungry to bed. Peaches were ripe; so were tomatoes. I loved them dearly, yet a steady diet of nothing but peaches and tomatoes left something to be desired. Day in, day out, my job was to stand in line, any line, in hopes of finding a potato. Stores advertised all the goods which they did not have. No sugar. No butter. No tea. No coffee. No chocolate. No lard. No bacon. No eggs. No milk. No meat. There was no white bread at the bakery. Bread had a sickish gray color and felt pasty, like glue.

Mama and I went apartment hunting. Toulouse was a delightful, red-roofed town not far from the Pyrenees. The sun smiled at us. Not so the inhabitants, suddenly overwhelmed by thousands of refugees. We walked miles and rang hundreds of doorbells. "Sorry. No rooms to let."

Two rabbits in a cage in a courtyard caught my eye. Where there are two rabbits, there will soon be more. "We are looking for a room," I told a woman feeding the rabbits. "I could let you have my son's room," she said. "I could put in another bed and a hot plate."

"We'll take it." The room was sunny and clean. Twice in the three months, we feasted on rabbit stew.

Mama made the rounds of military establishments in search of Max and found him in a hospital perhaps an hour's bus ride from Toulouse, in a small town perched in the foothills of the Pyrenees. We spent a week there. Max's roommate was African, from Senegal. He was black, the first black man I had ever seen. He was rich in his country, Max explained: he possessed four wives and seven sheep. The two, an unlikely pair, hobbled their way up and down the uneven cobblestones of the main street. "Who sleeps there?" asked my brother's companion with a puzzled look, pointing at a bed in a furniture store. Max taught him *belote,* a popular French card game, and the rudiments of a money economy, which meant counting in hundreds and thousands of francs. The African was a thoroughly likeable person, strong and confident, having gained immeasurably in social status as a returning war hero in the French army. Unlike my brother, he had a country, a tribe, a village, and several wives to come home to. He wasn't sure of the number of children he had.

When the last of the stitches came out and Max was declared fit for convalescent leave, we returned to Toulouse. Max cut a fine figure of a wounded veteran in uniform, one jacket sleeve casually draped over an arm in a sling, his stiff leg helped by a cane. But no amount of charm could coax food from housewives' empty shelves. Toulouse and the surrounding countryside had been systematically drained of victuals headed north.

I learned what happened to the butter, the ham, the lard, the bacon, the lovely wheat when I went on sabbatical to Germany in 1973. "We never went hungry during the war, only afterwards. Our troops were well supplied. My husband brought me the prettiest silk scarves, blouses, and lingerie from Paris," recalled my hostess in Freiburg, sighing with nostalgia for the good old days. She added, "You have to admit, der Führer gave us pride, a sense of honor."

The children of the Group, erstwhile playmates in Berlin, then in Paris, were now well into their teens. Every day we congregated at the central marketplace to stand in line and to study the lost and found notices tacked to a lamppost. I distinctly remember a tall, narrow post, though since lampposts are made of cement or metal, I don't see how the notices could have been tacked to one. Mostly, these notices announced lost and found people. Something like, "Michelle Dubois is looking for her brother, Jacques Dubois, last heard of in Mulhouse. Please contact at (address)."

Max had vanished to look for Margot. French authorities had thoughtfully opened the gates of alien internment camps just before the Germans took over, to let inmates fend for themselves. Margot's camp, somewhere near the Spanish border, was empty. Max scoured the countryside. How he chanced upon Margot, hidden in a monastery, remains clouded in mystery. Margot had shrunk from a buxom size fourteen to a fashionable size four. At eighty-five pounds, she was a shadow of her former self. She had no money, no papers, and no spare clothes. Like the people who posted notices on lampposts, Margot had lost her boyfriend, the same young man she had followed from Berlin to Amsterdam, who had left Amsterdam to fight in Spain, and who she had miraculously encountered recuperating in the infirmary in her camp.

Margot's affair with my brother was over; but you don't let a stray kitten starve on your doorstep. (Papa, who had found shelter in another part of town, had no words to describe his exasperation.) We rearranged our room as well as we could and added an extra cot. Mama must have found some bones. I returned from my market expedition triumphantly with a large potato and some greens. At any rate, Mama managed to produce a fairly nourishing soup. She established a rigorous routine of enforced bed rest for Margot, and prescribed vitamins and iron supplements, the origin of which remained a closely guarded secret.

Margot's spirits revived to the point that she could entertain us with funny stories—tales of courage, hope, and quiet determination. It seems that the internees at the camp organized classes in their spare time, mostly language classes, but also mathematics and science. There was no lack of academic talent among self-professed teachers, as well as highly acclaimed university docents. Students were highly motivated. I gathered that between ten-hour stints at the infirmary and classes, Margot was kept too busy to reflect upon her fate. Only now did boredom raise its oppressive head. Mama contrived a sort of patchwork summer dirndl out of remnants of different fabrics for Margot, who could no longer be restrained. Off she went, and left us agonizing about what would happen if she were questioned by the police.

Sometime in July, I presented myself for the baccalaureate exams at the University of Toulouse, totally unprepared, since I had left my notebooks and textbooks behind. The exams measured six years of sequentially accumulated knowledge, as well as writing and reasoning proficiency, so that cramming was of questionable use at best, except to organize material already mastered. I managed the series of three-hour written exams in French literature, composition, Latin, mathematics, English, and history (which were spread out over three days), not as brilliantly as I would have liked, but with a fair sense of accomplishment given the circumstances.

The orals were my downfall. Each candidate had to face several examiners seated behind a green felt covered table, a most intimidating spectacle. In chemistry, I blanked out. The professor, an elderly gentleman, sought to come to my rescue. He held up a brown colored liquid in a stoppered glass vial. "What is the first thing you would do to identify the contents?" "I don't know." "Here, I'll unstopper it. Now what do you smell?" "Nothing."

The following week, I found my name on the list of candidates who had passed. I had not only passed, but had received an honorable mention. I can only assume that I earned better than an F in chemistry on the strength of unflinching honesty.

America was becoming a reality. One of the Group had been dispatched to Washington. I am not sure of the political connections involved, but the mission was successful: an executive decision at the State Department level made it possible for political refugees to enter the golden shores of the United States on an emergency visa. It was only a question of time until the visas would be issued.

There was a party to celebrate this joyful news, which assembled all of the members of the Group present in Toulouse. Lola Dallin, formerly Estrine—perhaps in her late thirties, no beauty but radiant in a clinging black gown, her black shiny hair parted in the middle—did the honors. She introduced us to the marvels of American technology: a long zipper in the back of her dress, reaching from the neckline to below the waist, took the place of the clumsy hook and eye arrangement which Mama used on the left side of tight-fitting dresses. I recall being slightly shocked as every gentleman demonstrated the smooth operation of Lola's zipper.

We spent the better part of August in Toulouse waiting for our visas. This entailed heated discussions about life in America, most of it pure fantasy. My friends devised a new game called "my first meal in America," which became a daily ritual. Boys concentrated their culinary expertise on the best way to enhance a steak, came to blows because their dream meal was accompanied by the wrong sauce, and had to be separated by force. Girls (I recall only Zina, who used to live on rue Jullien near the Lycée Michelet), including myself, concentrated on desserts (but even my wildest concoctions of cake covered with chocolate sauce, heaps of chocolate mousse, and mounds of truffles, did not begin to approximate my first real-life banana split in New York, which left me speechless). I am not sure whether these daily food fantasies increased our hunger or helped to satiate it. I had never paid much attention to food; now the lack of it was the focal point of each day.

In preparation for our journey to America, our family was advised that the only way to save Margot from a paperless destiny in France—which meant certain deportation to Germany and even more certain death— was for my brother to marry her. As his wife, she would qualify for an emergency visa and entry to the United States.

A small religious ceremony was thus arranged, according to Jewish custom, which satisfied the American authorities but which was not considered legally valid in France, where births, deaths, and conjugal unions were strictly in the civil domain. The understanding was that the marriage would be annulled on those grounds once we landed safely in America.

August was coming to an end. My one pair of shoes were worn beyond repair. I recall acquiring a cheap pair of rope-soled cotton espadrilles at the central market, with a stacked heel then in fashion, and which I realized too late were downright perilous in negotiating uneven sidewalks and cobblestoned streets.

Our teenaged group were giddy with hunger and expectation. Coal, oil deposits, gold and silver mines, copper, and iron beckoned like mirages beyond the sea. They would drive the cars. They would pilot the planes. They would build the freeways. They were masters of their destinies. I wasn't so sure.

America was a land of doers, not of dreamers; of fierce competition, not of solidarity. "Getting ahead" was not the becoming thing to do for a young lady of modest means and genteel upbringing which my French education had succeeded in casting upon me in spite of my vehement protests. It is ironic that my idea of freedom in Paris at age twelve was to sit down on the curb on a busy street wearing slacks. I was careful never to act out this preposterous ideal. Yet when friends and colleagues routinely made themselves at home sitting on the floor some thirty years later, I was the only one left sitting primly on a chair, and not because I was then too old or too sick. To this day, I do not feel comfortable sitting on the floor, at least not in a western European setting. I was still weak from major surgery when I booked a flight to France in 1985. Jacqueline and I had left our rental car parked in the historic old district of Nice and embarked on a mile-long stroll along the famous boardwalk by the beach. "Could I sit on one of those beach chairs?" "No," Jacqueline responded, "They are for rent." "Well, I'll sit down on the step then." "You can't do that!" she said, horrified at the impropriety. I sat down anyway, about to faint, very conscious of my American mode of behavior suited to the circumstances.

News came at last, the best possible news. We were to travel to Marseilles to pick up our American emergency visas. We forgot hunger, heat, and sagging spirits. Our travel was sponsored by a rescue committee whose name I have forgotten—the American Jewish Rescue Committee?—courtesy of the powerful friends of the Menshevik group in America. Train tickets appeared like manna from heaven, with a small allowance for the necessary stay in Marseilles.

For the occasion of the trip, we faced the world as a united family Papa, Mama, Max, Margot, and me. I believe Max wore newly acquired civvies; being on convalescent leave and not discharged from the French army presented serious problems. Margot, although by now fairly fluent in French, had lost none of her German accent or mannerisms, and was condemned to the strictest silence. Mama and Papa got on best by concentrating on views from opposite windows.

Of the three-hour or so train ride, I distinctly remember burning fires: flames four, five, six stories high, perhaps a mile off to the right of the tracks in the flat lands along the Mediterranean coast, from a dozen or more giant cylindrical oil refinery reservoirs. Could this be sabotage? It was a stark reminder of war in a deceptively enchanting landscape. The next reminder of war came a few hundred feet from the railroad station in Marseilles, when Max and Margot prudently left their seats, silently made their way to the exit of the coach, and jumped off the train as it slowed down before entering the station, in order to avoid any hassle with passport control.

We met later that day in a small hotel. Marseilles was a wonderland compared to Toulouse. There was actually white bread available at a price. Do I recall two lumps of sugar? We spent our time "guarding" Margot, who was not let outside. The historic old city in Marseilles had always had a reputation for hosting the worst of the Corsican mafia, spies from every conceivable corner of the world, plain thieves and cutthroats, drug traffickers, and now French Resistance fighters, who found shelter in the labyrinthian streets and secret hideaways, and who attracted in their wake French authorities beholden to their German command. As Margot developed a serious case of cabin fever, we finally relented; late one night, Max, Margot, and I ventured forth into the infamous "old city," which bore in many ways earmarks of what I later came to recognize as the medinas of Moroccan towns: whitewashed walls, recesses upon recesses reaching into hidden inner courtyards, and narrow alleyways, all in steep ascents and descents.

We were used to sirens and police cars, but these sounds were different. Loudspeakers blared warnings to evacuate the old city. "Everybody leave. We are preparing to explode the old city." We left. The next day, the old city was in rubble; at least, I presumed so. Later, I thought this event had been one of my nightmares. After thirty years, I could not be sure, though when I visited Marseilles in 1967 and 1969, the old city was gone. Once, at the Prytania Theater in New Orleans, I chanced upon a French film set partially in Marseilles during World War II and saw the old city go up in flames. A classic way to flush out undesirables. (Actually, the old city of Marseilles was exploded by the S.S. in 1943.)

There was one last hurdle before our meeting with the American consul: obtaining a French exit visa, that is, permission to leave France. Transit visas for our sojourn in Spain and Portugal could be obtained only after securing our American emergency visas, and would be a minor formality. As a veteran of standing in lines, I was elected to secure a place for the family in the wee hours in front of the police station before it opened at eight o'clock in the morning. I overslept my wake-up hour of 5 A.M., hurriedly dressed, gulped down a cup of make-believe coffee, and ran to find a line four people abreast winding around the block.

I stood and stood, not a morning person in the best of times. The sun started beating down on us; my empty stomach turned flip flops; I grew faint. A classic recipe for heat stroke: stand hatless in the broiling sun on an empty stomach, preferably in a state of high anxiety guaranteed by the proximity of the police. I came to in the inner sanctum of the Commissariat surrounded by secretaries with smelling salts and bottled water. My exit visa application was expedited in a matter of minutes, even before the first of the line was admitted through the open doors. When Max retrieved me shortly after eight o'clock, Mama's and Papa's papers had been stamped as well. "Congratulations!" my brother said. "Well done! I didn't think you had it in you. That was a splendid idea." I was too weak to protest and took his mistaken compliment in stride.

The next day, the family Israel were summoned to appear at the offices of the American consul in Marseilles. We had splurged on hot baths at considerable expense, as baths were luxurious extras in hotels. Otherwise, the public bathhouse was the best alternative. We had decided to present a unified front and sober appearance, predicated on silence, which was not difficult to enforce since neither Papa nor Mama understood a word of English. This was a great relief to me, as I was terrified of a public argument. Poor Margot, who had been reduced to whispering in German behind closed doors, was in her natural element. I was appointed the official interpreter.

Monsieur le Consul, a blond man of hefty proportions, true to American form, faced a model family of diminutive stature with impeccable credentials. Seated in a semicircle around his desk from left to right: Miss Israel, a recently successful candidate at the feared baccalaureate exams; her parents, Dr. Ida Israel, M.D. from the University of Moscow, resident in gynecology at a well-known Berlin hospital, and Mr. Jeffim Israel, writer and editor, with a law degree from the University of St. Petersburg, a member of the Soviet Minority (Menshevik) Party in exile; Mrs. Margot Israel, the charmingly demure young bride of Mr. Max Israel; and Mr. Max Israel, recovering from wounds received while serving in the French army near the Maginot line.

On the wall behind the desk, a portrait of Franklin D. Roosevelt welcomed us with a dazzling smile. The Stars and Stripes discreetly proclaimed our presence on American soil.

Monsieur le Consul, having politely waved us to our seats, wasted no words. "I see you are eligible for emergency residence status in the United States, until such time as it is safe for you to return to your native country or to qualify for permanent immigration status. Since there are many more applicants born in the Soviet Union than our quota system allows to immigrate, there may be a wait of three to five years. I must warn you, Mr. Max Israel, being a citizen of no country, you will be subject to the draft upon arrival in the United States."

All of this I dutifully translated for my parents' benefit.

"Are there any questions? No? Then may I have your Nansen passes, please; birth certificates, marriage certificates, French exit visas. And yes, who will vouch for your financial support upon arrival in the United States?"

A quick consultation with Papa produced a paper from the American Rescue Committee, which was footing our transportation costs, and a letter from a Jewish organization in New York City that was ready to assist us until we found employment.

"Mrs. Israel," the consul addressed Margot, "we find you eligible for emergency status as the wife of Max Israel. However, we need some photo identification to prove that you are indeed the individual described as Margot née 'Kraemer' on your marriage certificate."

As I translated, I was greeted by stunned silence. All eyes were fixed on Margot, who clutched her purse and whispered, "I have no papers."

The consul was not ignorant of Margot's plight. "Think," he kindly interrupted our silence as we sat transfixed. "Anything with your maiden name and a photo on it."

"Do you have your youth hostel card?" I finally ventured in Margot's direction.

A sad little shake of the head.

"Your swimming pool card?" She shook her head again.

"Your library card?" Margot stopped shaking her head. From the recesses of her battered purse, she extracted a dog-eared, ink-smeared, miserable piece of thin cardboard with a faded likeness of her formerly plump self and handed this to the consul.

"Thank you. This will establish your identity." Then, addressing the whole family, "Your papers are in order. You may proceed to the United States." He stood up, handed us back our precious documents, and wished us well.

I cannot describe the collective sigh of relief as we silently left his office in single file. Only later did we hug each other, exhausted by the suspense of it all. Much strategic planning remained to be done, of which I was only vaguely aware. Our ship would leave from Lisbon, and we needed transit visas for Spain and Portugal, which apparently posed no problem since we had been promised legal entry to the United States. The trick was to get Max and Margot safely across the French/Spanish border, since neither of them had a French exit visa—Margot being an alien without any residence papers, and Max being a soldier on convalescent leave from the French army. An exit visa served as proof of a clean police record in the country which one desired to leave, so I suppose that the American authorities accepted as a clean record the fact that my brother had spent the last year in the army and that Margot had been interned in camp.

Two or three days later, early in September 1940, we were on the train to the Spanish border. Friends had surprised us at the station with a farewell package of boiled eggs, a loaf of genuine white French bread, and—unbelievably—a piece of sausage, the result of a week's assiduous scavenger hunt in the surrounding countryside. Max and Margot had to circumvent controls at the station. We held our breaths until they appeared safely on our coach. Hours later, just before the Spanish border at Port Bou, they would jump from the slowing train and make their way across the Pyrenees and Franco's Spain according to a detailed underground route. If all went well, they would rejoin us in Lisbon.

French and Spanish trains rolled on different-sized tracks, so we had to change trains at the border. This entailed an overnight wait. I remember sitting next to Mama the following day, a tight squeeze in a crowded, third-class coach compartment. I think Papa was in the same coach with his good friends, the Wolosoffs. There were a number of the Group on the same train and on trains following, and I ran into members of our teenage "first-meal-in-America" gang from Toulouse at every overnight stop. I had the distinct impression that train schedules were arranged to "accidentally" miss the only available connections and in this way provide a much-needed source of local income, since the civil war had ravaged the tourism industry.

My trusty brown bag and Mama's larger suitcase had been hoisted into the baggage net above our heads by the smiling, bowing Spanish gentlemen facing us. The first blow of culture shock in New York was to be the sheer unimaginable size of everything. It still is a shock for first-time arrivals from the old country. Adjectives had to be redefined. My suitcase was the size of a large briefcase. Mama's larger bag was the size of a carry-on.

In Toulouse, I had ditched the Latin dictionary that I had bought seemingly a lifetime ago from a *bouquiniste,* or street vendor, on the Left Bank. The dictionary had been no bargain, I discovered during the three-hour written Latin exam, as all the *c*s were missing, beginning with Caesar, a most important letter in Latin. Mama's German-French pocket dictionary would be of no further use to us, nor had we invested in a Spanish dictionary. We smiled to our left, we smiled to our right, and settled back to enjoy the enchanting scenery, the boiled-egg package securely in Mama's lap.

A German ditty from grade school days kept running through my head in time with the chugging train: "Erika, Erika, wir fahren nach Amerika" ("Erika, Erika, we're going to America"). In this game, children lined up on the playground. They had to march underneath an arch formed by two pairs of uplifted arms in rhythm with the song. When the song ended, the arms came down and an unfortunate child was caught and advised, "And you stay here!" before being turned out of the game to wait on the sideline. I couldn't believe I had won. I was going to America.

The train stopped. There was a big sign with the name of the town, but no town. There were remains of stone walls, heaps of stone rubble. On the rubble, small boys were pulling empty cans by a string. A boy hopped on one leg, because the other one was missing. He waved a stick at a boy with two legs and one arm. They were having fun. It was a scene out of a Hieronymus Bosch nightmare.

We rumbled through several more such ghost towns. In the bright sunlight, these were scenes of utter ruin and desolation, peppered by specters of black-clad women disappearing behind unidentifiable remains of walls. Again the train stopped. This time there was a solid station house attached to the name of the town. On the platform, young men were offering what looked like scrumptious cakes for sale. On closer inspection, they turned out to be round loaves of darkish bread decorated with slices of sausage stuck into clockwise slits on top.

A young, very pregnant woman was seated to the right of Mama. She bought one quarter loaf through the open window, then turned a sickish green. Mama got out her handkerchief just in time. The bread was strictly make-believe, coarser and heavier than the pastiest stuff in Toulouse; the sausage had the telltale smell of spoiled meat. Mama was tempted to throw it out the window, but one of the men seated across from us made a grab for it.

After awhile, Mama opened our precious package, took out one egg for each of us, broke off six inches of the white bread, then stopped. We felt the stare of eyes on us.

"Qué es esto?" ("What is it?") "Why, French white bread."

In the doorway of our compartment, hungry eyes were feasting on our bread; word had spread in a flash, up and down our coach; we saw at least ten people, shoved by many more behind them, crowding to witness this miracle for themselves. We couldn't eat. Distribute the bread equitably? That would yield at most a generous crumb per person. Discreetly, Mama covered up the broken length of French baguette. The hungry crowd slouched away in silence.

There were overnight stays in Barcelona, in Saragossa. We spent at least two nights in Madrid, where members of the Group met, exchanged news, and studied travel orders for the remainder of the trip to Lisbon. Zina, who was fifteen, was enchanted by the Spanish custom of after-dinner promenading by the light of the moon. She was flattered by compliments from handsome young men who were lounging about, seemingly untroubled by bullet-riddled houses, beggars, black-veiled women in deep mourning, and gentlemen of obvious standing in threadbare clothes.

Seated at an ice cream table in Madrid on the terrace of a less than fashionable café, we were surrounded by a horde of hungry children as we attempted to put a lump of sugar into our teacups. There were two lumps on each saucer, four lumps in all for Mama and me. The lumps disappeared in a free-for-all.

People were friendly. Gentlemen in suits and ladies in high heels had learned French in school. Assuring themselves that the police were not around, some would attempt to talk to us in French. "Kiss the American soil for us, the land of liberty," and, "We would fight if we had the strength," meaning against Franco and the Germans. This from starving men propped up against the walls of buildings, too weak to move. I was looking for a mailbox to post a card. "Let me put the stamp on, like this." Carefully, a lady licked my stamp with the likeness of the Generalissimo on it and stuck it on the card upside down. "There, you'll be safe mailing it. It will send a message to America."

We were invited to visit prisons in Madrid, part of an unlikely sightseeing program, which we politely declined. I have no explanation for this, but I recall it distinctly.

Mama, as always, dispensed free medical advice, mostly for nervous stomachs. At the top of her list of health care hints was the serious warning, "Do not, I repeat, do not eat a full meal upon arrival in Lisbon; eat clear soups and increase your food intake slowly over several days." She did not, however, elaborate on the consequences.

After a long train journey, uninterrupted by overnight stays, we arrived in Lisbon famished as usual. We were greeted by a whitewashed city of Disney World proportions, orderliness, and cleanliness. Cheerful crowds of well-dressed townspeople strolled along wide avenues paved in wavy patterns of black and white stones; storefronts gleamed with lights and elegant displays. Our small hotel featured a dining room with enormous menus, to be held in two hands and studied with care. Mama's advice fell by the wayside, as we succumbed to one mouth-watering dish after another.

After dinner we joined the crowds for a stroll on the brightly lit avenue. For the first time since I had left Berlin, I heard German spoken openly with aplomb and confidence, as well as every other European language I was acquainted with and some I was not. Lisbon, the only major Atlantic port in a neutral country, was reputedly a hotbed of every spying operation imaginable.

The next morning, everyone in the Group was sick. And the next. And the one after that. For eight days, we slouched around, fearful of leaving the proximity of the toilets, heaving and vomiting, clutching our cramping stomachs. Everyone, that is, except Mama. She dosed us with charcoal (where did she acquire that?), which she dispensed with a gleeful, I-told-you-so shake of the head.

For three blissful weeks, war was forgotten; our teenage gang regrouped for walks along the main avenue, to the port, for trolley rides to the zoo. We gawked unashamedly at colorful street scenes like any tourist, played guessing games as to the national origins of our fellow strollers, and conversed freely in whatever language came to mind, thus adding to the linguistic melee.

Max and Margot reappeared with accounts of hair-raising adventures and were welcomed as heroes of the Spanish underground trail. Not everyone had made it. One lady of their small group had drunk a bottle of eau de cologne to ward off the worst bout of dehydration during a perilous descent down a mountain pass. She passed out and died.

Max's friend Horst, from Paris, had lost his girlfriend, Mäuschen, to a Spanish jail. Horst was inconsolable. He went on drinking sprees and had to be watched every minute, as he alternately threatened to jump into the sea or to throw himself across the railroad tracks.

There was a gentleman related to the Group who had had no news from his wife and daughters. For some reason, they had returned to Paris to retrieve some belongings. He was told they had been shipped to Germany and had perished in the gas chambers. He hanged himself.

All was not gloom. The Group were expecting two, no, three "blessed events" in very short order. These included my friend Vivi, who had indeed married her Spanish prince. It was imperative that we sail as soon as possible, for the babies would be condemned to a paperless, countryless limbo if they were not born in the United States. I fished out my stainless steel knitting needles (which I had thrust into my small bag in Angers), went hunting for bargains in baby wool at the local market, retrieved a popular pattern for baby soakers and vests from photographic memory, and went to work.

Another of the mothers-to-be was a young woman whose French fiancé, an officer in the French army, had joined the Resistance. She had had no news of him. After the war, she returned to Paris with their child, found him, and married him.

The third future mom was Sylvia Garvi, the young girl who had had her middle finger amputated in Berlin. She was radiant with expectation, her husband Shura by her side. Her mother was driving her nearly crazy by flitting around constantly, fidgeting with pillows, handing her glasses of milk and vitamins, and not letting Sylvia move.

Our ship came in. Compared to the ocean liners in Hollywood films, it was an old crate, a converted pre–World War I freighter with a Greek name and a Greek crew. To us it was the most beautiful sight in the world. As we crowded the gangplank to board, there was a big commotion. Howling and screaming, Horst was being forcibly carried on board ship by four of his friends. Determined to get him to America, they had sat with him all night, packed his few belongings, and gotten him thoroughly drunk.

In the end, Mäuschen, released from Spanish prison, rejoined Horst a year later and married him. I saw Horst in Hamburg in the 1970s. He had become a prosperous businessman and had divorced poor little hardworking Mäuschen to marry an energetically optimistic German lady with impeccable connections in Hamburg.

There may have been a fourth class even more packed than our third class, I am not sure. Mama and I, and perhaps Margot, shared a six-berth cabin the size of an old French coach train compartment, which was perhaps twenty feet from the showers and toilets and an equal distance from the engine room. The noise was deafening. Everyone experienced at least some seasickness, but no matter how sick we were, Mama insisted that we climb up to the deck for fresh air.

The deck, at least the third-class section, was nearly as crowded as the train station in Bordeaux. Nevertheless, there were a few reclining deck chairs for the elderly, the obviously infirm, and the very pregnant. The young mothers-to-be were waited on hand and foot since they were not allowed to move. Their friends kept constant vigil by their sides, plied them with tidbits from the kitchens, and distracted them with funny stories. The strategy worked. Sylvia was delivered of a healthy eight-pound American boy the day after we landed in New York harbor. Another baby boy arrived a few days later.

All other available deck space was squatted on unceremoniously by groups of happy people singing, laughing, and talking, each group in their own language. One simply stepped over or in between legs from one group to another, from Polish to Czech to German to Hungarian, Rumanian, Russian, and Spanish until one found one's own language. I kept stopping to sample one group after another.

Besides singing old folk songs, socialist songs, and new freedom songs from the Spanish civil war, everyone was intent on learning the American anthem as well as the words from some of the better-known American songs. I remember "Swing Low, Sweet Chariot," "John Brown's Body," and "Clementine." We learned some of Walt Whitman's prose poems. There were impromptu lectures on the American diet, the American monetary system, and the American transportation system, but mostly there was singing. Our twelve-day voyage was one long celebration which neither foul weather nor rumors of submarines could dampen.

A mystery lady in a tan raincoat, stringy blond hair, and no makeup made her way from group to singing group introducing herself as an American and either a Christian Scientist or a Quaker. Armed with menus, subway tokens, detailed maps of Manhattan and greater New York, and money such as pennies, nickels, dimes, quarters, and dollar bills, she offered each group in turn lessons in American English. She explained how to obtain food from an automatic dispenser, how to get served in a cafeteria, how to shop in a self-service store. Simple, clear, uncluttered, and matter-of-fact, she explained that the first floor was the second, that ones were sevens, that the month is given before the day, and that decimals are marked by points, not commas. We practiced making change and telling time. We repeated ordinal numbers, as in Eighth Avenue, Forty-fourth Street, and the fifteenth floor.

It turned cold at sea. I became acutely aware of the fact that my prize possession, a pair of heavy, crepe-soled oxfords, tinted dark red and navy blue, were the wrong shape, the wrong color, the wrong weight, and that they didn't match my two pairs of knee socks. Since my cheap, rope-soled espadrilles had threatened to unravel in Marseilles, Mama had offered up a significant portion of her travel allowance for this one pair of solid shoes that I had set my heart on for the occasion of our interview with the American consul. Now, with safety and normalcy, guaranteed meals, and the prospect of a future in America, ordinary teenage concerns took over. It was okay to wrap up in one's blanket to keep from shivering on deck, okay to wear old downtrodden flats. It was not okay to wear brand-new shoes of the wrong color.

Unlike my acquaintances from the Group who had been born in France and were therefore French citizens, I knew I could never return to France to live. The others considered their journey to America a temporary escape until the war was over. I could never be French, as much as I had learned to love the language and as much as I loved Paris. Nor would I ever marry a Frenchman. I had no intention of ever cooking a decent French meal, nor of spending two hours in the middle of every day at the dinner table. One look at a French cookbook intended for innocent beginners had convinced me of my total ineptitude. I had survived seven years in the land famed for its wine and cheese without tasting either, thanks to Mama's plain cooking and our pecuniary deprivation.

Food was not what I would miss. It had taken seven years of concentrated effort to master the French language to the point that I felt literate in it, sufficiently so for formal written discourse. My mode of thinking, my literary and artistic tastes were indelibly programmed in French. I would have to master American English, to learn what I could about America, but I would not abandon France. My mission in the New World was clear: to interpret France to the Americans. My friends in France would say "to teach them about French civilization." Thus I resolved the language dilemma to my satisfaction.

I had met two German girls aboard ship. We felt free to converse in German. The father of one was a well-known German novelist; the father of the other was a socialist delegate in the German senate during the Weimar Republic. Like my French-born friends, they planned to return

home, which in their case was Germany, as soon as Hitler's Reich collapsed. The vaunted beauties of Prague and Budapest shimmered with
nostalgia in other teenagers' recollections. They would add American English to their arsenal of languages and return home, teach law or philosophy, and write. This they did; but I knew my home to be elsewhere. Elsewhere in America. And we were almost there!

New York, 1940–1942

The sweet air of liberty hit full blast, refreshingly cold, ablaze with lights, shamelessly wallowing in a parade of every new fad and fashion in a gluttonous display of self-indulgence. America was at peace. News from London crumbling under German air attacks was an unwelcome ripple in the frenzied race to succeed.

The map of Europe had been redrawn securely under the Nazi boot, every attempt at resistance ruthlessly crushed. Norway, Denmark, and the Low Countries were occupied. Italy had joined the Axis powers and attacked the British in North Africa, attacked Greece. In April 1941, Germany, aided by Hungary and Bulgaria, invaded Yugoslavia. On June 22, the anniversary of the fall of France, Hitler launched the invasion of the Soviet Union.

There were those who felt that an isolationist America would profit most from seeing the two evil empires destroy each other. Still, Congress approved the Lend-Lease Act, giving aid to England. On December 7, Japan's attack on Pearl Harbor left no room for compromise. America declared war. The Group supported the war effort in every way they could. It was the only hope for freedom and democracy to survive.

Of the landing on October 12, 1940, I only retain two vivid images. I was hanging onto the railing, shivering with cold, my blanket billowing in the wind as we caught sight of the Statue of Liberty. We must have jumped for joy as much as the crowding allowed. There was a spontaneous outburst of song and hilarity, shoulder slapping and bear hugs. Though Lady Liberty had been a familiar sight in Paris, I was not prepared for the sheer overpowering hugeness of her American replica. This was big as no newsreel, no documentary had been able to convey.

I next remember myself standing on solid ground, still shivering in my blanket, clutching my precious navy purse crammed with documents, my small brown bag by my side, in front of a long table covered with coats. Someone was saying, "Help yourself," and "Pick one." It was an incredible sight. People in summer clothes, blue with cold, shrank away from the table as if it had been booby-trapped. Pride, modesty, a law-abiding civilized upbringing had the upper hand; then the cold sank in, and a statuesque figure of a woman in mink started holding up coats for all to see and choose. I opted for an olive-green cloth wraparound affair and put it on. Carefully, I folded the blanket, very much aware that it did not belong to me. Did I carry it off over my arm or deposit it inconspicuously on the table?

Predictably, the cold had its effect, and there was a rush to the restrooms. I had never seen such gleaming splendor. Ladies in mink coats, not a hair out of place, were touching up their unblemished makeup in front of a row of mirrors above giant-sized washbasins, where hot water gushed forth in steady streams at the turn of a tap. There was only one thing missing: towels. I was introduced to the second wonder of American technology after zippers, the hot-air hand-drying machine.

Mama had carefully counseled members of the Group and other friends in matters of health and medical history. Three weeks of feasting (after the initial bouts of indigestion), basking in the sun, and leisurely promenading in Lisbon had restored even the most cadaverous to seemingly glowing health; everyone's smallpox vaccination was up to date. Yet poor Mama's singlehanded antismoking campaign had fallen on deaf ears. All she could do was to plead with heavy smokers to keep their coughing in check. Tuberculosis and inexplicable rashes were a surefire prescription for quarantine. Since they could not be deported and shipped back during this wartime emergency, it was unclear what would happen to those who were quarantined: stay in limbo on Ellis Island, I supposed, until they recovered or the war was won, whichever came first.

My brother's symbol of personal liberty, American style, was the glaring hole in Papa's cousin Moses Israel's lovingly polished, expensive new shoe. Moses, a white-haired sixty, did not share Papa's good looks, due to a protruding lower jaw, though his prominent cheekbones and delicate stature marked him as a member of the Israel clan. His father was Papa's uncle. Since Papa's parents were first cousins, Papa had only one set of great-grandparents. It had been a very close-knit, traditional, Orthodox family. I gathered that Papa had rebelled at an early age, rejecting all forms of Orthodoxy and plunging into a life of political activism. Moses followed a scientific bent and, not being able to come to terms with Communism, Bolshevik-style, emigrated to America. He was a well-read, liberally educated chemist, a gentleman to the core. We would owe him much.

So here was Moses, his diminutive sister Gittel and cousin Sarah by his side, welcoming us at Ellis Island. Max could not take his eyes off the offending hole in Moses' shoe. "Oh, that," Moses explained. "I suffer from an inflamed bunion, so I just cut a hole in my shoe." While Papa shared the same suffering, it was unthinkable for him to relieve the pain by disfiguring the shoe. Only in America! (This bit of Americana, which had taken place in Russian, was related to me by Max only much later.) Eventually, I came to know Moses' unusual tri-bachelor household in the Bronx very well, but on this occasion, I was either engrossed trying on my new green coat or in the midst of hasty good-byes to my old gang of friends, each intent on pursuing a separate version of the American dream. My premonition about America putting individual achievement above family loyalty proved correct. The glue that had held our Menshevik family together through exile in Berlin and Paris was to dissolve in the sweet air of liberty, at least for the younger generation.

There was a brief formal welcome organized by officials of the organization that had sponsored our trip, friends of the Group in New York. We were each handed a crisp $5 bill with the explanation that it was illegal to wander the streets of Manhattan without minimal funds. (Multiply this by ten in today's currency.) We were handed a map of the subway system, a map of Manhattan, and important telephone numbers. Each family was allocated the munificent sum of $25 for the first month's spending money, and assured of help in finding remunerative employment. This was a most ticklish point, since we were not eligible for permanent resident status nor for the all-important green card which makes it legal to earn money by working for a salary.

It was evening by the time the formalities were over. We were declared mentally, physically, and financially fit to enter the United States, and were handed a slip of paper duly stamped and signed attesting to our right of temporary residence on an emergency basis.

New York, i.e., Manhattan, greeted us with blazing lights, flashing sirens, neon signs, fleets of giant cars, crowds of richly clad people moving through vast canyons of cement, people who were vibrantly alive, striding along with purpose, vim, and vigor.

For two months or so, home was an elegant residence on Riverside Drive, I believe near 96th Street, with a view of the Hudson, a few blocks from Broadway. Mama and I shared a small room furnished with matching twin maple beds (covered with matching plaid bedspreads), and a maple dresser. Very nice! We shared a big bathroom with eight or so other residents and had one cupboard assigned to us in the kitchen. I learned what the American teacher on my way to Tours had meant by working hard. Every evening at 5:30 the bathroom was occupied for exactly ten minutes by a young lady with a mannequin figure who apologized, "I have to freshen up and put on my face." This was a job that required at least one full hour by my French classmates' standards and which I had decided to forgo entirely, having neither the money nor the time. After emerging from the bathroom and in the twenty minutes left until six o'clock, our housemate prepared and ate a light supper with her young husband, then rushed out the door, briefcase under her arm, to attend evening classes at New York University after a full eight-hour workday at the office. She looked smart, not a hair out of place, in high spirits, forging ahead to a successful career as a veterinarian. Et voilà! That is what America was all about.

The morning following our arrival, after counting our money and spending some time figuring out the difference between dimes, nickels, and quarters, we plunged down a scary fifteen floors in an express elevator and braved Manhattan traffic. The incredible assault of bumper-to-bumper cars actually came to a full stop at the red light and started off again the second the light turned green. It reminded me of Berlin. We crossed the block-wide street with confidence. Miracle of miracles, by pacing oneself at a comfortable steady gait, it was possible to reach each crossing at the precise moment when the little green man said "walk." Broadway was positively dizzying, with luxurious displays in small welcoming boutiques—perfumes, jewelry, furs, fine leather goods, hosiery galore, evening wear, and sportswear. Most amazingly, people actually were wearing what was in the shops. Mink, sable, and astrakhan coats. Smartly tailored outfits, color-coordinated accessories, spiked heels, silk stockings. (Nylon was reserved for parachutes.) Maybe this was just a sampling of a well-heeled clientele?

Not so. The young lady who dispensed fresh orange juice for one nickel at a breakfast bar did so with a flourish of her scarlet, perfectly manicured nails, which matched her perfectly applied lipstick. Her blond curls were mysteriously kept in place by an invisible net. She wore a spotless uniform outfit in a becoming color which could have doubled as an acceptable summer dress on the Côte d'Azur—not one of those shapeless black smocks, hopelessly gathered at the waist, which branded her European counterparts as lower class in similar circumstances. Indeed, the famed wealth of America, as popularized by Hollywood extravaganzas, hit me full blast as we entered the Woolworth store near 80th Street, our morning's destination. We emerged with a brilliantly colored set of matching Fiesta plates, bowls, and cups, our first unchipped, uncracked, and size-coordinated dinnerware since we had left gold-rimmed porcelain soup tureens and platters behind in Berlin. Four glasses decorated with unlikely orange cherries, or perhaps some sort of exotic miniature oranges, completed this color feast. With the cheapest of stainless steel silverware made in the United States and a couple of aluminum pots, our purchases came to under $5, expertly wrapped by smartly attired, perfectly dressed shop ladies whom I suspected of higher aspirations in the world of fashion.

There was only one explanation for Americans' predilection for cellophane wrapped cake which was mislabeled "bread." They had taken Marie Antoinette's well-meant advice to the starving crowds to heart, and had baked accordingly. Luckily for Mama, there was no shortage of German rye, pumpernickel, and Russian black bread on Broadway, nor of grapefruit, bananas, and oranges, nor of yogurt ready-packaged in a self-service supermarket, nor of ready-to-drink pasteurized milk, though why grown men would want to drink milk seemed puzzling.

I recall sitting down in a self-service cafeteria with a bowl of thick brown soup served in a French breakfast coffee bowl with a round spoon, and accompanied by two pale wafers unlike any cookies I had ever seen. In a land where bread was cake, it seemed plausible to dunk cookies in one's soup. "Those are crackers," a passing patron informed me. "But what do you do with them?" "You eat them with the soup."

I indulged myself at the Woolworth soda fountain by spinning around on the well-padded stool, totally unladylike. The dispensing of foaming pink liquids and bubbling caramel-colored carbonated concoctions never ceased to fascinate me, though twirling on the stool in rhythm with the rapid-fire jets of weirdly hued beverages from hissing machines cut short any desire to partake of them.

Max, who registered for the draft the day of our arrival, or possibly the next, was the first to find a job. He spent his days glued to a small battery-operated portable radio, sporting earphones, which he took off to talk to people on the street. This marked the beginning of a lifelong career in audience research, courtesy of a friend of Mama's, a cadaverous-looking genteel lady cast adrift in a no-nonsense, do-it-yourself America. Katya Adler was the widow of a great friend of the Mensheviks, and the mother of Felix Adler, Jr., a brilliant student racked by asthma and handicapped by an evident ineptitude at the simplest tasks of daily life. At twenty-five and six foot four, he looked the part of a gently bumbling, ashen-faced Frankenstein. Mrs. Adler, in gratitude for Mama's caring medical concern, referred Max to her husband's friend, Professor Lazarsfeld at Columbia University, who was then laying the foundations of public opinion research.

Mama and Papa separately enrolled in English classes at the YMCA, keenly aware that without a competent command of American English, employment commensurate with their training, experience, and intellectual abilities was out of the question. Papa eventually mastered the written word by dint of assiduous reading of newspapers and journals. His spoken English, after two years, would sound no better than his German and his French, which he quickly relegated to the back burner. Mama picked up everyday conversation by ear. It was to take her ten more years to master the written and technical language sufficiently well to pass her medical board exams.

A tall, middle-aged, thoroughly Americanized woman somehow connected with the Group took me aside for terse Dutch-uncle advice. I was to forget about higher education and start working, any job would do, to gain experience and much-needed cash. No, I would not forget everything I had learned in the lycée; besides, most of it was irrelevant, truth be told, and counterproductive to survival in the American marketplace. One or two years, even three, would not set me back. In the meantime, she handed me a reading list: Upton Sinclair, Sinclair Lewis, Walt Whitman. She pointed me in the direction of the nearest public library, scribbled down the address of the YMCA, where an ethical society held weekly discussion meetings for young people, and took leave without shaking hands. Not a wasted word, not a wasted gesture, a busy executive with no time to spare.

I was introduced to Nora, a self-assured freshman at Hunter College. Nora lived in the Bronx, in a spacious apartment with giant sofas and easy chairs slipcovered with a splash of exotic flowers against a grim background of dark walls, two different shades in the same room: dark reds, dark greens, dark blues. Her father was the editor of the *New Leader,* and Nora had definite literary ambitions. Hunter College, on the east side of

Central Park, was an easy half-hour walk from where we lived. Yes, through Central Park, bravely, with no thought of danger lurking behind every bush, free to enjoy the city's amenities. Nora had arranged for me to sit in on an advanced English class in Hunter College high school as a sort of student guest, something unheard of in a French educational institution.

I sat down at a long table with a dozen or so neatly scrubbed teens in sweater sets who were conducting the class with their teacher looking on! It appeared they were discussing a paper, a report on a Shakespearean play, skillfully tossing out comments, for which their silver-haired mentor unobtrusively sought clarification with a nod, a lifted eyebrow, a "how?" or a "why?" It was to take me several weeks to understand American English with ease, several months to speak it with a fair degree of fluency, two years to achieve sufficient mastery to follow lectures and write papers of my own.

In the meantime, this seminar felt like home. The complete works of Shakespeare in German translation were probably still lined up on Mama's wobbly shelves in our Paris apartment. I had struggled through a number of his plays. Miss Duncan had taught us several sonnets. By listening very carefully, I could follow the gist of the arguments. I tried to remember a few of the expressions that were new to me; later I would ask Nora what they meant.

The English teacher, a soft-spoken, self-effacing lady who came to life in the classroom with sparkling eyes and incisive comments, invited me to her house, which turned out to be a large studio apartment in a brownstone on the east side of Central Park, as vast as Maud's entire apartment on rue du Théâtre in Paris. Over a bit of conversation, she quickly assessed my predicament: I loved to read and write, had a sound academic foundation in the classics, but for the second time in my life I had lost a language to do it in.

She invited me to audit her English course for the remainder of the winter term, sketched a quick outline of the American educational system, and seemed to concur with my previous adviser that hands-on experience in the real world would be a most beneficial thing for me. Aside from the urgent need to earn money, it had something to do with a "well-rounded personality."

Shortly thereafter, I met a young woman two years older than I, who had arrived from Germany a year earlier and was happily engaged in work.

She lived in a tiny rented room with piles of half-sewn ties which took up the space between her cot and an ironing board. "All I have to do is stitch these ties together vertically in the middle and press them. It's real easy. I listen to the radio, to the wind outside, get up whenever I feel like it, walk in the park." "How many hours a day do you have to do this to earn enough money?" "Maybe ten. Sometimes more, sometimes less. It pays the rent, groceries, subway fare, stamps. Best of all, no one tells me what to do. You don't starve in America."

She was paid by the piece, or rather tie: expensive, hand-stitched silk ties. With practice, she could sew and iron at least five ties an hour with the greatest of ease. If worse came to worst, so could I. It didn't.

Word had spread about my knitting ability, possibly as a result of the baby soakers. At any rate, I was approached by a Polish American woman who specialized in designer hand-fashioned knitwear. I was responsible for the fronts and backs of garish pink garments which I never saw in their entirety, a most frustrating state of affairs. I assumed they were destined to be some sort of sweaters. The pattern was quite intricate. I found myself gladly donating the first front and back as a free sample, then calculated my time as being worth roughly ten cents an hour. After two more sets of ghastly fronts and backs, I quit knitting. I had earned $5.00, of which I spent $2.75 plus tax on a long-sleeved, button-down, soft, pale pink shirt: my first ever very own purchase.

Papa's cousin Moses had us over for dinner. At this point, I am rather hazy as to who "us" might have been, since Mama and Papa were very careful not to meet except for emergencies involving papers and our legal status in the United States. Max, who had had his marriage to Margot annulled as planned, was not talking to Papa. Margot had disappeared. Mirrha told me many years later that she knew Margot well and saw her occasionally. Margot established herself as a capable seamstress, thrived on hamburgers and sodas, regained her rosy cheeks and her curves well short of plump. She married an American engineer and raised three sons. I never saw her again after we landed.

Moses, Sarah, and Gittel lived in the Bronx in a two-room apartment, not counting the kitchen. Sarah and Gittel shared a spacious enough, sunny bedroom and Moses slept on a divan in the corner of the other room which was a combination living-dining room. That is, the living room was speedily transformed into a formal dining room by moving a gateleg table to the center, opening it up, adding leaves, and arranging all available chairs around it. A fine white linen cloth, linen napkins, white porcelain, silver silverware, candles in silver candlesticks, and flowers arranged in a crystal vase, gave the room an air of festive good taste. I admired the polished mahogany of the Windsor chairs, a style quite new to me, and a diminutive mahogany china cabinet. Moses' family had wisely chosen to downsize their possessions to fit their own small size, a problem I was to become well aware of in oversized America. Of the meal, I only remember giant grapefruit halves, each with a maraschino cherry in the hollowed-out center.

Gittel worked full time in an office. Sarah stayed home to shop, cook, and keep house. Theirs was a carefully ordered household, with every minute and every penny thoughtfully accounted for. Moses was an avowed atheist, to the left of Papa; he had made a stab at returning to the USSR in 1935, when Stalin's purges were at their height, and had quickly beaten a retreat to the good old United States. Unlike our emigrant families in Berlin and Paris, who spoke German and French under duress only to communicate with the outside world, all three cousins conversed in English amongst themselves, with a heavy Bronx accent overlaying traces of Slavic intonation.

Their mission became one of Americanization and focused on my hemline, my klutzy red and blue oxfords, my limp and scraggly hair, my bare freckles devoid of makeup. I was enjoined to attend night classes at the YMCA for typing as a starter; then I was whisked off to a Saturday afternoon shopping spree at Macy's, which produced a brown Chesterfield coat with a velvet collar, a pretty scarf to match, and my first pair of long stockings to complement a lovely pair of high-heeled dark brown pumps size 7½ AAAA.

I met a determined girl from Prague. Of average looks, she made no effort to disguise her slightly plump figure, her ungainly bouncing gait, her long strands of straight hair unceremoniously chopped off below the nape. She dragged me to lectures at the New School for Social Research. "You'll see, Jacques Maritain is a good friend of Papa's; he's propounding a new kind of philosophy." I went to hear his elegant French, but the gist of the presentation escaped me.

Each morning, as we walked through Central Park, my new friend entertained me with the latest theatrical news, and tried her best to introduce me to the French theater of the absurd.

"What will you do?" I asked her.

"Study philosophy and write." She did. She never doubted her superior powers of intellect, and predicated her career on a return to Europe as soon as was feasible.

When Mama came to visit us in Iowa City in Finkbine Park, she found me struggling with frozen laundry, ice on the bedroom floor, snow waist high outside the door. "I don't recall Moscow ever being that cold," Mama said. "My friend from Prague constantly complains about her daughter's hardships. The girl insisted on returning after the war. She has to scrub, deal with busted pipes, a finicky stove, can't afford help. I told her my daughter in America has a much harder life." Mama had been appalled at my efforts to scrub a black iron frying pan, on the bottom no less.

Some twenty years ago in Paris, the name of the girl, which I never retained, cropped up again. "Yes, she lives in Paris. She's quite a well-known writer. Married a Frenchman after her divorce in Prague." How my brother knew, I didn't ask.

I made a brief foray into the theatrical world, courtesy of the same plain girl. We were to be something called ushers at a theater somewhere east of Central Park. No purveying of cigarettes and candy, just showing people to their seats. I rehearsed my "lines" carefully, trying not to trip over the impossible ordinal numbers of eighth and tenth rows, those unpronounceable *th* endings, and put on a happy stage smile. When a gentleman handed me a $10 bill I was convinced it was a mistake and tried to return it, but was assured it was not. With the rest of the quarters and dimes, it turned out to be a most fortunate evening. I could sympathize with the heroine of the *Glass Menagerie;* best of all, the consummate acting carried me over the hurdles of the English language. I was left with the impression that I had understood every word. It was the ideal situation for testing my oral proficiency. To this day, English has remained a "wooden leg." I use it to write and talk, but the sound of poetry does not move me, my ear misses the rhythm; words have meaning but they fall flat, they do not touch the senses. I can taste the brine of salt in German, I can feel the cold of shivers in French, I can feel the pain and joy in Russian when only a sprinkling of words carries precise meaning.

Mama would disappear after a hasty, if not hearty, breakfast on mysterious rounds of friends and friends' connections. Without English, without permanent residence papers, without any hope of passing the state board medical exams, her future looked bleak. She settled for work on the fringes of the medical establishment, working as an orderly, sitting with the sick. Papa, who was boarding with a family further uptown near Riverside Drive, was bursting with pride: incongruously, thanks to cousin Moses' intervention, he had landed a full-time job in a chemical laboratory performing a routine, mind-numbing, and dangerous task which he was careful not to describe to me. I had never seen Papa use his hands except to type with two fingers and dial a number on the phone. Newspapers and cigarettes were handed to him, clothes were laid out for him; through the worst of the lean years in Paris, Papa managed to avoid learning how to boil an egg, prepare tea, or purchase fruit at an open market; he survived on his wits, badly. By the time the war broke out, he had built up a small, faithful Russian-speaking clientele to whom he sold insurance.

So this was a veritable metamorphosis. This most grueling of demeaning tasks did not in the least impinge on Papa's self-image; on the contrary, he was following in the footsteps of hardy pioneers in the best tradition of *homo Americanus*. He could pay his landlady, decline any further help from the Rescue Committee, face the future with confidence. At night, he diligently studied English with newspapers and dictionary, wrote articles for a Russian-language newspaper, and pursued correspondence with far-flung cousins up and down the coast, long-distance calling being a privilege of the super-rich.

Besides Moses, there was another, more prosperous cousin who lived in the upper reaches of the Bronx. Since Papa's parents were first cousins, all of his relatives were doubly related on both his mother's and his father's side, which made for intricate family relationships. We were duly impressed by the overstuffed chairs, the thick carpets, the clashing wallpaper colors, the new, lovingly waxed and polished car—in short, unconditional success of the kind that rendered my parents' selfless struggles for social justice crushingly inappropriate.

The black sheep of this family was a thirtyish young man devoted to the education of young children, a career noted for its lack of pecuniary rewards. He and his young expectant wife, a snub-nosed blonde with healthy good spirits, resided in a refreshingly bare two-room apartment. He set the table, helped with the dishes, cheerfully sat down on the floor to sandpaper unfinished shelves, all the while explaining his prospects for promotion to assistant principal and his plan of saving enough money for a down payment on a house. A similarly unfinished pine chest of

drawers would be his next task. I was fascinated. This was my first en-
counter with do-it-yourself America, based on a "share the chores as well
as the laughter" kind of family values.

A younger brother, Sol, nineteen going on twenty, a perfect charmer
with polished manners and accent, made no secret of being headed for
the big time. To his credit, and in spite of mutually frustrating outings
to the Cloisters and Riverside Park, Sol included me for a memorable New
Year's Eve celebration with a few of his friends. I wore my precious high-
heeled pumps as far as Central Park, then tossed aside all social constraints.
Prompted by excruciating pain, I took off my shoes and marched on
cheerfully barefooted the rest of the way, swinging the offending footwear
vigorously back and forth. At the stroke of midnight, we reached Times
Square in a frenzy of lights and densely packed crowds.

A feeling of overpowering guilt at being alive came crashing down on
me. Tears streaked down my cheeks as we swayed with the crowd to the
entrancing and mournful melody of "Auld Lang Syne." My companions
did not take kindly to this display of spoilsport misery. I could not help it.
How could they dance when little children in Spain hopped about on
rubble with only one leg?

Blinded by the garish lights, I couldn't stop thinking of western Europe blacked out, drained of food and sustenance to feed Hitler's armies.
These were not figures of speech. People stumbled in the dark, braved
curfews, risked arrest if light shone through a hole in their blackout curtains. How long could London withstand the Blitz? Children fought over
a lump of sugar. Adults lost weight. No wonder movie idols were then
pleasingly plump. Women shed their corsets and hiked up their hems to
be more comfortable and save fabric and money. There was no way to
convey the overpowering sadness I felt on this New Year's Eve of 1940,
when America was at peace, cheerfully pulling out of the depression while
revving up its defense industry. "Come on, let's have a banana split!" In-
credulous, I stared at this concoction through my tears. A banana split
lengthwise, piled high with four giant scoops of ice cream, set off with a
generous helping of freshly whipped cream, garnished with nuts and
chocolate shavings, a maraschino cherry on top. The reality of it surpassed
my wildest ice cream fantasies of our Toulouse food-dreaming days. It
struck me as monstrous, as obscene. I drenched the hapless mounds in
tears, choking on a mistaken dream. "Take me home. I can't eat this."

I had to get out of New York, go elsewhere, see America. It took me almost two years, urged on by the overpowering conviction that I had to face America on my own terms, cut loose from the distressing quagmire of distorted, broken lives which Mama seemed compelled to nurture, cut loose from all the well-intentioned helping hands pointing me in contradictory directions. But first we moved to the Bronx. How or why, I never knew. Mama disappeared at eight every morning, leaving me with a pile of zippers. I had become an expert at zipping zippers, since someone had recommended this unlikely job as paying a nickel more per hour than knitting pink hats. The job entailed a grueling subway ride to Brooklyn, where I retrieved a gunnysack full of old zipper halves. These had to be matched by length and, more importantly, by the size of the zipper teeth, then zipped back together by pulling halves through a zipping machine anchored to the edge of a table top. I returned the gunnysack full of zipped-up zippers to be dyed and sold as new, in exchange for a weekly ration of unzipped zipper halves. When all my fingers and both thumbs were bandaged to protect the precious zippers from blood dripping from my damaged digits, I had to give up zipping zippers.

Eventually, I graduated from zipping zippers to making clay "leaves," an endless subway commute away in Queens. It had something to do with my perceived artistic ability. I had managed to sell a few hat pin designs to an acquaintance thrice removed, though the connection between fashioning leaves at the rate of sixty leaves a minute (I kept count) and artistic inspiration escaped me. A crew of about ten leaf-making young ladies with varying higher aspirations sat around a long table and filled cookie sheets with rows of thumbnail-sized leaves fashioned from tiny clumps of gray putty. The cookie sheets were whisked away as soon as they were filled. Once I caught a glimpse of the finished handcrafted product in a first-floor display case: a sort of misshapen eight-inch-high tree trunk sprouting leaves like a wild mop of hair, with one or two little birds fetchingly pecking away at it. The whole thing was in shiny Technicolor—destined, I presumed, to adorn mantelpieces and coffee tables.

When I asked for a raise from $7.50 to $8.00 a week, the kind and understanding designer of the product shook her head. "Julia, let's face it. You'd be a lot happier in college. Frankly, I see no future here in leaf-making for you."

Neither did I. I dimly suspected that I had been let go because of my less than cheerful attitude around the leaf-making table. I showed a woefully inadequate response to the light and airy repartee about weekend dates and impossible romances; instead, I clouded the atmosphere with mournful calculations of the disparity between wages and profits. I was no team player.

Just once in New York, I was privileged to watch a successful small business take off from scratch. I had enrolled in a silk-screening evening course, where a dozen or so adults of varying ages, backgrounds, and languages painfully mastered the art of transferring cherished patterns onto fabrics through a silk screen, each color being applied separately. The object, I recall, was to create original fabric designs. One small, wispy blonde, severely angular woman of uncertain age and accent stood out by the fierceness of her determination in spite of the incredible naiveté of her designs: a ball, a spade, a pail, a bear, all in vivid primary colors on a white background. Feverishly, she raced against time to practice the technique of printing these on sturdy preshrunk white cotton. "I'm making a baby book. Here is my phone number. I may need your help." She left the class, leaving me to struggle with an array of red roosters which entailed only one application of the silk screen. I managed three yards of roosters, which were transformed into play shorts several years later, to my daughter's great amusement.

When I called this woman a couple of weeks later, she told me to come over to help. I found her with two other girls cutting yards of fabric into nine-by-nineteen-inch rectangles, which she proceeded to stitch together, five rectangles one on top of the other, smack through the middle. Her bed was stacked high with piles of these; she did not cut the thread from one stitched rectangle pile to the next, just let them dangle attached to each other from her sewing machine.

"These are pinking shears. When I cut the books loose, you are to pink the edges all around, very neatly and evenly. Then stack them in piles in the other room." Her optimism was infectious. I pinked and pinked and watched the stacks of washable cloth baby books grow until there was no more room.

Six years or so later, a friend in Finkbine Park asked me to come over. "Look at the curtains I made for the nursery." And there they were, billowing gaily, the pages from the erstwhile first cloth baby book. Finkbine Park was a haven for returning veterans on the G.I. Bill busily fathering the baby boom generation, and I had no trouble visualizing babies in a good number of the three hundred Quonset huts chewing with pleasurable concentration on the cloth baby books come to full fruition.

Encouraged by my silk-screening prowess, I ventured forth into the depths of lower Manhattan's garment district with a colorful collection of my original fabric designs. To my utter astonishment, I met with immediate success: Could I return with several shower curtain designs the next morning? "Of course," I offered, neglecting to inform myself of the precise dimensions of the designs and method of eventual payment. I tossed and turned all night. My experience with shower curtains was nil, never having taken a shower until we moved to the Bronx. The lone shower curtain I had ever seen was imprinted with a school of improbably white and totally uninspiring glassy-eyed fish. I woke up drained of inspiration, my mind a blank.

Soon thereafter, I was rescued from total desperation by a grim, gray-haired figure of a woman in sensible shoes, bravely peering at the world through thick glasses, a spinster named Pinson, who kindly offered to engage me as an assistant file clerk on a volunteer basis, in the McGraw Building on 34th Street or on the 34th floor, or possibly both. As I understood it, I was to volunteer my services under Miss Pinson's stern supervision in exchange for a trifling nominal payment out of petty cash, thus sidestepping both union regulations and my no-work emergency residence status.

Miss Pinson sat me down at a shaky typewriter table hidden behind her desk, with a stack of small index cards on which I was to type every address of every piece of correspondence, to be filed in a maze of file cabinets occupying a space of perhaps forty by fifty feet. This is how I became acquainted with an American geography based on a strictly alphabetical sequence of the then forty-eight states. This was to have some unforeseen consequences. I committed the capitals of every state to memory, which helped enormously in solving crossword puzzles. I had no trouble with Boise, Idaho, or Springfield, Illinois. Relocating wayward states from west to east, such as Virginia, and from east to west, such as California, was a more painful matter, akin to switching to the left hand when one is right-handed. While Washington and Wyoming were properly relegated to the far left, that is to the far west of my fantasy map, and Idaho, Illinois, Iowa, and Kansas roughly occupied the middle region, California naturally stood to the far right, that is on the East Coast, next to Connecticut, and only a file cabinet away from Delaware and Florida.

I suppose that the correspondence stashed away in this labyrinth of green filing cabinets would be stored in a few computer discs today. Both Miss Pinson and I would be out of a job, as would 80 percent of the staff of the American Jewish Congress, which occupied the entire floor, or perhaps two floors, in a deafening clatter of mechanical typewriters. Nor would I be stalking the files, dimly aware of lurking danger in the hastily penciled missives detailing secret meetings of American Nazi groups and other activities supported by the enemy.

The date that would live in infamy was long past; to the relief of the Group, the United States had joined the war. My brother had been duly drafted and was now wearing a G.I. uniform, relishing his newly acquired mastery of American slang.

Aunt Mirrha, with Uncle Karl and Cousin Joe, had arrived after a memorable sea crossing entailing numerous stops, the last two in Caracas and Havana. They were drained, penniless, seasick, and deliriously happy to set foot in the New World. Within a week, Mirrha was stitching army uniforms ten, twelve hours a day and making serious money.

One file in Miss Pinson's domain was devoted to the correspondence of agent X and read like a spy thriller. I sped up my typing. I couldn't wait to get back to the files with a stack of correspondence, expertly sorted, to save time for the next "installment." Periodically, a team of solemn gentlemen threatened to take the files away. Miss Pinson stared at them in innocent disbelief; her assistant concentrated on the laborious task of inserting a recalcitrant index card on the typewriter carriage; both sighed with relief when the gentlemen, presumably from the FBI, trooped away empty-handed. This must have been early in 1942. We had moved back from the Bronx to an apartment on the corner of Broadway and 81st Street, something to do with Oskar, the superintendent of the building, who was Austrian and known to Karl.

My most prized possession was a poorly typed, officially stamped document attesting to my passing the baccalaureate exams with honors at the University of Toulouse, as a displaced student from the Lycée Joachim du Bellay in Angers, now in the occupied zone. There was a notarized translation and a transcript of corresponding American high school credits. I presented these papers to the dean of Barnard College, who had graciously agreed to a personal interview.

"Have you thought of applying to NYU?" Yes, I explained, but I had been told that I did not qualify because of my nonresident emergency status. The lady, an alert, scholarly, and elegant version of Miss Pinson, studied the documents with genuine interest. "These are excellent academic qualifications. I can appreciate your sincerity and motivation. However, we do have a quota." I was puzzled. I realized there was a quota to immigrate to the United States, I was not aware of a quota to enter university or college.

"Unfortunately, you see, our quota for Jewish students has been filled. I'm terribly sorry, but there is nothing I can do. I suggest you apply for scholarships elsewhere."

This is where the alphabetically geographical filing system of Miss Pinson's department collided with physical reality. Diligently, I wrote down addresses of universities targeted for possible international student scholarships and tried to locate them on the map. Ohio turned out to be much more to the east than the initial O would indicate. Colorado, which I confused with literary allusions to El Dorado, conjuring up visions of gold and emeralds, was in the Wild West. Only Wyoming, a vast, sparsely populated area, was as far to the west as its alphabetical position would indicate. I studied the scale, translated distances from miles to kilometers, confronted the vertical barrier of the Rocky Mountains and the horizontal expanse of deserts as vast as France, and concluded with an irrepressible conviction that my good fortune lay elsewhere than in New York.

I sent off several applications. The process of acquiring them and filling them out impressed me as a very adequate competency test for college admission. I was rewarded with three responses in the same week, one from Ohio, one from Colorado, and one from Wyoming, each generously offering tuition plus room and board. Again, I looked at the map. Ohio was awfully close to New York State, part of the industrial east. Wyoming was too far away. That is, transportation by bus or train would cost too much. Colorado seemed to be the golden mean.

As it happened, my brother had been working closely with a young lady in audience research at Columbia University who had studied in Boulder, Colorado. With close-cropped black curls, a ready laugh, and twinkling eyes, Rose proposed to smooth the way by writing to her erstwhile adviser, a Dr. Stone (as I'll call him here), who would meet me in Boulder and help me get settled.

Mama stayed up late at night to stitch two wool skirts, one a pleated red and green plaid, the other a flared Irish green, with a green wool jacket to match both. Saddle shoes, half a dozen pair of bobby socks, a red corduroy raincoat lined in baby blue cotton, my two blouses and blue skirt from France, my own purchased pink cotton shirt, a pair of jeans, and two sweaters pretty much completed my wardrobe.

At work, the girls with whom I shared lunch organized a surprise farewell party. I felt embarrassed to be so happy at leaving them. They had been a neat bunch, explaining intricacies of labor law, "closed shops," and union policy, which left me baffled. Unless one belonged to the union, one could not get hired. To belong to the union, one had to have experience. The one seemed to preclude the other.

My friends presented me with a magnificent leather briefcase, a badge of my new identity which I toted around for the next thirty years until it ruptured at the seams. My brown bag proved too small for my newly acquired possessions. Mama let me pack her battered veteran weekender.

My brother, who was home on furlough, had two pieces of curt advice: "Don't get married. Don't join the Communist Party." I thought this rather odd, since I had no intention of doing either.

Mama handed me an envelope with three ten-dollar bills, a small fortune meant as an allowance for the first month of settling in. As I climbed into the Trailways coach, her good friend Mrs. Scheiner, whom I remembered from Berlin as the new mother of an infant daughter (now a reedy, shy teen), unfastened a cameo from her suit lapel and impulsively pinned it to my blouse. "An old family heirloom. Take good care of it." As my only piece of genuine jewelry, I wore it on every special occasion until it melted in the Painted Cave fire in Santa Barbara, together with all of Carl and Pam's belongings, in June 1990. It can be seen at my neck in a faded photograph on my naturalization certificate.

I clambered into the bus, avoiding Mama's soulful good-bye look. My journey elsewhere had begun.

Elsewhere in America
The Heartland, 1942–1956

My instincts were right. I needed to cut loose from the cocoon of intellectual concerns, the shielding arm of the Group's American connections, my Bronx cousins' dismay at my lack of interest in youthful pursuits, the string of recent arrivals invading Mama's kitchen in New York as they had in Paris, reciting their litany of woes.

I would not find America on Broadway, not in Aunt Mirrha's favorite Hungarian restaurant, not in the Viennese bakery, not in the Polish deli.

I went west in search of American roots and was greeted with a can-do spirit beyond all expectations—the same vaunted childish optimism, ready to tackle any obstacle and to take any risk, which Europeans thought naive and which had propelled generations of settlers to conquer a continent against all odds.

Imbued with newfound independence, equipped with some twenty advanced credit hours, I informed my adviser, the dean of the College of Sciences, that I was planning a medical career and registering in a pre-med curriculum. "You are a girl. You are Jewish. You have no money. I'll be frank: your chances for admission to medical school will be nil. However, a foundation in the basic sciences will round out a liberal arts education."

I went ahead with a hefty dose of physics, chemistry, and biology, relieved by philosophy, French literature, and social science.

Halfway into my sophomore year, I met Fred; we were married six months later, on January 15, 1944, disregarding such well-meant advice as, "Think what it will do to Fred's prospects. He has a brilliant career ahead of him." News from Enrico Fermi's laboratory in Chicago made the possibility of atomic war a reality. The then-unknown extent of damage from an uncontrollable chain reaction was constantly on our mind. "Expect the worst, hope for the best." The best was our daughter, Tanya, born November 3, 1944, a year ahead of the avalanche of returning veterans and the ensuing baby boom.

Franklin Delano Roosevelt died on April 12, 1945, Fred's twenty-fourth birthday. Germany surrendered in May. Truman dropped the first atomic bombs in August. Japan surrendered on September 2.

Fred finished his master's degree in biochemistry that same summer. There

*followed two years of strenuous, thoroughly exhilarating graduate work at the
University of Chicago, funded by a Lederle research grant, which earned Fred
a doctorate in pharmacology. This was his ticket to "freedom in the lab"; he
now could pursue his own research in drug design.*

*In 1947, Fred accepted an offer to teach at the University of Iowa Medical
School in Iowa City, assured of ample laboratory space, a flexible schedule,
fresh air, and clean living for his family. Our son, Carl, was born two years
later, on November 10, 1949. By the time we left Iowa for the Deep South in
1956, both our children had acquired an indelible midwestern accent, a laud-
able dose of self-reliance, and an open, trusting disposition, the enviable earmarks of an American childhood.*

I cannot recall how long I sat on the bus that took me west. A day and a
night? And another day? Bleary-eyed and weary to the bone, I arrived in
Chicago, where I was to take the train the rest of the way to Denver, then
on to Boulder.

True to my clumsy self, I found myself running to catch the train
when Mama's suitcase, expertly packed to hold twice its intended load,
burst open. Like a good scout, I was prepared. I fished for a length of
twine in my purse, hastily stuffed my belongings back into the recalcitrant piece of luggage, somehow tied it together, and jumped on the train
just as it started huffing and puffing out of the station.

I was used to nightmares, but never got used to the sound of sirens.
After two years in New York, I still fought the urge to hit the floor, preferably underneath a desk, whenever I heard the sirens of a police car. On
the way to college in Boulder, I splurged on the luxury of a berth for the
overnight portion of the trip from Chicago to Denver. Sure enough, I
had one of my usual nightmares. Explosions, fire, smoke, people yelling
and scurrying about. I was catapulted from my upper berth into the fray
and pinched myself. This couldn't be real; I was in America. "Get out!"
someone yelled. I did, and joined a crowd of passengers standing outside
as the train crew ran up and down along the tracks, inspecting the rails.

There had been a small explosion and minor damage caused by a
homemade bomb. We were delayed five hours until the train was declared
safe. How was I going to explain my late arrival to Professor Stone?

"Julia? We were expecting you earlier this afternoon. I'm Scott Stone."
I found myself shaking hands with a tall, red-headed, balding gentleman

in his early forties, carefully attired in casual dress: an expensive tweed jacket with fashionably worn leather patches. It was late evening, past nine o'clock. I had arrived in Boulder bedraggled, red-eyed, a sorry spectacle carrying Mama's suitcase held together by a clumsily knotted string. "There was a bomb on the rails. We were held up for five hours," I blurted by way of an excuse. This must have completed Dr. Stone's impression of me as a troubled young lady, scarred by her war experiences. Matter-of-factly he switched to mundane matters as he strode by my side, carrying my despicable bag. "I'm afraid I have some bad news. Your scholarship only covers tuition, not room and board as you were led to believe. Do you have any money?" "Twenty-eight dollars." "Well, don't worry. You can stay with us. Give my wife a hand with the children; help me in the office."

The Stone household turned out to be a spotless abode carved out of pink rock, barely distinguishable from the surrounding foothills, perched on its own acreage, a marvel of modern architecture and efficient design. I was met by vast expanses of deep-pile white carpeting set off by a few stunning statues, bare wood surfaces gleaming like polished mirrors, windows bending in an arc from wall to wall to catch spectacular sunsets. The house was a triple split-level, with a wing for the children and another for the parents. A path led down to a corral where the children, a girl and two boys, kept their horses in nearby stables.

I was shown to an immaculate guest room with an adjoining bath and left staring at a can of cleaning powder after being told to scrub the tub after taking a bath. I had never scrubbed a tub. Such knowledge is taken for granted, but unless one has actually watched the procedure and paid attention while watching, it is possible not to know how to move a just barely wet sponge with just a dab of powder in circular motions along the inner wall of the tub, rinse out the sponge, and start over again with clear water. Bent over at an unaccustomed angle, my efforts left me panting, confronting streaks of white powder zigzagging across a mean gray ring— the accumulation of dirt gathered on my three-day journey west.

The next morning, Mrs. Stone, a lithe blond woman in her thirties, wearing blue jeans and a flannel shirt, showed me the marvels of her kitchen: double stainless-steel sinks, built-in electric oven, built-in gas range, built-in cabinets, built-in electric refrigerator and freezer. There was a big island counter with an additional sink and a warming oven. The pantry was as big as a corner grocery in Paris, stacked with neatly labeled preserves, jams, cans, and every imaginable supply necessary to feed a family and assorted dogs, cats, and guests.

After a few days of my getting tangled in yards of vacuum cleaner cord, letting dogs in and cats out, Dr. Stone arrived at a solution to everyone's satisfaction. The International House had agreed to feed and lodge me for $20 a month, which I would earn by acting as Dr. Stone's receptionist and typist for five hours a day. Dr. Stone generously offered to let me study when the phone wasn't ringing. He also accepted a flexible schedule adjusted to my course requirements, with the exception of the hour from four to five in the afternoon. During that time, he paced the floor while carefully dictating his daily radio talk, the content of which totally escaped me, as I was concentrating on typing it triple-spaced on yellow paper. I became a passable typist in the process, but ever after could not think while typing and always wrote in longhand.

The International House, a stately three-story bungalow mellowed with age, stood on a tree-lined street in a comfortable residential section a few minutes from Main Street and forty minutes' walk uphill to the Boulder campus. The only international thing about it was me. The house was a cooperative experiment in diversity, or American pluralism, which neither the dormitories nor sororities were equipped to handle at that time. Twelve or so young ladies of impeccable academic standing (not everyone went to high school in those days, let alone college) ran the house with the help of a cook. Although there was a housemother, an appealingly delicate and erudite graduate of Bennington College, her guidance was strictly nominal. The young ladies ranged in hue from freckled, sunburned white, to yellow, copper, tan, brown, and black, and confessed to as many religious faiths; yet they were all American, and all proud of it.

As an aspiring immigrant, I couldn't have landed in a better place.

Cheerfully, I took up residence in the attic, where I was helped to prop up a worn-out box spring on stacks of bricks. Two cartons—one for books, one for clothes—completed the furnishings. A small window recessed in the slanting roof let in dazzling sunshine. I learned to descend the narrow ladderlike steps backward without stumbling, even in the dark.

As my share of the Saturday housecleaning, I offered to polish the banister and dining room table and chairs, mindful of Mrs. Ducky's teaching exactly six years earlier.

Dinner was a daily feast of lovingly prepared meals. Everyone tried to be Jo the cook's best friend, sharing recipes and darting into the kitchen for previews of meals before being shooed out good-naturedly. Our house-mother, Miss Lauralie Saunders (not her real name), presided at the dinner table. She was a model of exquisite manners; she had a way of guiding the flow of conversation effortlessly, bouncing ideas back and forth, getting everyone to participate while remaining demurely self-effacing. I admired her charm, her wit, and her scholarship, unsuspecting of a deadly triangle developing behind the scenes. Miss Saunders turned out to be the prototype of the professional victim who managed to victimize her benefactors, leaving a trail of broken lives behind her.

Miss Saunders had a fiancé, a naval officer who was enrolled in the Japanese-language program, and who was the reason she elected to continue her education on the Boulder campus. He willingly accepted her frail health, footing the bills for her bouts of pneumonia, allergies, and depression. As Miss Saunders' liaison with Professor Stone became common knowledge, her fiancé left on assignment in the Pacific, inconsolable, not sorry to face the enemy. Stone's wife, the no-nonsense athletic blonde in blue jeans, whose family's estate had paid for the horses and the dream house nestled in the foothills, killed herself, leaving three motherless children. Miss Saunders' nurse, hired by a distraught Stone to help him cope with his lover's latest bout of sickness, was a strong-boned, strong-willed woman; she too succumbed to Lauralie's siren song. This nurse neglected her work to devote herself body and soul, day and night, to the caretaking of Lauralie. She and Stone had come to some sort of strange understanding, Stone paying the bills to keep the object of his undying love alive.

The last news I had of Miss Saunders was in the late forties. We were living in Iowa City, where the nurse had moved with an adopted five-year-old girl to rebuild her life after losing Lauralie to dreams of a literary career in France. Once there, Lauralie had fallen ill, had been cared for by a French family, and promptly had repaid their kindness by claiming the love of both father and son. Many years later, when Fred and I had moved to Louisiana, I noticed a lukewarm review of a novel by a Scott Stone. I read it in the library: an infinitely sad account of Stone and Lauralie's ill-fated affair, dreary beyond belief in spite of the writer's exquisite prose.

Coralie Dudley, a new recruit from New England, bounced into this murky atmosphere like a breath of fresh air. Her fresh scrubbed looks matched a candid and straightforward outlook, which saw problems as challenges to be met in a can-do way, mincing neither words nor effort. As an aspiring nursing student, she volunteered at the community hospital and devoted herself to Benny. Benny's life was an extraordinary feat of courage, a lesson to all in the triumph of the human spirit over pain and adversity. A handsome young athlete, he had been rescued from a mining accident with a broken back, severe internal injuries, and an arm torn off at the shoulder. Because of his wounds he lay on his stomach, covered by a sheet, resting on a gurney which was moved to the doorway of his room so he could watch the comings and goings of hospital personnel. He could move his head and his one arm, and had assumed the role of a one-man cheering section. A steady stream of aides, nurses, orderlies, and technicians went out of their way to unburden their troubles and Benny would listen, laugh at his own predicament, and make *them* feel good! The cure for the blues, according to Coralie, was to "go see Benny."

For me, the academic year 1942–43 was a year on the run. I ran up the hill to save bus fare, lugging pounds of books. I ran from one building to another to save five minutes to review notes. I had registered for eighteen credit hours, some of which entailed double lab sessions. Under the mistaken belief that a reading list of some thirty authors was a requirement in each of several subjects, I ran breathlessly to and fro between the library, Dr. Stone's office, and classes. I had not allocated any time for study, relying instead on disciplined note-taking, a photographic memory, and years of practice cramming for exams at the lycée.

The Boulder campus of the University of Colorado was a dream of sun-dappled lawns, tennis-playing coeds, clean-shaven young men in ROTC uniforms. Only a few miles west, the foothills of the Rockies played out a symphony of blazing lights and colors as the sun set.

I kept running. I crisscrossed this peaceful scene as if I were dodging bullets from the small plane that kept circling over the square in front of the Aguilés' house. London was blitzed to smithereens, American troops were fighting on unpronounceable islands in the Pacific, Mama had had no news of her family in the USSR since a laconic postcard implied "don't write." In an unheated castle in the unoccupied zone of France, Mirrha had worked with displaced children, many of whose parents had perished in Hitler's death camps. The news filtered through secondhand, numbing, not yet the stuff of headlines, not a topic for polite conversation.

I kept running. I was almost twenty. I was getting old and there was no time.

Since I had checked "no religious affiliation" on a student activities form, I was wooed by every denomination in town, which took care of picnics, barbecues, square dancing, and potluck suppers on a long string of Sundays, services not included. I didn't smoke or drink, at the time a serious liability at social gatherings; this made me a perfect candidate for any number of churches, but no one bothered to explain the religious aspect of it. "We have great outings, a swell group of young people." This did not strike me as a convincing argument to join a church.

I don't recall when a new resident—I'll call her June—joined me in the attic. A young woman in her twenties, of Rubenesque proportions, shoulder-length red curls, an abundance of freckles on pallid skin, an all-knowing smile, June was careful not to disturb the decorous equilibrium of our multiracial household. Having learned of my questionable antecedents, she started to confide in me, in evenly measured tones that belied the stark reality of child abuse, juvenile delinquency, and teenage pregnancy (the oldest of her three children was then eight, she barely twenty-four). June was the most generous and brilliant person to cross my path. She also displayed a frank disregard for accepted social behavior, and did her best to initiate me into the seamier side of life. This included a sad evening of bar-hopping, sad because I cried into my half mug of beer and cut short June's attempt at picking up a likely companion for the night. It was a good thing June told me about her frequent need for male companionship, as I took in evidence of nightly visitors in the attic without undue surprise. (I was only taken aback one morning when the person in June's arms turned out to be a woman.) June dispensed her favors indiscriminately, as she did other people's belongings, to "those in need." As she would say, echoing the motto of the Communist Party, "from each according to his ability, to each according to his need." She was selflessly dedicated to the Communist cause. I was not altogether as naive as my big brother presumed, but as always, curiosity got the better of me. I played along.

Russia was our ally, faltering under shock wave after shock wave of aerial bombardment as German tanks continued their relentless progress inland. It was imperative that America open a second front in Europe.

The mood was ripe for June and Co. to recruit patriotic sympathizers for the cause.

She was quite up front about it. "There is a fellow in chemistry I'd like you to meet. Fred. He gave me this book. Why don't you read it and let him know what you think of it." The book was *Mathematics and the Imagination,* and was a marvel of lucidity. "I knew you would like it. I'll tell him." Sometime after third trimester finals, June mentioned a picnic. "Will Paul be there?" I asked. (Paul was French, with disarming good looks that melted hearts left and right.) "O.K. then, I'll go." Paul was there all right, but paid me no attention, surrounded by a bevy of suntanned coeds.

"There is Fred Schueler." June pointed to a stocky young man sitting on a solitary rock. A shock of unruly ash blond hair, massive shoulders, a thick neck, and piercing green eyes filled with such ache and longing that I blurted out to myself, "I'll never marry you!" and ran up a perilous hillside strewn with boulders, braids flying, trying to escape that look.

I had to sign up for inorganic chemistry, one of the requirements for the pre-med curriculum. My plea not to be in Fred Schueler's lab session fell on deaf ears. As I spilled and splattered, broke equipment, burned my fingers, Fred appeared gleefully at my side, picking up the pieces, bandaging my fingers. My partner kept nudging me, "Ask him. He likes you," when instructions seemed unclear.

Dr. Stone, whose expertise was Greek, Latin, and ancient history, was sufficiently intrigued by my acquaintance with the Cyrillic alphabet to pass me on to the library as an expert file clerk who could transliterate Russian titles, some of which I understood. This saved me from running back and forth between library and office to check out my own books, and gave me precious quiet moments until there appeared a Dr. Thompson, who was in desperate need of my talents to help with a bibliography for his quarterly journal devoted to Eastern Europe. Had I taken the time to read the journal, I would be less confused now by events in the former Yugoslavia, for example. As it was, I kept my nose to the grindstone, perusing every newspaper and journal in every language I could decipher, including Polish and Russian, for articles dealing with the situation in Eastern Europe. I typed out a list of these, which, to my horror, Dr. Thompson included at the end of each issue of his journal sight unseen.

I had moved to a rooming house closer to the campus at the start of the summer session, where I shared a room with a congenial brunette, a cheerleader intent on climbing the corporate ladder via Mr. Right, which explained her careful grooming sessions and twelve sweater sets to match her every mood. In this rooming house, there were hot plates and tables covered with gaily colored oilcloths available in the basement, but no organized meals. As my cooking experience extended to raw vegetables and fruit, with the occasional boiled egg, I boldly accepted a "hashing" job which paid me three full meals a day, including a copious western breakfast, in exchange for clearing the tables and preparing the dishes for the dishpan. The dishwasher was a young man, not a machine, an efficiency expert who tossed the gleaming, newly washed plates like frisbees to his assistant dryer, who caught them with his towel. They never missed a beat. The trick to keeping this job was to get myself up and running by 6:30 A.M.

Just before summer finals, an official directive reached me from the Naturalization and Immigration Service, informing me that the deadline to pick up my immigration visa in Winnipeg, Canada, was on Saturday. This was Monday. The post office had neglected to forward this letter for six weeks, in spite of a carefully printed request to forward mail to my new residence.

I dug up the address of a Jewish committee in Denver supplied by my brother "in case of emergency," took the train to Denver, and pleaded my case. The young woman who saw me was quick, efficient, and sympathetic. Within thirty minutes I was handed an envelope with a round-trip ticket to Winnipeg and $20. "That should do it for the weekend." I promised myself to repay this loan, caught the train back to Boulder, and started packing—not the weekender, that was too cumbersome, just my briefcase. My train left Wednesday at 4 P.M. On Tuesday, I ran around getting assignments from all my classes. I was going to miss my chemistry lab exam. "Don't worry, you can make it up in my lab when you return." Fred fished around in a pocket and came up with a stained $5 bill. "I want you to have this. It's all I have. You'll need it," he said. "I wish I could go with you." I tried to reach Dr. Thompson, but his office was locked (there were no answering machines then). Wednesday at one, a distraught Paul stood at the door of my rooming house. "A terrible thing has happened; you have to come with me; there is no one else."

"I can't. I have to catch a train at four."

"It's a matter of life or death; I'll explain on the way."

"Okay, but we'll have to run. I have to get back before two o'clock."

Paul lived with his parents in a handsome house a forty-minute walk southeast of the campus. Halfway down the hill, Paul stopped. "Not so fast. My heart." Speaking French, he gestured dramatically, clutching his chest. I had to laugh. "You're a real pal, Julia. I can talk to you as a friend, not a girl."

I had been ready to melt into his arms. Now I froze, close to slapping him.

"You see, I had this dream. My canary is sick. If he dies, I die with him. You must have a look at him; we must make him well."

Paul's canary wasn't exactly chirping in his cage, but then I knew nothing about canaries. "He looks fine to me, Paul. Really, I have to get back." And I ran.

Winnipeg was an unexpected place elsewhere half a continent north, it seemed, day and night and day again through endless fields of corn and wheat. I befriended a shy Mennonite girl on the train, and we agreed to have lunch in Winnipeg. In Boulder I had splurged on a reckless pair of red suede ankle-strap shoes. By the time I checked into my hotel, I realized that they sent entirely the wrong message. "You're not with the swimming team?" the desk clerk ventured, handing me my key. The next morning, Friday, I stopped at the first shoe store on the way to the American consulate and bought plain brown pumps. The hotel cost $5. The shoes cost another $5. I had barely $15 left. The consul looked at my papers with interest. "You understand we are in a state of war emergency. It will take at least a week for Washington to send the necessary authorization by surface mail. It cannot be handled by wireless. Come back in a week."

I went to see the Mennonite girl. I found her in a tiny and sunny room that was furnished with a cot, a chair, and a hot plate on a small table. She was overcome by the confusion and bustle of a big town. I took her by the hand to walk down the main avenue, showed her the shops, the streetcar. I knew my way around a city. At the end of the car line, there was a zoo.

That afternoon, I walked, map in hand, in search of cheap lodgings. About two miles from the center, houses grew more modest, stuck together without side yards. Women wore cotton housedresses, their hands red from scrubbing. Their sons were in the army, probably overseas. There had to be some empty spare rooms.

I started ringing doorbells. On the fifth try I got lucky, as a housewife considered my outlandish explanation (stranded in Canada to gain legal residency in the United States) in good faith. "Well, there's my boy's room under the attic, but it's very small, not really suitable for a young lady. I could let your have it for fifty cents." I noticed the woman's fingers, swollen with arthritis. "I'll help you with the dishes," I offered.

"That would be wonderful. You could share our supper."

For ten days, I crisscrossed the city, walked along a riverbank, went to the zoo. No longer would I be without a country; my immigration visa assured me of American citizenship within five years. Life was glorious, everything was possible; I was overcome by the sheer wonder of it, the vastness and luxury of the land that had whizzed past the train, the exhilarating feeling of freedom from fear. I had to write. Paul would not understand. Fred would. I wrote to Fred.

The following Saturday, I picked up my visa, hugged my landlady, said good-bye to the Mennonite girl (now settled in a clerical job), and took the train back to Boulder. June met me at the station. "Paul died last week. He was buried Saturday. Did you know he suffered from a rheumatic heart? Let me walk you home."

Fred and Julia

When my brother, Max, came to visit in late August, cutting a dashing figure in his new American army uniform, I didn't know how to explain Fred. We had lunch—a festive occasion—in the Sink, a student hangout sunk, as the name implied, three feet beneath ground level. I had invited Fred and one of my girlfriends. The men shook hands. Fred shone with a presence that belied his plain appearance, radiated confidence, pulled out all stops to impress my brother. I knew him to hold an audience of several hundred bored students in his gaze, who hung onto his every word as he demonstrated the drama of a chemical reaction. Max was a pretty shrewd knower of men. "I see you're in good hands, Julia." He turned to my girlfriend, I think Darlene. "Shall we go?" On a recent visit to Orléans, Max thanked me. "I had a terrific time on that last furlough in Boulder. Your girlfriends were great."

He and my parents had retrieved their immigration visas in Montreal, only a day's train ride north from New York City. "Here's my army address. Don't expect any mail. I'll be with the OSS in London. By the way, I had to change my name. Max Ralis."

When we first met, while I espoused a spartan lifestyle under the eaves of an unfinished attic, Fred had found refuge in a dark and comfy basement next to a furnace, which he kept faithfully stoked in exchange for a rent-free sleeping space, a precariously sagging cot surrounded by piles of books.

After I returned with my immigration visa from Canada, Fred helped me make up work in chemistry. He then used a passkey to gain access to the biology lab where my rabbit, carefully preserved and partially dissected, had defied any attempt on my part to identify the structures of its nervous system. We wrapped it up in some dreadfully foul-smelling cloth and carried it to the cooking basement of my rooming house, where it yielded its secrets and became an object of beauty as Fred expounded on the wondrous workings of it all. Like a pair of furtive thieves cradling some precious loot, we returned it to the biology lab that same night. Although I earned a top grade in my make-up practical the next day, my professor informed me curtly that he could award me a passing C at best, since missing an exam to go to Canada for my immigration visa was no excuse. Besides, I was a girl and had no business wasting his time and mine in pre-med. All things considered, and with considerable hindsight, he turned out to be right. Dr. Thompson was not so kind. I had left him in the lurch without a bibliography for the latest edition of the his journal and was fired on the spot. This left me without a job except for the three-meal-a-day hashing for the rest of the summer, with ample time to read, study, attend classes, and spend evenings in the rat house or in the lab with Fred. We explored every building on campus, besides the library and student union, which might possibly conceal a piano for our musical entertainment. Thus was I treated to enchanting concerts, as Fred played his favorite classics and his own latest compositions.

Days grew shorter, snow capped the foothills, the campus was transformed into a winter wonderland. Driven into each other's arms by the cold, we decided to marry. That is, Fred decided; I saw no purpose in it. "You've got to marry me. I can't do my work without you. I may have to go to Chicago; how can I be sure you're coming with me, unless we're married?" Oh, but I would! Elsewhere with Fred spelled home, no matter where.

Here I must thank an unlikely benefactor, Fred's former roommate at the dorm, who initiated him into the secrets of Cantonese cuisine and the use of chopsticks in exchange for help in chemistry and math. Po Yum Fok had the ideal physique for a jockey, a receding chin with protruding teeth, a wardrobe of tailor-made suits, a Cadillac, a racehorse, and a heart of gold. He let Fred drive his car on special occasions—a picnic in the mountains, a day out in Denver—temptations I could not resist. When Fred and I were married on a Friday, January 15, 1944, Po let us have his car for an idyllic weekend honeymoon in Estes Park. I still have a slender hand-bound book of Chinese characters printed on rice paper. His porcelain soup bowls, spoons, and chopsticks are long gone. In Chicago a few years later, Fred and I received a family photo celebrating Po's son's first birthday in Hong Kong. Po had married a tall, attractive Japanese American woman from San Francisco. When we lived in Rome, Fred enjoyed startling would-be panhandlers by responding in a pretty good rendition of Chinese speech. I always thought he made it up, but come to think of it, it may have been Po's legacy. The following year, my brother was traveling in the East; I gave my Max Po's address and asked him to look up Po in Hong Kong on his way to Bangkok. Max was informed of Po's death under mysterious circumstances; his widow and son had returned to San Francisco.

In Boulder, the Communist Party had targeted Fred early on as a promising scientist, and while, with June's help, they had succeeded in getting him interested in me, they didn't count on my keeping him out. This was easy, as he was too occupied in the lab, until curiosity threatened to get the better of him. I need not have worried. At a student election there was a box on a chair just outside the lecture hall where student speakers held forth; June's friends, recruited by the dozen, many of them nonstudents, trotted by the box dropping in their ballots without ever setting foot in the lecture hall. When Fred witnessed this unabashed stuffing of the box, he became outraged at the flagrant disregard for the democratic process and convinced of the uncompromising nature of Communism in a way no amount of explaining on my part could have achieved. He did, however, commence a reading program in the social sciences in his idle moments. From then on, when June urged me to attend a meeting and bring Fred, I could reply in good conscience that we were too busy.

At the end of the spring term 1945, June gave a party to celebrate her doctorate in physics. For the occasion, she had custody of her youngest son, perhaps twenty months old, who spent the entire evening howling inconsolably in his crib. For me, the great attraction was cookie sheets loaded with precisely aligned stuffed bell peppers, each topped with a perky green hat. There were forty of them, one per guest. June took pride in her cooking, which she mastered with the same unfailing precision, when the need arose, as she had mastered Russian, French, and mathematics. I was no judge of her scientific expertise but could vouch for her uncanny, mind-chilling ability to commit to instant memory every new phrase, idiom, and grammatical structure of the French language. Within six months she achieved commendable fluency in French, complete with a Parisian accent; she could read French scientific abstracts with pleasure and without recourse to laborious translation, having devoted exactly thirty minutes a day to the study of the language with the help of a dog-eared old text and no other formal instruction.

June's thesis adviser in physics was a Dr. Lubovitch, who had left Russia with his wife under difficult circumstances. The couple, near retirement, had lost their only son in the Pacific. The shock deprived Mrs. Lubovitch of the ability to speak the broken English she had so painfully acquired over the years. As June explained it to me, Mrs. Lubovitch was on the brink of losing contact with reality, confined by her grief into a world of silence. June's solution was simple and direct. She helped Mrs. Lubovitch prepare borscht, stuffed cabbage, and other Russian delights, while learning to speak Russian with the same deliberate attention she had bestowed upon French.

Sometime in the fall of the previous year, I had visited a girls' reform school an hour's bus drive from Boulder as part of a sociology project. I was introduced to the resident nurse, a formidable giant of a woman with graying braids twisted in a crown atop her head, an intimidating figure with an equally intimidating name: Wilhelmina Schueler. Did she know a Fred Schueler, a chemistry student at Boulder? Yes indeed; Bud, as he was called, was her nephew. Wilhelmina offered a brisk ten-minute tour of the premises, of which I recall a near-empty library with few books, kept under lock and key. Did she remember a redhead by the name of June, who was an inmate some ten years earlier? Yes indeed. June kept to herself and read all the books in the library. She got out at fifteen, when an old gentleman offered to be her guardian and marry her.

According to June, she felt sorry for the old man (old has gotten a lot older these past fifty years; as I recall, the man was in his fifties). She married him, bore him two sons in two years, cooked and washed diapers, and found consolation in a set of encyclopedias, later an assortment of math books. She read these volumes assiduously, seated on a park bench, while keeping an eye on her progeny playing in a sandbox nearby. Whether she left, or whether the babies, abandoned for hours at a time, were taken from her, was never clear; nor how she came by her third boy, whom she nursed long enough to wean to cow's milk, then used to leave alone with his bottle while entertaining a questionable string of gentlemen free of charge. "How did you know that about June?" my friend Julie asked. I believe June told me.

Fred and I saw June one last time, shortly after her farewell party. She came to us in brazen need of a sizable sum of money, representing one half of Fred's monthly instructor's salary in the chemistry department. June's grant for postdoctoral research at Columbia University had come through; she needed the money for train fare, having spent her last penny on liquor for the party. A loan, of course, to be repaid when next we visited in New York. We should have known better, but felt it impossible to refuse.

The Party didn't give up easily. Fred never knew that June's contact in Chicago knocked on our basement door at regular intervals—a polite, well-dressed young gentleman who introduced himself as June's friend and beseeched me to bring Fred along to "our next meeting." I could truthfully reply that Fred was too busy. As far as I know, they gave up when we moved to Iowa.

Fred's culinary specialty was beef hearts with Chinese vegetables: thin slivers of lightly precooked beef, tossed and steamed with chopped celery, Chinese cabbage, and whatever other veggies, cut into fine strips, were at hand. Fred cooked with loving care, with the same precise, agile gestures he used in maneuvering and adjusting delicate lab instruments. I was grateful for his beef heart experiments. We relied on the occasional rabbit to round out a meager diet, and sometimes frogs' legs as well, sacrifices from experiments to test the effect of new compounds on the heart and nervous system. Fred even tried to cook a rat. At the end of every month, there was a frantic search for mislaid pennies under the sofa cushions. A dinner invitation was a memorable event. Dr. E. K. G. Geiling, the head of the pharmacology department and a confirmed bachelor, had us over for an elegant repast served by his houseboy in a vast expanse of dining room. Dr. Geiling's specialty was the pituitary gland: the whale had the biggest. He entertained us with stories of his whale-hunting days. It took a leap of imagination to combine sport with science. A South Afrikaner from Johannesburg, Dr. Geiling spoke Dutch and English, but no French. A call to Abbott Laboratories produced a steady trickle of translation work for me, pharmaceutical advertising from English to French. He generously welcomed our baby in his office. Tanya was a self-assured, pudgy, blond-curled toddler who went straight for the candy jar.

Dr. Chen, a tall Chinese American, Fred's thesis adviser, graciously asked us to share supper with his family. Five or six little Chens crowded around the dining table while Mrs. Chen put the finishing touches on several of a dozen dishes. I sat in awe of this young woman's accomplishments. She had no help, lived in relatively spartan walk-up faculty housing, had finished shampooing the living room rug that very morning, and still managed a look of poised elegance in a simple Chinese frock. Dr. Chen later left the University of Chicago to head research and development at Eli Lilly. He and Fred continued a friendly and scientifically fruitful relationship.

One of the research assistants Fred befriended was a gentleman in his forties, who had retired from business to devote his energy to a youthful passion for science. He and his wife invited us up to their penthouse with a starlit view of Lake Michigan. There was a small gathering in honor of a young artist whose paintings our hostess was promoting. Her frank and open look went beyond social niceties and begged to go to the heart of the matter.

She took me aside. "Tell me, what do you do to keep from being bored?"

"Bored? I don't have any time. There is work. There is school. There is the baby. There is Fred. Don't you work?"

"No. I have money, and it is a terrible burden. John loves his experiments, but I don't know what to do. I am helping this young man with his painting career."

I tried to console her. "It's very generous of you to help a young artist."

It did not occur to me to add, "and a young scientist." (In retrospect, Fred may have mentioned her husband's generous financial contributions to the pharmacology department's laboratories.)

We spent the winter of 1945–46 in a nightmarish tenement crawling with rats and roaches. I couldn't decide whether to carry the baby up the three flights of stairs, leaving the groceries to be sneezed, coughed, and spit upon by a gang of sickly looking preschoolers, or get the groceries up first, leaving the baby in the care of said grimy crew. I wisely opted for the baby first, which meant leaving her unattended in her playpen while I dashed downstairs to carry up the groceries. In spite of constant scrubbing, the floor bore the indelible traces of the aforementioned nightly visitors; Tanya, now a year old, was confined to her playpen all day long. Mama arrived from New York, took one look, and took Tanya with her back to New York. We hugged them both all the way to the railroad station.

By moving down, we moved up in the world. Our new basement apartment, which had served as a polling place, had been condemned because it regularly flooded during heavy rains. Fred convinced the owners that this was a minor inconvenience and absolved them of all responsibility in return for an affordable rent. He furnished it with $100 worth of Salvation Army chic, painted it in pastel colors, and phoned me in New York, where I had gone after six months to fetch our daughter. "The place is ready. You've got to come back right away."

"I can't. The diapers are all wet." But I went. A brightly mottled linoleum set off the pastel walls. A pail and a mop by the entrance steps ensured periodic and thorough floor washing when it poured cats and dogs at unpredictable intervals and the rainwater, as promised, cascaded down our basement steps.

Charles Post, Fred's high school buddy, had returned from service in the Pacific. Reddish blond, slight of build, he sported a mustache and a passion for opera and precious gems. He and Fred were the original odd couple, Charles being the meticulous dresser, while Fred covered up in stained, acid-punctured lab coats. Charles, blessed with a rich tenor voice, felt under obligation to pursue a career in pharmacy. He continued to share our new basement quarters, as he had the tenement. Secure in the knowledge that his family was not alone, Fred often spent nights as well as days in the lab, since some ongoing experiments entailed injections at four-hour intervals.

Fred got hold of an old practice piano. Unattached young graduate students dropped in for musical evenings, flute or clarinet in hand. Fred improvised at the piano, loud and clear. At midnight, strangers stumbled down the steps, thinking they had discovered another bar.

The streetcar was another matter. It rumbled by our half-sized windows—which were flush with the sidewalk, revealing only boots and small dogs on leashes—at unpredictable yet frequent intervals, with the startling effect of a mini-earthquake. A cacophonous clanging and banging left us speechless in midsentence and interrupted Fred's impromptu musical gatherings—leaving startled guests with their bows in midair, leaving Charles choking on a high note, and shocking assorted drop-ins from the rarefied atmosphere of the Rockies about the reality of urban living.

I found the streetcar soothing and less threatening than the steam locomotives which seemed to roar through Mr. Mousy's railroad station. Looking back, the Chicago streetcar served as a welcome apprenticeship for teaching some twenty years in a New Orleans public school, the windows open to waves of hot, moisture-laden air, with the noise of the famed streetcars rolling through students' recitations. Only the then thrice-weekly trash compactor, parked beneath the classroom windows, brought any thought of teaching to a complete twenty-minute standstill, while I hastily chalked a written assignment on the board, mouthing and mimicking the lesson. My students became adept at lip reading.

Our little darling, perched on the back of the sofa or on the piano bench, was fascinated by wheels and feet and little dogs chasing each other down the street. Between passing streetcars, an ice cream parlor beckoned from the other side of the tracks, where father and daughter mischievously spent loose change when I was safely occupied struggling with the laundry in the "basement" part of the basement. Change dropped through often-mended holes in trouser pockets, or lab coat pockets, rolling under the bed and under the chest, where I hoped my broom would find the coins before the baby ate them.

Such was the fascination of the ice cream parlor that one morning, as we turned the corner to access the enclosed yard space in back of our building, Tanya, a goal-oriented two-year-old charmer, escaped my grasp to run across the street. Cars screeched to a stop, bicyclists swerved, I flew to snatch my baby inches from a passing streetcar. I spanked. I cried. I hugged. I remembered Mama snatching me from under the horse on the Wittenbergplatz in Berlin. Fred found us both in tears. Magnanimously, he offered a visit to the ice cream parlor, his daughter riding safely on his shoulders.

At Easter 1947, Fred surprised us with a white fluff of fur stuck in his coat pocket, the first of many experimental pets borrowed from the lab. Wisely, the real live bunny escaped our daughter's squeals of joy and attempts at hugging, cowering instead in dark, inaccessible corners. After two weeks of pining away, refusing to nibble on lettuce leaves, the bunny had turned into a melancholy shadow of its erstwhile hopping self. He was transported back to the animal quarters at the medical school, where he recovered his former spirits and good health.

One day, our peaceful family scene was interrupted by a long-distance phone call, an event to be reckoned with in 1947. It was Mama. "Basia jumped out the window; I left her for a minute to answer the door after bandaging her slashed wrists in the bathroom. She was convinced spies were after her. You must come right away, Julia, I cannot talk on the phone."

Anything was possible. Basia, a chemist by profession, a vigorous, short-legged maiden lady with a pronounced limp, straight steel-gray hair, and sharp incisive eyes, known to all of us as "Shura's aunt," had lost all contact with her family left behind in the Soviet Union. In Berlin and Paris, her mission had been to raise her nephew, Shura. There had been vague allusions about Shura disappearing during the Occupation to make his way to the eastern front.

Mama had taken pity on Basia, an old friend, and invited her to share her apartment. I held on to the receiver, turned my head, and told Grandma Mabel, who was visiting with us from Colorado, "It's my mother. A friend killed herself; I have to go to New York."

"She must be mad," was Grandma Mabel's curt response. "How can she expect you to leave your baby, your family, at a drop of hat?" No, of course I could not leave.

Mama's whispered agony would continue to haunt me. Basia's demons never let go and eventually caught up with her. By 1952, when I met Mama at the train station in Iowa City, she was too terrified to speak, surrounded by imaginary phantoms.

Our little yellow house in Coralville was not safe enough. Silently, on tiptoes, fingers pressed to her closed lips, Mama checked every door, every window, pulled down every blind, turned off every light. Fred was out of town. I fed the children, shooed them to their room, into their pajamas, and into bed. Mama burst out of her silence into an uninterrupted stream of the vilest language I had ever heard, language I never knew she knew, until she fell down exhausted on her bed. It was one in the morning. I was terrified. I phoned a colleague, a psychiatrist, and found myself whispering on the phone, "I can't talk, it's an emergency, it's my mother." "I'll be out in ten minutes. I'll park in the driveway, without lights. Come to the car."

We sat in the car. I briefly recounted Mama's behavior. "She cannot stay. It's dangerous." "Is there any help for her here?" "No, not as a New York resident. You must get her back to New York. I'll help make the arrangements. You must not leave her alone with the children." For a year or two, Mama managed to control her behavior for short periods of time, sufficiently conscious of what was happening to her as to fool any doctor friend brought in to help. When she refused to eat, accusing her sister and best friend of poisoning her, when she could no longer keep at bay the blue phantoms threatening to choke her, she was mercifully committed to an institution for her own safety. With the help of treatment and drugs, she was able to continue in her special world without being a threat to others or to herself. Thirty years later, she embraced her great-grand-sons, Réda and Amin, then five and one year old, who had come with Tanya from Morocco to spend the summer in the States. Sixteen years ago, my son Carl and his wife Pam sought her blessing for their firstborn, my older granddaughter, Janelle. On the photo Carl sent me, the baby beamed at my mother, who beamed back in unmitigated delight. Mama died peacefully the following year, at the age of ninety-two, on Janelle's first birthday, February 11, 1983.

Back in Chicago, in the spring of 1947, where Grandma Mabel had pulled me firmly back to solid ground, I registered for some courses in child development, sociology, and economics. I was shocked to discover that we were living below the poverty line. Dr. Havighurst, renowned for his research in educational psychology, asked me to supervise a blackening team for one of his graduate students. I was in charge of a dozen or so would-be historians, sociologists, anthropologists, and economists, whom I seated around two long tables with stacks of IQ tests in front of them. Their task was to blacken all the answers already blackened, but perhaps not blackened enough, by children possibly unaware of the importance of blackening a spot with vigor and precision; after which the stacks of book-lets were whisked away, much like the trays of clay leaves in Queens, to be analyzed and compared to preblackened test results.

It took a team of highly trained, motivated graduate students to sur-vive the monotonous tedium of blackening. There were lively discussions, interrupted by inhuman shrieks as hapless social workers from Dr. Bet-telheim's orthogenic school for autistic children chased their unruly charges through the portion of the basement that had been allocated to us.

Early one evening, I answered an imperious knock at the door of our apartment. Facing me stood my cousin Joe, spouting German and En-glish in a state of unaccustomed excitement.

"Trudi," he repeated. "I rang the wrong doorbell on the first floor and Trudi opened it."

"Trudi?"

"Trudi, my kindergarten teacher in Vienna. We hugged and cried. She married a Dr. Bettelheim, a psychologist."

That was a good thing, I thought, because the raven-haired little girl from the apartment above, who played in the backyard under her nanny's supervision, was wont to stomp and cry when things did not go her way, to our own little darling's wide-eyed astonishment.

Joshi, who had hitchhiked from New York at seventeen, an old hand at this perilous mode of transportation, joined us at the kitchen table, rav-enously hungry and eager to partake of Fred's latest culinary experiment.

I don't recall how I joined Dr. Bettelheim's support group for young mothers. I believe it was called "conversations with mothers." The most re-assuring aspect of it was to hear of other young women's struggles with recalcitrant eaters and sleepers, this being before the advent of Dr. Spock's liberating self-demand schedule. These were problems I had been bliss-fully unaware of, as our two-year-old ate everything in sight. On the Mid-way, she invariably toddled back from making the rounds of picnicking families chewing on a cookie. We had full confidence in the decency of strangers then.

Iowa City, Iowa, 1947–1956

There was a flap in the lower part of our door in the Quonset hut in Finkbine Park, which a previous animal lover tenant had intended for his cat. We weren't aware of this until a toddler surprised us in our bedroom at an ungodly hour of the morning, and we realized he did not belong to us. We returned him to his parents—no small feat, since he apparently exited his abode by similar means and his family were not yet aware of his absence—after which Fred did the prudent thing and nailed the flap shut.

So we were not quite as shocked when there was an unexpected knock at our door about 8 A.M. some time later, though we were not in the habit of receiving guests that early in the morning. I opened the door, but being amply pregnant I saw no one there until a small girl with flaming red hair, perhaps four, tugged at my skirt and demanded in composed tones, "May I play with your little girl?"

"Why, she isn't up yet. Who are you?"

"I'm Michelle, and that's my daddy over there." Michelle's father appeared out of the shadows, soft-spoken and civil, yet barely able to hide a great distress. "I'm LeRoy Eyring. I had to leave my wife in San Francisco with our new baby. She had a caesarean three days ago and was unable to travel; my first lecture is scheduled in half an hour. Could Michelle play here until I pick her up at eleven? We arrived yesterday and she noticed your little girl playing outside."

"Of course."

This is how Michelle and Ruthie (Tanya had become Ruthie in Iowa, her middle name being Ruth, which we had carefully chosen in case Tanya proved too exotic) became fast friends, and how we met the Eyring family.

War in the Pacific and Mormon missionary work had set LeRoy back in his career. He was almost thirty, with a fresh Ph.D. from Berkeley. Iowa City was his first teaching assignment, in physical chemistry.

Michelle's mother, with eight-day-old Tricia, arrived a few days later by plane, a relatively rare event in the forties, direct from the hospital in San Francisco. Petite, incredibly narrow-hipped, with huge blue eyes and an expressive face framed by cascades of golden auburn waves which she tossed about like the mane of an impatient steed, LaReal always reminded me of a sort of western jean-clad Lady Godiva, all the more as she shared a passion for horses with LeRoy, galloping over mind-boggling expanses of desert scenery in Utah and Arizona. The oldest of seven children, LaReal had married at seventeen, shortly after Pearl Harbor, then wisely waited for LeRoy's safe return to start her ideal family of a dozen children. Three more precarious pregnancies and caesareans—two girls and a boy within the next four years—were to put a halt to this prodigal dream. In between nursing Tricia, LaReal scrubbed floors, baseboards, and furniture; she baked fresh bread, made casseroles, and did the washing but did not iron anything. LeRoy fashioned a miniature picket fence for the twenty-by-ten bit of lawn in front of their half of Quonset hut where Carl and Tricia could be left to play in relative safety a year and a half later; relative, because Carl loved his shovel and made little distinction between the top of his upside-down pail and Tricia's inviting head. Michelle and Ruthie were free to play in half a dozen halves of Quonset huts up and down our "block," behind and in front, a veritable haven for preschoolers free to sample any number of lifestyles, toys, dolls, and picture books; best loved by Ruthie, was the never-ending sampling of homemade fudge, taffy, cookies, brownies, and cupcakes, all baked from scratch.

In November, the Eyrings started baking in earnest, a mass production of candied nuts, fruitcakes, and gingerbread men. "LeRoy is the youngest of twenty-three. His brothers and sisters are all married with at least five children each. It's the best we can do by way of Christmas greetings." (Another Christmas season was devoted to the mass production of decorative candles.)

Polygamy was a concept I was familiar with from the study of primitive tribes in Africa and in the Pacific. I had even met a polygamous man face to face, my brother's African roommate from Senegal; but I admit I was a bit stunned to discover polygamy in America. Still, it seems LeRoy's father, who had married two sisters, had not had an easy time of it. He managed to raise all twenty-three of his children in the Mormon faith. The oldest had recently been awarded a much coveted prize in chemistry. I had the distinct impression that LeRoy, for all his imposing strength à la Yul Brynner, labored in his famous brother's shadow. For someone like me, whose parents had avoided all religious training apart from the basic ethical morality of a Judaic tradition, this was a brusque introduction to the multiplicity of sects in America and a prime example of what is meant by freedom of religion. Fred and LeRoy discussed the tenets of the Mormon faith alternately with problems in physics whenever one or the other was dispatched by a nursing wife to fetch their older progeny. I was content to be astonished by LaReal's unwavering enthusiasm in producing babies against considerable odds while keeping the proverbial spotless house; she continued to bake bread, paint furniture, and several years later, steam layers of wallpaper off twelve-foot walls in a magnificent three-story Victorian red brick home which she and LeRoy transformed from an abandoned relic into a prized and valuable possession, doubling its value in the process. In his spare time, LeRoy set to work removing an inner wall to reveal an impressive expanse of open living space, set off by a free-standing double fireplace; he built cabinets in the kitchen and bookshelves in the library, while LaReal rescued crawling baby girls from plaster dust and flakes of chipped paint. She tended to soups, stews, and casseroles in restaurant-sized receptacles to feed an ever-growing clientele of steady boarders who joined the family for dinner, which helped defray the cost of the ingredients and some of the staggering costs of the carefully planned renovations.

Surrounded by paragons of domestic virtues (the Eyrings were a prime example, but no exception), I felt crushed. Sightseeing in Iowa City consisted of admiring the latest basement workshop installations, or the most recently built ranch-style houses with picture windows framing frozen lawns. Going out meant dinner at friends' houses which we were in no position to reciprocate. I had survived our first Iowa summer in a darling cottage, spanking white and trimmed in blue, with a stone fireplace in the living room, dark blue linoleum on the kitchen floor, a brand-new washing machine in the basement facing a sizable yard, completely furnished in sturdy no-nonsense maple, courtesy of the pharmacology department; but I had no place to go. Fred quickly solved his transportation problem by acquiring a well-used and very solid black bicycle. I was left with a two-year-old toddler in a red wagon to negotiate the two miles or so across the Iowa River to the nearest grocery store. The yard next door was inhabited by a very large young woman, her mother, and possibly a grandmother as well; they were usually hidden behind billowing sheets and diapers on multiple laundry lines, busy with the youngest of several children, which left the oldest, a feisty almost four-year-old, free to pummel my little girl when no one was looking. These were not ideal neighbors. Two or three miles to the east, I discovered a landing field—airport being too formal a designation for a hangar and a couple of landing strips with cows grazing contentedly nearby. This airfield, and later, when Carl was a little boy and I had learned how to drive, the railroad station, were to be my favorite outing destinations, beckoning with the promise of unknown elsewheres.

Elsewhere in New Orleans, 1956–

It doesn't seem like it, but I am from New Orleans. I've lived here well over half of my life. New Orleans was Fred's gift to me. After fourteen years of blizzards, snowdrifts, frostbitten fingers, and frozen diapers alternating with torrid summers in small Midwestern towns where my accent, mismatched with my misunderstood south-of-the-border looks, aroused suspicion, slammed doors, and left me in a sea of silence, I stood with Fred in front of St. Louis Cathedral in the French Quarter on a mild December day in 1955. Peeled away from furs, boots, scarves, gloves, ear muffs, and woolly hat to a plain shirt-sleeved dress, I stared at the palms in Jackson Square. I heard bells ringing, horses' hooves on cobblestones, echoes of my childhood; people were talking everywhere, unhurried, in a rich miscellany of accents; artists at easels—a small Montmartre—sat on the periphery of the square. Framed by the red brick Pontalba buildings, enclosed by a suspiciously French-looking wrought-iron grill, Jackson Square seemed a tropical replica of my beloved Place des Vosges in the Marais, on the Right Bank of Paris. It too had been a swamp, just like New Orleans, minus the snakes and alligators. Fred had been raised in Colorado, a day's ride or two from Cheyenne on horseback. Stone houses, narrow streets, and city crowds crushed his spirits. He needed space, an uncluttered horizon, unsullied by people's marks of civilization. "Long Island or New Orleans?" The offer in Long Island was prestigious, and double the salary, but we gave it not a thought. Fred chose New Orleans, with the freedom to build his own laboratories in the new addition to the Tulane Medical School, and granted me a city I could love.

These past forty years, especially since Fred died and the children left home, New Orleans has been my springboard to fly out to far-off places, always to come back refreshed, renewed, happy to call it home. In a city that thrives on diversity, it is easier to melt into the background; a foreign accent does not alarm, rather it is welcomed with mild interest.

Some twenty-five years ago, an ad in the "room wanted" section of our local newspaper sparked my interest: Japanese seeks home with American family to learn English. Shigeru Ohara, meaning "big mountain," I was informed, was a slight young man from Nagasaki, whose histrionic talents made up for his inability to communicate in English and helped him overcome his natural shyness. Over a period of some three years my spare bedroom acquired a distinctly sparse oriental look—chairs pushed aside, a small desk transformed into a makeshift altar, the daybed serving as a permanent repository for books and tapes, while my thick wool rug from the Atlas Mountains provided an ideal sleeping space.

Perched cross-legged on a chair in my kitchen, Shigeru acted out his father's military career: his father's shared shame in a defeated army, his disappointment bordering on dishonor when his only son, he, Shigeru, failed his university entrance exams. So vivid was Shigeru's mimicry that I could see his grandparents, bowed by age and cares, tending to a small vegetable garden, tying twisting vines to makeshift bamboo sticks, tenderly fertilizing the soil around each plant. With a suggestive wave of the hand, my kitchen was transformed into a bare space with sliding rice paper partitions, a small brook rippling through the middle, alive with exotic fish shimmering in ever-changing hues. While Shigeru's English improved but haltingly, I was afforded a privileged glimpse of a mode of life inaccessible to the ordinary traveler.

In the wee hours of a spring day in 1973, I was startled by a phone call from Tokyo. So dramatic was the message that Shigeru exploded in unaccustomed speech: "Yen, bank, dictionary, vely important." Perched on his kitchen chair, armed with graph paper and pencil, Shigeru demonstrated the unthinkable. As of that morning, Tokyo time, the buying power of the U.S. dollar had almost shrunk by half. "Vely good, vely good, make more money." Indeed, the dollar value of his salary (paid in yen by his Japanese company) would almost double overnight, while my dollar purchases for my upcoming trip to France and Germany would be cut in half. "Go to bank; change money," Shigeru advised, painstakingly double-checking words in his dictionary.

At the bank, my financial adviser greeted me with bored disbelief, but obliged by selling me enough francs and marks at the still current rate for an extended sabbatical stay overseas. The next day's financial page confirmed the devaluation of the U.S. dollar.

Henceforth, my vaunted expertise at traveling on the cheap was to be sorely tested; dreams of retiring on a modest pension which would provide double the amenities abroad while the dollar was king evaporated. Sony, Kawasaki, Toyota, Toshiba, and Ricoh became household words in the

States, and American companies went global to survive. France fought a losing battle against American idioms such as "le stress" and "le weekend," which were perceived to threaten the purity of the French language. Vaguely I realized the potential of my spare bedroom. I would concentrate on tenants from exotic places, welcome outlandish elsewheres in my home.

Shigeru's parents in Japan, hearing of their son's weekly exploits in the French Quarter, had arranged a speedy marriage for their progeny by telephone with the fiancée of their choosing. After three days of fasting, devoted to meditation and prayer, a much chastened young man emerged from his room and sought my advice, not on his upcoming state of matrimony, but on his qualifications as the future father of a son. My fervent good wishes were to materialize beyond Shigeru's wildest expectations: his newly arrived eighteen-year-old bride, a shyly giggling apparition all of four foot ten, teetering on platform shoes and lugging an enormous suitcase in her husband's wake, gave birth to a strapping nine-pound baby boy a year later, while I was overseas.

On a weekend shortly after my return, a proud father invited me to his new apartment for tea, where I was to witness his parenting expertise while the baby's mother was out shopping. I stood in the bathroom in awed admiration, watching a fully dressed Shigeru crouching in an empty tub, his gurgling baby boy held securely in his arms. The infant was gently soaped, rinsed off, tapped dry, oiled, powdered, diapered, and dressed. I was awarded the honor of holding him while his father heated a bottle. I handed him back to Shigeru to be fed and gently lulled to sleep. "Good father?" I was asked. "A-one father, A-one son," I responded truthfully. (The Oharas returned to Japan with their American-born baby a year later; I am sorry to have lost track of them.)

On another occasion, I had rented house, garden, and pet dog to a racehorse trainer from Colorado whose devotion to his wife ("How she would love this little house!") convinced me of his rectitude. Suntanned and soft-spoken, with crinkly blue eyes, I could imagine him riding into the sunset as an extra in any number of westerns. I never met his wife, a small rotund Navaho Indian, nor his four-year-old daughter, who delighted in playing with my dachshund, Maya (this according to neighbors down the street). The family had moved out the day before my return. The kitchen floor gleamed, windowpanes sparkled, curtains were starched, parquet floors had been waxed and buffed to an unaccustomed shine. My house smiled at me in the reflection of the tender care bestowed upon it by an unknown, loving family.

Soon thereafter, an emaciated, swarthy, dark-mustached young man who introduced himself as Ricky, "short for Rachid," beseeched me in such soul-wrenching terms to rent my spare room to him—he was a true believer, upholding the tenets of the Koran—that I found no words to turn him away. While he fetched his suitcase from a friend's house, I checked my atlas to verify the location of Pakistan relative to Iran and India, then placed a call to my sister-in-law in Paris, whom I considered an expert in matters both geographic (she having worked as an agent for Air France) and Islamic (since she had briefly been married to a Tunisian gentleman of that persuasion). We wasted no words, transatlantic calls being quite costly then. "You may trust him to tell the truth if he is a true believer."

As outrageous as Ricky's boasts seemed to me, each one of them eventually turned out to be true. To begin with, he told me that he had left behind in Pakistan a young fiancée of ravishing looks, good family, and impeccable academic standing, who was currently completing her medical training in Karachi. How this could be, given Ricky's sullen yet cocky demeanor, less than average looks, and dismal financial and academic prospects, was baffling indeed. Subsisting on a diet of bananas, peanut butter, and sardines washed down with thankful gulps of fresh water from the tap, Ricky punctiliously paid the agreed-upon rent, while I prayed that the necessary funds had been acquired in a legal, if perhaps unconventional, fashion. When Ricky discovered my sturdy blue bicycle in the shed, he swallowed his pride and asked if he could use it to ride to class at the community college, thus cutting his commute in half. I had assumed that he was taking the bus, when in fact he had been walking one and a half hours each way, more often in rain than shine. He knew he cut a derisory figure on my lady's bicycle (actually a girl's bike to suit my small size), perched uncomfortably on a hiked-up saddle, wearing a billowing garbage bag to keep dry when it poured.

In time, pictures began to emerge. He had been hungry until he was seven; he didn't know what not being hungry felt like until he was fed proper food at an uncle's house in Karachi. He had to learn to wear shoes, painfully. He almost drowned in a rushing stream; the details were not clear, after which, "I was not afraid of anything; I was not afraid to die." With single-minded ambition, he directed every effort to escape a bleak future, to avoid following in his poor father's footsteps, who had labored in the fields from dawn to dusk without being able to feed his children.

I wasn't sure I wanted to know how Ricky came to America. I would have been suspicious of whatever he told me. He said he had come by boat, by freighter, with lengthy stops in Saudi Arabia and in South America, eventually landing in Texas. His passport seemed genuine, as did his most-prized possession, a fiercely guarded green card.

Over a year of residence my spare room—now furnished with an exquisite prayer rug, one wall adorned with a festive tapestry featuring intricate calligraphy—I gathered from snatches of conversation on the telephone that Ricky exchanged his hard-earned knowledge about immigration, specifically the acquisition of a green card, for a variety of favors. A sadly dented vehicle was parked in front of the house one day, "a loan from my friend the mechanic who is teaching me how to drive." Ricky's diet now included the occasional orange, apple, and cereal; he was not bashful about asking to use my iron to press his shirts, being a rather fastidious dresser.

In due time, I was introduced to his friend "the engineer from Turkey," his friend "the agronomist from Egypt," his friend "the navigator from Jordan," and several other gentlemen, all of whom treated Ricky with awe and respect, even though some were twice his age with dignified beards, dispensing advice in a variety of Middle Eastern accents.

At the end of the school year, as I prepared for summer abroad, Ricky pleaded with me to leave him in charge of house and dog. "I am a true believer, you can trust me, I will take care of your dog." Taking care of Maya, I knew, did not come naturally to Ricky who, I feared, may have viewed her dog food with some envy when he first moved in. I made sure Maya was comfortable riding in a basket attached to the handlebar of my bicycle, left detailed instructions, her veterinarian's address, and an ample supply of special food. Upon my return two months later, a proud Ricky greeted me with a tail-wagging, sleek, and happy pet sporting a fancy new collar. "She was a big help. I took her to City Park where we made many friends. People have confidence in a man and his dog. I met a girl who loves her, she gave her baths and bought her a new collar."

I recalled somewhat similar circumstances, when Maya's predecessor, her exact replica of a medium-sized red dachshund, charmed her way out of a perilous destiny as a laboratory subject in the medical school. Fred had left early in the morning for work in a flurry of activity, papers, airline

tickets, lecture notes, tie and suit coat tossed on the seat as an after-
thought. In the afternoon he phoned from the airport, in great distress.
"Have you seen Elli? I want you to put an ad in the paper; I'm afraid she
jumped in the car this morning, but I couldn't find her when I left the
car in the Tulane parking garage. She may have gotten out! You know I'll
be gone ten days." A week passed with no news of Elli, when an apolo-
getic voice informed me on the phone that Elli had found a new home. "I
saw this little dog wandering around the Tulane parking garage and took
him up to the lab. We are always on the lookout for healthy specimens.
But she was so cute and cuddly I decided to give her to my girlfriend instead and propose to her. I took her to the vet for a checkup, shots, sham-
poo, and manicure, bought her a red collar with a new red leash. Won't
you reconsider and leave your pet with us? My fiancée will be heartbroken." I was adamant. When Fred returned, he was greeted by a frisky little
princess of a dog, auburn coat gleaming with good health, breath positively sweet smelling. This was to be Elli's first and last free ride to the
medical school; Fred established a ritual of checking-for-Elli every morning to avoid any further potential disaster.

Some twenty years later, while Elli's successor, Maya, gently snoozed in
her basket under the kitchen table, daily news about a shaky truce in the
Middle East intruded upon my peaceful household. Ricky's invectives
against Israel made clear his fanatic allegiance to the Palestinian cause. I
told him my maiden name was Israel; I would no longer tolerate such language in my house. Ricky held his tongue, with difficulty. I was not sorry
to see him go.

My next tenant was a refreshingly simple-minded young man from
Bogotá, whose family, aware of his limitations, sought a safe haven for
their son, turned eighteen and thus threatened by induction into the
Colombian army or, worse, kidnapping. Paul, whose mother was American, had been raised behind the sheltered walls of a grand villa, protected
by an army of servants, and within the confines of a well-known American school in Bogotá. Maya became his bosom friend. He hugged her,
fed her, ran with her, met all the neighborhood kids who knew her. Once
again, my sturdy blue bicycle was called into service, as Paul, a hefty two
hundred pounder, pedaled mightily, dodging traffic along a four-mile
stretch of highway to reach his destination: an eight-hour stint as a busboy
in a newly opened Steak and Ale restaurant.

Clearing tables did not come easily to Paul, who suffered from clumsiness aggravated by severe myopia. His good nature was sorely tested by the constant ribbing of his co-workers. Wistfully he confided that his dream of attaining a position as a waiter seemed beyond reach. Perhaps, if he studied mathematics at the junior college, he would improve his money-counting skills sufficiently to impress the headwaiter? Fortunately for Paul, all decisions were taken out of his hands when his family fled Bogotá. He rejoined his mother and little sister in Florida; his father sought to salvage the family's fortune in Caracas.

While Ricky had examined my recent acquisition of several smallish Persian rugs with a practiced eye and correctly appraised the most worn as the most valuable, Paul had spent blissful moments in my study, where the exotic collection of Colombian artifacts which Fred had carried home from his journey to the Amazon never ceased to soothe Paul's spirits. He would stroke the silken smooth alpaca rug which depicted a Spanish conquistador with prominent Indian features, admire a hollowed-out log drum, a polished hardwood bow, a quiver of arrows, a seven-foot blowgun, a feather headdress, and stand in silent awe before a black clay pottery vase shaped like a dancing maid with arms akimbo, fighting to keep his hands in check and not touch.

For a brief period my house was invaded by young people courting Heidi, an irresistibly exuberant young lady in blue overalls who arrived in tears one night, having traveled in a dust-covered red Volkswagen bug all the way from Houston. She had been introduced to me by phone as a budding geologist, newly appointed to a government agency a ten-minute drive from my house. Heidi cooked, sang, played the piano, washed her car in my driveway . . . and the young men came. Sheepishly, I knocked at my own kitchen door to ask permission to join in the fun; invited myself to impromptu musical evenings in my living room; enjoyed the food and the lively discussions—that is, until Heidi's mother flew in from Texas to check on her enterprising daughter. Heidi became subdued, if not terrified; the laughter drained out of her. Her mother, a handsome blond matron in her forties, was a formidable personage indeed. I suggested the Steak and Ale (in memory of Paul's valiant efforts) for a farewell dinner party, after which mother and daughter returned to Texas.

A succession of roomers and tenants were to inhabit my house for many more years. I recall a gentleman between marriages, a retired nurse between houses. Year after year I would bump into Ricky, barely recognizable in a smart suit and tie. First there was the discreet knock on the door, a broad smile, a proffered business card, "export, imports," with an address in the French Quarter. One day a shiny Cadillac passed my car, with a happily grinning Ricky at the wheel. Another year, same car, same Ricky, with an enchanting, slender, doe-eyed beauty at his side—his fiancée from Karachi. Several years later, a letter arrived with a family photo, the same young lady with two little girls. "Business doing well in Florida. This is my family. Ricky."

My conservative neighbors had become used to my exotic guests. No eyebrows were raised when a young Vietnamese gentleman with a shiny new sports car moved in an impressive collection of high-tech instruments to help with his advanced studies in dentistry. Trinh, dressed in the height of collegiate fashion, was a model of decorum caught, as he expressed it, between two worlds. He was grieving the death of his aged grandfather who had insisted on a traditional Vietnamese upbringing in a small Louisiana town where Trinh's family were the only Vietnamese. Of Saigon, which he left when he turned seven (or six by our reckoning), Trinh remembered little, save the servants' concern to keep him sheltered in a big villa. He owed it to his family to succeed in his studies. His older brother was a pathologist in Texas. His sister, a biochemist, had rebelled against an arranged marriage and been disowned by the family; she was living in Germany with a German boyfriend. He, Trinh, could not stomach American food. His mom had prepared his school lunches all through high school. That is why he responded to my bulletin board notice in the University of New Orleans student center, which mentioned "use of kitchen." Every weekend, Trinh returned from a visit home with a trunkful of frozen Vietnamese dinners lovingly prepared by his mother, which I am afraid I did not appreciate, even though Trinh offered to share these delicacies. For once, my olfactory deficiency stood me in good stead, as friends sniffed the air in my kitchen with disapproving looks. "What have you been cooking?"

To our mutual relief, Trinh was engaged and married to a Vietnamese young lady with his parents' heartfelt approval. I wished him well.

For three years, an exceedingly bashful young athlete—a black belt in karate, expert golfer and tennis player—lived in my house without speaking. Masao Umeki, from Tokyo, was the epitome of discretion, helped by a minimal English vocabulary and an inability to express himself by acting out his wishes. I had carefully drafted a rental contract which included the clause, "Mr. Umeki will let me know when he does not understand," based on my previous experience with Mr. Ohara, whose negative nods I had misinterpreted as meaning "no" while his positive nods apparently signified the opposite. Trinh's expensive wardrobe, microscope, and instruments gave way to a closet full of golf clubs, tennis rackets, and weights. Appropriately and in due time, I was introduced to a muscular Japanese American young lady who shared Mr. Umeki's passion for golf and tennis, and spoke English. Theirs was a match made on the tennis courts of City Park.

On the occasion of their wedding, while I was traveling overseas, I invited Mr. Umeki's parents to stay in my house for the duration of their two-week visit. I have always wondered what impressions of America they took back with them from my house in Metairie, but unfortunately missed my golden opportunity to ask them. I was undergoing aggressive chemotherapy, and was very ill. When the doorbell rang, I forced myself to make the few steps to open the door, and there, smiling, bowing, stood an elderly, elegantly dressed, Japanese couple with a prosperous, English-speaking Mr. Umeki by their side, and an energetic five-year-old boy unceremoniously leading the way. "Please, I know the house, I want you to meet my parents and show my son where I used to live." I excused myself with a wave of the hand, too weak to speak or stand, and sat down in the nearest chair while the Umekis inspected their erstwhile American quarters.

One of my last roomers was an all-American boy in fringed shorts, high-top hiking shoes, neatly groomed blond ponytail, with a collection of band instruments, including drums, which he stashed in his closet for safekeeping. Lester was a part-time student and laborer, a refugee from Silicon Valley in California, determined to show his parents he could make it on his own without their help. He had worked on the oil rigs in the Gulf before deciding to go back to college, and lifted heavy weights in a warehouse on the wrong side of the tracks. For some reason, I had more inquiries about Lester's somewhat unaccustomed appearance than about any of my foreign guests, whose strangeness was to be expected. Lester spoke with a broad western accent, jogged during early morning hours, lovingly washed and polished a well-used car, and carefully programmed his few free hours to accommodate friends he met for band rehearsals. He was not a southerner.

It took me two years after cancer struck to regain my former strength and confidence and accept paid assignments as a trilingual tour guide, in addition to volunteer work, showing foreign visitors the sights of New Orleans and surrounding areas. I considered I learned more from these guests than they did from me; this was the best of "tourism in reverse." After all, what chance did I have to visit Devil's Island? Yet here I was in a bus with a dozen denizens of every hue chatting away in French, each explaining their very recent ancestry to that infamous island. No, they would prefer shopping to a swamp excursion, their jungle was more tropical, their birds more colorful. On another occasion, I had the privilege of accompanying a refined group of ladies from Martinique, in the French West Indies. We stopped in Lafayette, the capital of Acadiana, in time for dinner and an impromptu shopping spree at a popular discount store. I alerted the manager to my group's needs, i.e., only a few of the ladies understood English. To my surprise, I found them chatting away in Creole, the French dialect of the Islands, with several of the store's employees, who greeted them like long-lost friends. Everywhere we went the following day—the Avery Island jungle gardens, St. Martinville, the Acadian Village—they were welcomed with open arms in French, in Cajun, and in Creole. I learned that they belonged to a travel club and had decided on this Louisiana venture only a week earlier. "You know, one gets tired of white sand beaches, blue skies, and sunshine. Always the same." To me it sounded like escape from paradise.

One of my more challenging groups was a busload of French Canadians who were under the impression that a plantation was a kind of meadow planted with trees. They happily skipped the scheduled visit of Houmas Plantation, one of my favorites, searching for lost cows on the levee instead. We had lunch at the nearby Cabin restaurant, a collection of slave cabins filled with old tools, milk cans, washboards, saws, and other memorabilia of a bygone age. They were entranced, recalling their own struggles and youth on the farm.

Not so long ago, scarcely a year after the fall of the Berlin Wall and German reunification, I escorted a group of German salesmen, still reeling under the shock of a recent tour of duty in the former East Germany. Their trip to America, fully funded by their Japanese employer (Ricoh), was to make up for the hardships endured in the former East Germany, with its lack of basic amenities taken for granted in the prosperous West. They were a merry crew, yet I noticed an unnatural reserve, until someone whispered to me, "That's the big boss in back of the bus, the tiny Japanese gentleman with his wife." When I greeted said gentleman during one of our stops, he handed me his card and asked for a favor. Could I phone one of their employees in New Orleans for him and advise him of his transfer to Atlanta? He had jotted down the name: Masao Umeki. "Of course, I know Masao very well. I will let him know." Somehow, the thought that the only Japanese person I knew in New Orleans was the one the gentleman on the bus was trying to contact felt very reassuring. It was a chink in Julia's elsewheres, a feeling that anywhere was here.

The Man under the Bridge

Nowhere was this feeling of being at home anywhere more succinctly demonstrated to me than on my second trip to Thailand, courtesy of a free frequent flyer ticket, early in 1992. I recalled my brother reminiscing about his work in India and Thailand in 1955. He had enjoyed his five-week stint in Thailand the most, directing some testing of cross-cultural opinion polls in an agricultural setting now part of the greater Bangkok urban sprawl. He had mentioned his interpreter, an American anthropologist, a Dr. Textor, a bit younger than he. I clicked in Dr. Textor's name on the computer in my branch library, found several scholarly treatises, checked one out, learned Dr. Textor had been teaching at Stanford in the 1960s, phoned Stanford, was told Professor Textor had retired and was living in Portland. My Delta flight to Bangkok via Seoul and Taipei had a two-hour layover in Portland. I phoned the professor from Portland. "This is Max Ralis' sister. Do you have any advice for me? I am on my way to Bangkok." "Yes; could you please give my greetings to my closest friend, an extraordinary human being, a philosopher and a sage, who taught me Buddhism and the Thai language. His name is Sin Saensuk and he lives under a bridge. He decided a few years ago to retire from his family and devote his waning years to meditation and prayer. Drive to the police station in Nimburi village, now a suburb some thirty miles northwest from the capital, ask the police chief to take you to him."

The next morning, or possibly the one after that, or the one before (I have never been able to figure out the time lag flying west to the Orient), I prevailed upon a young Thai colleague I had met years ago at a Tulane graduate party to drive me there. As it happened, she lived in a new sub-urban development not far from the erstwhile village where my brother had tested his questionnaires in an assortment of rice paddies with the help of his interpreter, Dr. Textor. I recalled my brother's description of the police station in said village, a rare old-fashioned construction of dark unpainted wood, with intricately carved eaves, a sort of humble down-sized version of a Siamese palatial abode; and sure enough, there it stood, incongruously set back from a busy highway lined with newly built lack-luster cement structures. We ascended the broad flight of stairs leading to the raised first floor with some trepidation. I was well aware of my colleague's sense of unease in surroundings not becoming a young lady of her social standing, but curiosity prevailed. I nudged her toward a room where several police officers were engaged in pleasant banter, to judge by their relaxed and informal manner. "Ask to speak to the chief. Ask him to direct us to the man under the bridge." After a few polite exchanges, Sri turned to me: "He needs to take a shower and change and will meet us in our car in five minutes." Five minutes later, a freshly scrubbed, neatly groomed diminutive policeman in a starched white shirt not yet wilted by the heat tucked his radio phone in his belt and invited us unceremoniously to proceed down the highway in Sri's car. We stopped just a few blocks ahead, rounding the corner of a busy shopping street. Our police chief disappeared to "talk to the village chief," then rejoined us to ask us to wait five minutes while said gentleman showered and changed. "We can't drive the car under the bridge, which is a short walk down the highway, so we will leave it parked here," Sri translated. Very much aware of muddied sandals, damply clinging and mussed frocks, we followed the two squeaky clean gentlemen down the four-lane highway, facing oncoming traffic on the left of the road.

We didn't see the bridge. We would have passed over it without notic-ing. It was just a short twin span of highway crossing a creek, perhaps forty or fifty feet wide. Our guides motioned us down a fairly steep em-bankment, then stopped. To our right, a white-haired septuagenarian sat in motionless meditation on a wooden platform. The sharp incline of the embankment left barely a foot between the top of his head and the ce-ment bridge span. To the steadily droning accompaniment of uninter-rupted traffic above, he had created his own world of silence. With a cal-culated economy of gesture, he turned his head. "Tell him I bring greetings from his friend in America. Tell him I am Max's sister." Sri du-tifully translated. There followed a polite exchange of bows, of clasped hands, whereupon the Man under the Bridge stood up, gathered his gar-ment about him, and left. "He excused himself to fetch clean water for his guests and to take a quick shower and change," explained Sri. In the dim light, I took in familiar objects displayed in incongruous surround-ings—a couple of tin cups, a radio, a faded photo of His Majesty—propped up and fastened to the pilings of the bridge, or set neatly upon wooden crates. On the embankment beneath the twin span to the right, a safe distance away, a handsomely carved spirit house sat securely perched on a makeshift pedestal. There seemed to be some sort of cooking arrange-ment, although I had been told that Sin Saensuk's oldest daughter cooked for him and brought his meals. He reappeared, stepping surefooted in bare feet, clad in traditional Thai garb, loose pants gathered tightly be-neath the knees, ample folds of a crisp shirt set off by a narrow band at the neck. His commanding presence was in no way diminished by the hum-ble surroundings, but rather enhanced by them. An assortment of old jelly or jam glasses was proffered round and filled with fresh bottled water, after which the Man under the Bridge resumed his cross-legged posture on the seating platform, while Sri proceeded to engage him in conversa-tion at my behest. I watched him take in the scene below with a sweep of his eyes and a broad swing of his arm: this was his domain, the rap-idly coursing water bearing an uninterrupted string of boat people, fish-ermen, traders, artisans, some in rowboats, some in small outboard motor craft. He knew them all. I tried to picture the rice paddies eaten up by the suburban sprawl, the endless cement structures, the new highways, the incredible noise and pollution and traffic jams, my brother's memories half a century away. The Man under the Bridge had kept his eyes on the past, but was firmly anchored in the here and now. He no longer moved from his perch under the bridge, people came to him. "Ask him what ad-vice he has for me, Sri." I watched him flip-flop his hands in an expressive gesture. "Everything changes; you must change with it." Did he remem-ber my brother? "Max, of course, very well, a fun-loving happy gentle-man." What about Dr. Textor? "My best student. Mastered Thai language 80 percent. Very difficult for a Westerner."

I left with an indescribable feeling of no longer being lost, of having found elsewhere right here, under this bridge, where Sin Saensuk had as-sembled the simple essentials of a meaningful life. Elsewhere could be anywhere I chose, and I had chosen New Orleans.

Ten years ago, I traveled to the outer reaches of Inner Mongolia in a vague search for ancestral memories handed down by my Aunt Mirrha as an ex-planation for my green slit eyes, memories of vast unbroken steppes whipped up by unforgiving winds. After several hours' drive through an eerily monotonous sea of swaying grasses, our jeeplike vehicle stopped in the middle of nowhere, surrounded by silence as far as the eye could see, a silence interrupted by waves of swishing grass, made more ominous by leaden skies above. Our guide pointed ahead to a slender pile of stones. "What is it?" "It is a marker. No one gets lost. It tells the directions, north, east, south, and west."

When friends or family find me fighting for breath, eyes closed, and wonder where I am, I am concentrating on that marker in the middle of nowhere to find my way back. I shall close my book now, and listen to the wind which marks the spot between past and morrow while I am here.

Epilogue

Writing *Elsewhere* was yet another journey of discovery, as I dealt with advanced breast cancer. Between waves of nausea and weakness, I concentrated on images from my past, intent on putting them on paper for my family. There were times when I couldn't stand, times when I couldn't speak, times when my pen escaped too weak a grasp. During almost three years of chemotherapy, I could count on perhaps a dozen days a month when my head cleared sufficiently, my spirits lifted from a chemically induced fog of the bleakest depression and its unnatural euphoric counterpoint, a roller coaster ride which threatened my sanity.

Elsewhere became a safe haven, scribbled hand-penned pages beckoning from my writing table six short paces from my bed. It got me up in the morning, and thinking about it helped me find sleep at night. My daughter, Tanya, was able to decipher my handwriting, type a major portion of the manuscript on her word processor, and catch the more obvious errors on the way.

Last summer, tired and spent, I sought out a support group at one of our local hospitals. It was on one of my good days. I felt confident I could park the car and walk to the entrance. I didn't count on a succession of hallways to the meeting room. No one noticed my leaning against the wall, gasping for breath. Clearly, no one expected sick people to attend this meeting. An uplifting presentation, something about "looking good, feeling well," made me feel bad instead, responsible for my illness, since positive thoughts had failed me. I became angry. Yet I couldn't afford to be angry; I was in too perilous an emotional equilibrium between the rise and fall of my monthly chemo roller coaster ride. I needed help.

That was when my nurse introduced me to cyberspace. "Have you thought of finding a support group on the Web?"

My life changed. I entered yet another dimension, elsewhere in cyberspace. I ordered the lightest of laptops, the smallest of printers. As soon as the worst of the nausea wore off, I struggled to master the commands which would take my beeping, blinking electronic wonder through its paces and do my bidding. Unseen people from every state, every continent, were sharing their concerns by e-mail on a breast cancer discussion list. Their caring, loving, and knowledgeable thoughts have buoyed my spirits and helped me live at peace with cancer, knowing that in this last journey I am not alone, here, elsewhere, and everywhere.